Willie,

With best wishes,

Neill

AT THE HEART OF THE UNION

Also by Neill Nugent

THE BRITISH RIGHT (*co-editor with R. King*)

RESPECTABLE REBELS (*co-editor with R. King*)

THE LEFT IN FRANCE (*with D. Lovve*)

THE GOVERNMENT AND POLITICS OF THE EUROPEAN UNION

THE EUROPEAN BUSINESS ENVIRONMENT (*co-editor with R. O'Donnell*)

THE EUROPEAN UNION: Annual Review of Activities (*editor*)

THE EUROPEAN UNION, Volumes 1 and 2 (*editor*)

At the Heart of the Union

Studies of the European Commission

Edited by

Neill Nugent
Professor of Politics
Manchester Metropolitan University

First published in Great Britain 1997 by
MACMILLAN PRESS LTD
Houndmills, Basingstoke, Hampshire RG21 6XS and London
Companies and representatives throughout the world

A catalogue record for this book is available from the British Library.

ISBN 0–333–67564–9

First published in the United States of America 1997 by
ST. MARTIN'S PRESS, INC.,
Scholarly and Reference Division,
175 Fifth Avenue, New York, N.Y. 10010

ISBN 0–312–17413–6

Library of Congress Cataloging-in Publication Data
At the heart of the Union : studies of the European Commission /
edited by Neill Nugent.
p.   cm.
Includes bibliographical references (p.   ) and index.
ISBN 0–312–17413–6 (cloth)
1. European Commission.   2. European Union.   I. Nugent, Neill.
JN33.5.A7 1997
341.242'2—dc21   96–46501
                                                              CIP

This book is printed on paper suitable for recycling and made from fully managed and
sustained forest sources.

10   9   8   7   6   5   4   3   2   1
06   05   04   03   02   01   00   99   98   97

Printed and bound in Great Britain by
Antony Rowe Ltd, Chippenham, Wiltshire

Contents

Preface

This book is based on two main premises. The first is that the significance of the Commission is such as to make it worthy of extensive and detailed study. The most obvious manifestation of this significance is the large number of key roles the Commission exercises within the European Union's system of governance. Particularly prominent are its legislative, executive, judicial, representative, and mediative roles. The second premise is that not as much has been written about the Commission as might be expected given its position as a key institution of the European Union. A considerable amount of research has been, and is being, undertaken on the Commission, but not enough of it has appeared in published form.

The aim of the book is to make a significant contribution to furthering understanding of the Commission by bringing together in one volume the fruits of new research and new thinking. Different aspects of the Commission are explored via a range of perspectives and with the use of both empirical and theoretical approaches. Many of the book's chapters focus on subject areas that have been barely touched upon, let alone rigorously examined, in the existing literature on the Commission.

I would like to express my gratitude to the contributors for producing, on schedule, what I believe to be work of very high quality. I would also like to thank Maureen Nugent for her invaluable secretarial assistance.

February 1997   NEILL NUGENT

List of Abbreviations

CAP	Common Agricultural Policy
CCP	Common Commercial Policy
CFI	Court of First Instance
CFSP	Common Foreign and Security Policy
CIS	Commonwealth of Independent States
COM/COM DOC	Commission Document
COREPER	Committee of Permanent Representatives
CSF	Community Support Framework
DG	Directorate General
DTI	Department of Trade and Industry (UK)
EC	European Community
ECA	European Court of Auditors
ECJ	European Court of Justice
ECO	European Cartel Office
ECSC	European Coal and Steel Community
ECOFIN	Council of Economic and Finance Ministers
ECU	European Currency Unit
EDF	European Development Fund
EEC	European Economic Community
EFTA	European Free Trade Association
EMS	European Monetary System
EMU	Economic and Monetary Union
EP	European Parliament
EPU	European Political Union
ERM	Exchange Rate Mechanism
ESPRIT	European Strategic Programme for Research and Development in Information Technology
EU	European Union
EURATOM	European Atomic Energy Community
EUREKA	European Programme for High Technology Research and Development
GATT	General Agreement on Tariffs and Trade
IGC	Intergovernmental Conference
IT	Information Technology

JHA	Justice and Home Affairs
MEP	Member of the European Parliament
MP	Member of Parliament (UK)
MTF	Merger Task Force
NESL	North East Shipbuilders Limited
OECD	Organisation for Economic Co-operation and Development
OEEC	Organisation for European Economic Cooperation
OJ	Official Journal of the European Communities
PASOK	Pan-Hellenic Socialist Movement
PHARE	Poland and Hungary: Aid for the Reconstruction of Economies (this abbreviation subsequently retained for aid schemes to Eastern Europe as a whole)
qmv	qualified majority voting
PSOE	Spanish Socialist Party
RACE	Research and Development in Advanced Communications Technologies for Europe
R&D	Research and Development
R&TD	Research and Technological Development
SEA	Single European Act
SEC	Internal Commission General Secretariat Document
SEM	Single European Market
SEP	Strathclyde European Partnership
SPD	Single Programming Document
SOID	Scottish Office Industry Department
TEU	Treaty on European Union
UCLAF	Unité de Coordination de la Lutte Anti-Fraude
UK	United Kingdom
VAT	Value Added Tax
VFM	value for money

Notes on the Contributors

Michelle Cini is Jean Monnet Lecturer in European Community Studies in the Department of Politics, University of Bristol. Amongst her publications is *The European Commission* (Manchester University Press, 1997). She is the co-author, with Lee McGowan, of *Competition Policy in the European Union* (Macmillan, forthcoming).

Desmond Dinan is Associate Professor of History and Director of the Center for European Integration Studies at George Mason University, Virginia. His most recent book is *Ever Closer Union? An Introduction to the European Community* (Lynne Rienner, 1994). He is currently editing and compiling *The Encyclopedia of the European Union* (Lynne Rienner, forthcoming).

Helen Drake is Lecturer in French and European Studies at Loughborough University. Her PhD (Aston), completed in 1996, consisted of a study of the legitimisation of authority in the European Union. Amongst her publications, she is the co-editor of *The Language of Leadership in Contemporary France* (Dartmouth, 1996). She is currently writing a biography of Jacques Delors and is researching in the area of France and Europe.

Liesbet Hooghe is Assistant Professor in Political Science at the University of Toronto. She recently edited *Cohesion Policy and European Integration: Building Multi-Level Governance* (Oxford University Press, 1996). Her current research includes a project on the political orientations of senior Commission officials.

Thomas Lawton is Lecturer in European Business and Policy at Royal Holloway College, University of London. His recent publications and his current research focus primarily on the nature and market effects of European Union industrial policy.

Roger Levy is Professor of Government and Head of the School of Public Administration and Law at The Robert Gordon University, Aberdeen. His publications and his main areas of interest are centred on the financial management of the European Union. He is a member of a Commission expert group on budgetary assessment in the European Union.

Andrew MacMullen is Associate Director of the Centre for European Studies and Lecturer in Politics at the University of Durham. He has published on several aspects of European politics. His research interests include the nature of European Secretariats and the personnel of the European Commission.

Maryon McDonald was formerly Reader in Social Anthropology at Brunel University, and since 1996 has been Senior Fellow in the Department of Social Anthropology, University of Cambridge. Amongst her publications she is author of *'We are not French!': Language, Culture and Identity in Brittany* (Routledge, 1989) and is the editor of *History and Ethnicity* (Routledge, 1989) and *Gender, Drink and Drugs* (Berg, 1994). Since 1991 she has pursued extensive ethnographic research inside the European Parliament and the European Commission.

Lee McGowan is Lecturer in Government and a member of the Public Policy Research Group at the University of Ulster at Jordanstown. He has published widely on aspects of competition policy in Europe and is the co-author, with Michelle Cini, of *Competition Policy in the European Union* (Macmillan, forthcoming).

Janne Haaland Matláry is Senior Researcher and Assistant Professor at the Centre for Advanced Research of the Europeanisation of the Nation State (ARENA) at Oslo University. Amongst her publications is *Energy Policy in the European Union* (Macmillan, 1997). Her research is focused on institutional changes in the European Union and their impact on the state.

Neill Nugent is Professor of Politics at Manchester Metropolitan University. Amongst his publications, he is the author of *The Government and Politics of the European Union* (Macmillan, 3rd edition, 1994), and is the co-editor of *The European Business Environment* (Macmillan, 1994). He is currently preparing a book on the Commission.

B. Guy Peters is Maurice Falk Professor of American Government at the University of Pittsburgh. Amongst his many publications he is the author of *The Politics of Bureaucracy* (4th edition Longman, 1994), the co-editor of *The Politics of Expert Advice* (Edinburgh University Press, 1993) and *Advising West European Governments* (Edinburgh University Press, 1993), and the editor of *American Public Policy: Promise and Performance* (Chatham House, 1995). His current research is mainly focused on comparing bureaucracies and administrative reform.

Mark Pollack is Assistant Professor of Politics at the University of Wisconsin, Madison. He has published on several aspects of the European Union. His current research interests include the European Union's supranational institutions and policy-making processes.

Mitchell P. Smith is Assistant Professor of Political Science at Middlebury College. He has published on the Commission and on democracy in the European Union. He is currently preparing a book on the Commission as a policy entrepreneur.

1 At the Heart of the Union

Neill Nugent[1]

DEFINING THE COMMISSION

The European Commission is commonly referred to simply as the Commission. Whether the full or the shortened version is preferred, usage of the name can create ambiguity, misunderstanding, and confusion. This is because the name can be, and frequently is, used in at least three different senses.

In one sense the name is used to refer to the whole Commission: to the Commission as a collective entity. In a second sense it is used to refer to the College of Commissioners: the body which is the Commission's highest decision-making forum. And in a third sense it is used to refer to a part of the Commission which deals with a particular aspect of the Commission's work: phrases along the lines of 'the Commission's view of . . . is that . . .' are frequently used, when what in fact is meant is that 'the Directorate General (or the unit) in the Commission which deals with . . . takes the view that . . .'.

Without engaging in laborious explanations of meaning every time reference is made to the Commission, there is no way of avoiding this definitional, or identification, problem. It is just not possible on all occasions to risk misinterpretations of usage. What can, however, be done is to minimise the risk of misinterpretations by always being sensitive to the potential problem and by being aware of the likely meaning in particular contexts.

DISAGGREGATING THE COMMISSION

The political and the administrative arms

Whatever meaning is being given in a particular context to its name, the Commission is usually portrayed as being a single, monolithic entity. That it is so is understandable enough. After all, its internal deliberations and decision-making processes are not open to public inspection or viewing but are conducted behind closed doors. From behind these closed doors a great volume and wide range of decisions, recommendations, opinions, and other measures are issued in the Commission's name: 'the Commission has decided that'.... 'the Commission is initiating investigations into . . .' 'the Commission proposes to take action against . . .'. No suggestion is ever given that deliverances of this kind are anything other than the agreed and collective view of the Commission. Rational decision-making processes may be said to be implied, in which the Commission is a united and coherent actor making decisions which advance European Union (EU) objectives.

But the Commission is not as united or coherent as it is often portrayed as being. Rather is it composed of many elements and interests. The responsibilities and the roles of these elements and interests vary considerably, as do some of their perceptions of what the Commission should be doing and in what ways it should be doing it. So although the Commission presents itself, and formally acts, as a collective entity, a full understanding of its nature – covering such matters as its composition, structure, procedures, functions, and aims – requires that it be disaggregated. The most obvious way of undertaking such a disaggregation is to separate what might be thought of as the two arms of the Commission.

The first arm is the political arm and consists of the College of Commissioners. One reason for thinking of the College as the political arm is its position and its functions. It sits at the apex of what is essentially a pyramidical Commission organisational structure and from this apex it is expected to provide, both as a collective body and through the portfolio responsibilities of its members, leadership and direction for both the Commission and the EU, and accountability for Commission activities. Another reason for thinking of the College as the political arm of the Commission is that its twenty members – two from each of the five largest EU Member States (France, Germany, Italy, Spain, and the UK) and one from each of the other ten Member States – are very much political appointees and are themselves almost invariably former national politicians, in many cases of senior rank.

The second arm is the administrative arm and consists not of the vast 'Eurocracy' of popular portrayal but of a (by comparison with the size of public sector agencies in Member States) relatively small number of officials and support staff. In 1995 the Commission's establishment of administrative related posts consisted of 15,001 permanent posts – including 1,763 assigned to translation and interpretation work – and 835 temporary posts (Commission, 1996a, p. 440). There is some politicisation of this administrative arm at its most senior levels, most notably in terms of appointments procedures, but for the most part it is based and structured along recognisable administrative lines and is engaged in recognisable administrative tasks.

Disaggregating the Commission need not be confined to differentiating between its political and administrative arms, for each of these arms can themselves be broken down into component parts and interests. That this is so is evident from much of recent research and writing on the Commission, where the focus is frequently not on the Commission as a whole but on particular actors within it. The picture that emerges is of, as Cram (1994) has described it, a 'multi level organization'. It is a multi level organisation, moreover, in which the various levels, and the actors and interests at each level, are not always pulling in quite the same direction.

Disaggregating the political arm

There are three main component parts to the political arm of the Commission.

First, there is the office of President, the standing and status of which has been so raised over the years that the occupant is now far more than just *primus inter pares*. The number of very important initiatives which came to be identified with the name of Jacques Delors during his tenure of office from January 1985 to January 1995 – most notably the 1988 'Delors I' and 1992 'Delors II' budgetary reform packages, the 1988 'Delors (Committee) proposals' on Economic and Monetary Union (EMU), and the 1993 'Delors White Paper' on growth, competitiveness and unemployment – is testimony to the presence, the status, and the influence which can be associated with the post. (On the Commission Presidency, especially under Delors, see Drake, 1995; Grant, 1994; and Ross, 1995.)

Second, there are the Commissioners, both in their collective capacity as members of the College of Commissioners and in their individual capacity as holders of portfolio responsibilities. In the first of these capacities, Commissioners are members of the body which must give approval to all significant decisions that are made in the name of the Commission, and in the second of the capacities they exercise responsibilities which are something of a cross between the responsibilities exercised at national levels by, on the one hand, ministers and, on the other hand, the most senior of civil servants. Although much of the research and writing which has been undertaken on the Commission has things to say about Commissioners, surprisingly little has been specifically focused on them. An area where some College-specific work has been done is in regard to the background of Commissioners, with Page and Wouters (1994) and Andrew MacMullen in Chapter 2 identifying a number of patterns and developments. A key point for MacMullen is that the post of Commissioner is attracting increasingly high-profile political figures. This heightened politicisation of the College both reflects and contributes to the considerable political status, role and influence that is now attached to the post of European Commissioner.

Third, there are the *cabinets* – or private offices – of the Commissioners. Consisting usually of six to eight senior advisers, plus support staff, their role is essentially to support and assist their Commissioner in his/her work. As such, it might be thought they hardly merit being regarded as a separate component of the political arm of the Commission, but in acting as a partial link and a partial buffer between Commissioners and the Commission administrative services they do, in fact, virtually constitute a separate policy and decision-making layer in their own right. Such indeed is the influence of *cabinets* that their staff and their activities often come to be the targets of resentment by officials in the Commission services. Like Commissioners, *cabinets* have not been studied as much as might have been expected, although Ross (1993, 1994, and 1995) has written interesting and informative insider accounts on the operation of the Delors' *cabinet* and Donnelly (1993) and Donnelly and Ritchie (1994) have produced more generally focused analyses of the functioning of the *cabinet* system as a whole.

Disaggregating the administrative arm

The administrative arm – which is commonly referred to as the Commission services – can also be broken down into component parts. There are two main such parts. First, the 25 Directorates General (DGs), which are mainly policy-based and which in some respects are similar in structure and function to national ministries. Second, a number of co-ordinating and servicing units, of which the most important in political and policy terms are the Secretariat General and the Legal Service. (See Annex for a listing of DGs and special units.)

No formal hierarchy exists within the Commission's services. However, it is clear that amongst Commission officials some parts are regarded as enjoying higher status and as being generally more interesting and desirable places to be located than others. In very broad terms it can be said that those parts of the services which are directly involved in policy development enjoy more prestige than those which are primarily concerned with policy implementation or with horizontal activities such as information dissemination or financial coordination. The prestige and standing of parts of the Commission services is also influenced by the extent to which responsibilities are seen as being at the EU's policy core and at the cutting edge of policy promotion. An example of a part of the Commission which has benefited in terms of prestige and perceived importance by becoming part of the core is DGIV (Competition): it used to be regarded as something of a backwater but since the mid 1980s it has, under the umbrella of the drive to complete the internal market and with the assistance of strong Competition Commissioners, established itself as one of the leading policy initiating DGs.

The administrative arm is subject to internal divisions and conflicts of various kinds. The differing national identifications of Commission officials is, for example, a problem area in this regard, as Maryon McDonald explains in Chapter 3. Cohesion and unity are also undermined by differences between DGs in respect of policy priorities and approaches. Tom Lawton and Lee McGowan provide illustrations of, and explore, such differences in Chapters 7 and 8 respectively. (Other studies which at least touch on such differences include Ross, 1993; Bulmer, 1994a; and Fuchs 1995.) Differences between DGs are especially difficult to manage when they are based on clashes of DG administrative cultures: clashes which, in a few cases, involve conflicts of DG 'missions' regarding what should be done and by what means. Michelle Cini explores two contrasting DG administrative cultures in Chapter 4. (Other studies of administrative culture in the Commission include Abélès *et al.*, 1993, and Bellier 1994.)

The DG which is most commonly at odds with other DGs over policy matters is DGIV. This is primarily because, as Cini shows, its treaty obligations and the mission culture of its officials incline it to non-interventionist economic policies and the removal of anti competitive business practices, whereas officials in other DGs – perhaps supported, or even led, by their Commissioner – take the view that there are circumstances in which market imperatives should be relaxed and other priorities should be emphasised. DGs with which DGIV sometimes clashes include DGIII (Industry), DGVII (Transport), DGXI (Environment), and DGXIII (Telecommunications).

THE COMMISSION'S POSITION IN THE EUROPEAN UNION SYSTEM

The Commission is at the heart of the EU system of governance. It is so by virtue of being a key actor in EU decision-making processes. The nature of these decision-making processes, and the Commission's role within them, varies, but in all of the major types of EU decision-making the Commission is a significant participant.

A useful way of differentiating between the Commission's decision-making roles is in terms of its position in relation to the main types of decisions that are produced by the EU:

Directional decisions

Decisions concerning the general direction of the EU – covering such matters as constitutional reform, EMU, accessions, and major policy innovations – are taken by the European Council. Because of the composition of this body (it consists of Heads of Government, Foreign Ministers, and the President and one Vice President of the Commission), because it (almost invariably) takes its decisions by unanimity, and because it is not subject to any treaty restrictions, it might be thought that the Commission's influence within it would be minimal. However, although there certainly are examples of the Commission being disappointed by European Council deliberations – it has long wanted, for example, a more integrationist position to be taken towards institutional reform – its influence within the Council has clearly been important on issues such as budgetary expansion and reform, the development of the social dimension, and EU policy towards Eastern Europe. The principal means used by the Commission to exercise an important role within the European Council have been the submission of policy papers of various kinds (sometimes on its own initiative and sometimes at the request of the European Council itself) and pro-activity by the President (especially during Delors' occupancy of the presidential post).

Legislative decisions

There are four main EU legislative procedures: consultation, cooperation, co-decision and assent. The ultimate decision-maker under the consultation and cooperation procedures is the Council of Ministers, and under the co-decision and assent procedures it is the Council and the EP. However, under all four procedures the Commission is strategically placed in three extremely important respects: it enjoys the exclusive formal right to initiate and draft proposals, (the Council and the EP only have the formal right to request the Commission to bring forward proposals); it is extremely difficult for either the Council or the EP to amend Commission proposals against its will; and, alone of the EU institutions, the Commission is physically present at every legislative stage, so it is extremely well placed to try to influence content and progress so as to suit its preferences and its advantage.

Common Commercial Policy decisions
Within the framework of the Common Commercial Policy
(CCP), the Commission negotiates on behalf of all fifteen
EU Member States with third countries in respect of trading relations. It is restricted in what it can do in that it is
obliged to negotiate on the basis of mandates laid down for
it by the Council of Ministers, and agreements which it reaches
with trading partners are subject to ratification by the Council.
Nonetheless, the Commission's room for manoeuvre is usually not inconsiderable, and evidence (much of it admit-
tedly anecdotal in character) abounds of the Commission
persuading the Council to its view of what is and is not
possible, and of when and when not to come to an agreement, in particular negotiating circumstances.

Pillar two and pillar three decisions
Under pillars two (Common Foreign and Security Policy
(CFSP)) and three (cooperation in the fields of Justice and
Home Affairs (JHA)) of the TEU, decision-making is mainly
intergovernmental in character and the Member States are
the dominant actors. However, the Commission can exercise influence under both pillars. It is, in the words of the
TEU, 'fully associated' with both pillars, it has a (non-ex-
clusive) right of initiation, and it is frequently asked to provide information and to tender advice.

Budgetary decisions
Two different sorts of decisions are taken about the EU's
budget. The first involves the setting of medium-term financial
perspectives which lay down a framework for overall income
and expenditure and which provide for the planned increase
and decrease of particular categories of expenditure. Two
financial perspectives have been adopted to date, covering
the years 1988–92 and 1993–9. Decisions about the contents
of financial perspectives are a matter for national governments, with final decisions being taken in the European
Council, but their deliberations are based in large part on
information and recommendations which are put before them
by the Commission. The second sort of decision concerns
the annual budget. This has to be agreed jointly by the EP
and the Council of Ministers, but negotiations start with,

and are largely framed by, the preliminary draft budget which is drawn up by the Commission.

Administrative decisions

Many different sorts of decisions are taken in regard to the implementation of EU policies. In one way or another, the Commission is involved in them all. This involvement takes three broad forms. First, the Commission has some powerful direct implementation powers. The most important of these are in the sphere of competition policy, where the Commission can, under the European Community (EC) Treaty, take direct action – including imposing very large fines on companies – in respect of a range of unfair trading practices, and where it also has the responsibility, under the 1989 Merger Control Regulation, to make judgements about proposed mergers between large companies. Second, many implementation decisions, such as those involving agricultural price alterations in the framework of the Common Agricultural Policy (CAP), involve minor 'updating' adjustments to existing legislation. These adjustments usually take the form of administrative legislation and are issued as Commission regulations or decisions. In respect of such implementing decisions the Commission normally has to work with, or through, specialised committees. There are three main types of such specialised committees and the Commission's formal powers vary under each: advisory committees, which are mainly composed of sectional interest representatives and national experts, only have – as their name suggests – the power to advise; management committees, which are composed of governmental representatives (usually officials from a relevant ministry), can block Commission decisions by a qualified majority; and regulatory committees, whose composition is much the same as that of management committees, must give their approval to Commission decisions by a qualified majority. In practice, the Commission is not usually inconvenienced by any of these types of committees. Third, the Commission has monitoring, watching brief, and legal guardianship responsibilities to ensure that the agencies in the Member States which undertake most of the day to day implementation of EU policies perform their tasks in a proper manner and in

conformity with EU laws. Much of this monitoring work is
undertaken on an informal basis, but formal powers – including the referral of cases to the Court of Justice and
(since the TEU) the imposition of fines on Member States
– are available.

The situation in which the Commission is positioned in regard to these different types of decision-making procedures
thus varies. Leaving aside administrative decisions, which are
a special sort of category, the Commission's position is strongest where legislative decisions are being made, for in respect of these it has full authority to be an active participant
at every stage of the decision-making cycle: conception,
agenda-setting, formulation, decision taking, implementation,
and evaluation. The Commission's position is weakest when
directional and pillars two and three decisions are being
made. This is partly because these decisions emanate from
procedures and structures which are predominantly intergovernmental in character, and partly because the Commission enjoys no exclusive rights under these procedures –
such as the exclusive rights it has under other procedures
to formulate the preliminary draft budget, to draft legislative proposals, or to negotiate on behalf of the EU (in the
context of the CCP).
  However, the Commission's potential for influencing EU
decision-making is not just a consequence of its positioning
and its formal powers in decision-making procedures. The
nature of EU decision-making is so extremely complex, with
a multiplicity of governmental and non-governmental actors
at national and EU levels interacting with one another through
a multiplicity of channels, that the Commission has many
opportunities to play roles and to exercise influence over
and above its formal responsibilities. So, for example, it can
be, and often is, an important broker and mediator of interests at many different points of EU policy processes: in,
for instance, the consultative and advisory committees that
are clustered around the Commission and which bring together – usually under its chairmanship – representatives of
sectional interests; in Council of Ministers meetings which
it attends at all levels (working parties, Permanent Representatives, and Ministers) and in which it is an influential

(non voting) participant; and in Council–EP exchanges and relations, where the presence of the Commission at all important meetings in and between both institutions puts it in an advantageous position to know what would probably be acceptable to both institutions and, therefore, what sort of agreements and what sort of progress may be possible.

Closely related to, and overlapping with, brokering and mediatory functions, the Commission also has the potential to be an important facilitator of EU decision-making procedures. This is so, for example, as a result of the many occasions in which it finds itself, or it can present itself, as the body which is best positioned and is best able to provide the necessary informational bases for decision-making. This ability to use its position as a key informational source to act as a facilitator of decision-making is seen in all EU decision-making processes, from European Council directional decisions – which are very frequently based on Commission papers embodying recommendations – to some pillar two CFSP decisions – most notably those which involve linkages to EC trade policy concerns.

CONDITIONS DETERMINING THE USE THAT CAN BE MADE OF THE COMMISSION'S POSITION

The Commission is thus extremely well positioned to exercise a range of very important formal and informal roles in the EU's decision-making system(s). But good strategic positioning is not enough if these roles are to be exercised effectively. If they are to be so, other conditions must also be favourable. Three such conditions are especially important: the Commission must have access to appropriate resources over and above the resource of favourable positioning; other powerful actors – most notably the European Council, the Council of Ministers, and to a lesser extent the EP – must be receptive, or at least not too resistant, to the notion of the Commission exercising important roles; and the Commission must have clear ideas as to what it wishes to do and it must be willing to assert itself to give effect to such ideas – particularly in those decision-making situations where it is not in command of exclusive rights and where its formal powers are circumscribed or are even weak.

It is beyond the reach of this chapter to examine these three conditions in depth, but brief observations on each of them are in order so as to further demonstrate how considerable is the potential, and often is the actual, role and influence of the Commission within EU decision-making.

Commission resources

The Commission can seek to make use of a number of resources to take advantage of its strategic positions in the EU's decision-making systems. The most important of these resources are:

Constitutional powers

The Commission has a range of constitutional powers available to it, some of which have already been referred to above. Two treaty articles which have not, as yet, been specifically mentioned, combine to give the Commission the power to bring forward proposals on almost any policy matter which can be construed as falling within the (very broad) remit of the EC Treaty. The first of these Treaty articles is Article 155, which charges the Commission with ensuring 'the proper functioning and development of the common market'. The second is Article 235, which empowers the Commission to bring forward proposals if 'action by the Community should prove necessary to attain, in the course of the operation of the common market, one of the objectives of the Community and this Treaty has not provided the necessary powers'.

Knowledge and expertise

The Commission is the main single source of knowledge and expertise about the content and impact of EU policies. It is a knowledge and expertise which takes many forms, ranging from an awareness of the opinions of transnational companies on existing and prospective EU policies, to an understanding of the issues involved in setting or revising EU-wide standards in highly complex technical and/or scientific areas. This knowledge and expertise is acquired not only from the Commission's own direct fact finding efforts, which in many policy areas are limited in scope because of low staffing resources, but also from a variety of other sources: from the agencies in the Member States which implement EU policies; from participation in networks of key policy actors in some policy areas – policy networks which, in some cases, it has itself promoted and encouraged; from the hundreds of officially established consultative and advisory committees which it manages; and from subcontracted work which is undertaken on the Commission's behalf by consultancy firms, research institutes, and academic institutions. The knowledge and expertise which these various sources provide for the Commission can be used for purposes such as promoting policy innovations, suggesting policy revisions, and resisting demands for policy changes.

Impartiality and neutrality
Since the Commission was established in the 1950s (initially as the High Authority of the European Coal and Steel Community), an important part of the thinking behind it has been that it should represent a Community interest or perspective, as opposed to the national viewpoints represented in the Council. Accordingly, notwithstanding the fact that Commissioners are national and political appointees, they are charged to act 'in the general interest of the Community' and to be 'completely independent in the performance of their duties' (Art. 157, EC). Most EU decision-making participants accept that in practice the Commission does indeed – for the most part at least – formulate its proposals in the general interest, does keep a reasonable distance from narrow national and sectional pressures, and does take its decisions with the EU interest as a whole in view. This perception of the Commission as being the 'conscience' of the Union gives it an advantage over other EU actors, who are usually viewed as being partial in their interests and who are thus regarded with some suspicion when they launch initiatives and seek to influence decision-making.

The motor role
Closely related to perceptions of the Commission as being the 'conscience' of the Union are widely held perceptions of it as the Union's 'motor' or 'engine'. That is to say, it is the EU institution that is most commonly looked to for ideas

and initiatives. Perceptions of this kind are so ingrained amongst EU decision-makers and would-be decision influencers that the Commission is sometimes criticised for lack of innovation and drive if it is seen as not bringing forward proposals which are judged to be sufficiently imaginative. This motor role is readily accepted by most Commissioners and Commission officials: before taking up office Commissioners-designate usually hope for, and often lobby for, portfolios in 'leading edge' policy areas, whilst the more thrusting and ambitious of officials usually seek appointment to DGs and to posts which are concerned with policy development rather than with policy implementation.

Relative cohesion

The Commission is, as was noted above, and as is further noted in subsequent chapters of this book, subject to internal divisions of various sorts at both College and DG levels. However, as compared with the EU's other main institutions – the European Council, the Council of Ministers, and the EP – it is relatively cohesive. When political and national differences give rise to difficulties within the Commission they are not usually as sharp or as enduring as in the other institutions, and they are certainly not as publicly proclaimed or as contested. This relative cohesion is clearly an important power resource, not least in that it greatly assists an ability to be proactive as opposed to simply reactive.

The standing and status of Commissioners

Commissioners are people of political standing and of experience. As Andrew MacMullen shows in his chapter, before their appointment most Commissioners have held senior political positions in their own countries, usually at ministerial level. On coming to Brussels, they join an institution whose profile has increased greatly since the 'relaunch' of the Community in the mid-1980s and they become a member of a body (the College) whose legitimacy has been strengthened by virtue of the TEU provision that it be endorsed by the EP before assuming office. Both the College and individual Commissioners thus enjoy standing and status, which have the potential to be marshalled with effect.

The position of the President
Over the years, a number of factors have combined to establish a high status and potentially very influential position for the occupant of the Commission Presidency. These factors include the generally increased importance of the EU, the attendance of the President at high profile meetings such as the European Council and Group of Seven (G7) Summits, the vigour and the dynamism which Jacques Delors brought to the post, and the assumption by presidents of important portfolio responsibilities. A forceful and clear-thinking president can, as Helen Drake shows in Chapter 12 in respect of Delors, do much to advance Commission views (which may have stemmed from the President himself) and to promote the position of the Commission in the EU system.

Perceptions by other EU actors of the role of the Commission

The ability of the Commission to make use of its resources depends in considerable measure on the ways in which its roles and its potential roles are viewed by the other main EU decision-makers. Notwithstanding the advantageous general perceptions which were noted above of the Commission as the conscience and motor of the Union, specific perceptions can vary according to circumstances, with consequences for what the Commission can and cannot do.

Perceptions are least important for what might be called the treaty based, regularised, administrative and quasi-administrative roles which are allotted to the Commission. So, for example, in respect of the preparation of the preliminary draft budget, the management and implementation of the CAP, and the conduct of negotiations to open up an overseas market, Member States may sometimes not like Commission actions and recommendations, but they do not normally query its right to be engaged in actions or to be making recommendations.

Queries, spilling over sometimes into resistance, can, however, arise in relation to broader and more informal Commission roles. Much depends on the mood of the times, as is demonstrated in the contrast between the 1985–92 period and the periods preceding and succeeding it. Before 1985 and for a time after 1992 the mood was not favourable in the sense that there was no great desire on the part of the Member States, or at least a sufficient number of Member States, to be pressing ahead with policy development at the European level. The consequence of this was that the Commission was hesitant about bringing forward ambitious or far-reaching policy proposals except where special circumstances were seen (by at least some key actors) as applying – as with, for example, the perceived need in the early 1980s to tackle Europe's lack of competitiveness in information technology (IT) and the perceived need in the 1990s to alleviate the problem of persisting high levels of unemployment. (The first of these perceptions led to the development of Commission promoted and sponsored IT research and collaboration programmes, and the second resulted in a major Commission White Paper [1993a] and a range of specific action programmes – the most notable of these being directed towards the development of Trans-European Networks.) Between 1985-92, by contrast, the mood was favourable in that there was a widely held desire to confront policy problems and policy failures and there was a willingness to seek new types of solutions. It was a period, as Wayne Sandholtz (1993a) has described it, of policy adaptation: 'Under such circumstances international organisations (like the Commission) can seize the initiative to supply new models and strategies and to promote bargains. Policy crises provide opportunities for activist, entrepreneurial IO (international organisation) leaders to marshal states behind a cooperative solution' (p. 252). The most important solution identified and pursued by the Commission during this period was the completion of the internal market, but others of great significance included the expansion and reform of the structural funds, the development of the social dimension, and rapid movement towards EMU (the last of these being associated not so much with the Commission as a whole but rather with Jacques Delors – who succeeded in persuading Chancellor Kohl to arrange for him to be appointed chairman of the committee of bankers and financiers that submitted a blueprint for EMU to the 1989 Madrid European Council).

The mood of the times is thus important for perceptions of the Commission, as a predisposition to integrationist advance means that the Commission is likely to be viewed as an important vehicle for progress – except in policy areas where the preference is for proceeding on an inter-governmentalist basis. However, factors in addition to the climate of the times can also shape perceptions of the Commission and of its role. So, for example, perceptions can become somewhat negative if the Commission is seen as having made misjudgments, as being ineffective (either generally or in a particular policy area), or as being divided. In this context, there is no doubt that the Delors II and III Commissions were undermined by well-publicised disputes between Commissioners and by the blame which was attached to the Commission for the rejection of the TEU in the Danish referendum of June 1992 (Delors, in particular, being accused of having been over enthusiastic in his integrationist rhetoric in the period leading up to the referendum).

Commission visions, resolve, strategies, and tactics

The visions, the resolve, the strategies and the tactics of the Commission must be tailored to the climate of the times, or at least they must if the Commission is not to experience recurring frustrations and defeats in unpromising times and accusations of not being up to the task in promising times. That said, the existence of clear visions and firm resolve, and the use of appropriate strategies and tactics, can do much to ensure that the Commission does not just follow events, but can do much to encourage, promote, and even lead them.

The contrast which is often made in this context is between the Commission led by Gaston Thorn (1981–4) and its successors led by Jacques Delors – or, at least, the Delors-led Commissions up to the point of the June 1992 Danish referendum. Criticism of the Thorn Commission has perhaps been overstated, not least since some of its initiatives and proposals were picked up and used when the climate was more favourable from the mid-1980s. However, there can be no doubt that the Delors Commissions were more forcefully led, did produce much more in the way of grand visions and major initiatives (notably those related to the Single European Market programme, EMU, and the social dimension), and did make fuller use of a wide range of strategies and tactics to advance progress with its ideas and initiatives. On this latter point, strategies and tactics which came to be more heavily used under Delors included: greater reliance on a regulatory policy approach (which tends to produce less political opposition than an approach resting on EU budgetary expenditure since the 'winners' and the 'losers' are not so obvious and since also the financial costs of implementing such policies do not usually fall directly on public exchequers); the mobilisation and cultivation of supportive policy networks with, as appropriate, European-wide, national, and subnational policy actors; the issuing of major policy discussion papers – often as White or Green Papers; and the use of 'soft law' – in the form of non-binding declarations, opinions, and recommendations.

It is necessary, however, to avoid making too many generalisations about differences between overall Commission behaviour at particular points in time because important differences in respect of vision, resolve, and strategical and tactical acumen always exist within the Commission. The thrust, the competence, and the imagination of Commissioners and leading Commission officials are important factors in making some parts of the Commission more dynamic than others. In this context it is striking how the 'Brussels circuit' is usually in broad agreement regarding which Commissioners and which DGs are providing innovation and drive, and which are, at best, treading water.

Perhaps the most cited example of a Commissioner, Delors apart, bringing innovation and drive to the job is Etienne Davignon who, in his capacity as Industry Commissioner between 1977 and 1984, was able to do much, despite operating in a relatively unfavourable climate, to generate interest and support for collaborative activity at the EC level in the area of information technology. As Sandholtz (1992a) has observed, 'The Commission's drive to win approval for a Community IT programme began with the appointment of Etienne Davignon as Commissioner of Industry' (p. 13). Other Commissioners who have successfully promoted and helped to carry through significant innovations and developments in their spheres of responsibility include: Raymond MacSharry, Agriculture Commissioner in the Delors I Commission, who led a drive for major reforms in the CAP; Peter Sutherland in the Delors 1 Commission and Sir Leon Brittan in the Delors II Commission who, as Competition Commissioner, both prompted the Commission to become much more active in using its powers under the EEC Treaty to outlaw unfair and uncompetitive trading practices; and Padraig Flynn, Social Affairs Commissioner in the Delors III and Santer Commissions, who succeeded a Commissioner widely viewed as being ineffective and who, assisted in no small measure by the TEU Social Protocol, helped to give social policy development a considerable thrust.

THE IMPACT OF THE COMMISSION ON EU DECISION-MAKING

With its favourable positionings in EU decision-making processes, with its extensive array of resources, and with its potential for marshalling vision and determination, the Commission would thus appear to be capable of exercising a very considerable impact on EU decision-making. Does it, in practice, make such an impact?

There is a considerable debate amongst scholars about this. It is a debate which is closely linked to the wider debate about the nature of the integrationist process as a whole in that those who propound, or have some sympathy with, neofunctionalist and supranational interpretations of European integration usually make much of the Commission's impact, whilst those who take a more intergovernmentalist view play it down.

This debate about the Commission's impact focuses primarily on the innovative and policy formulative aspects of EU decision-making rather than on the routine and the administrative aspects. That this should be so is understandable enough, for in undertaking its routine and administrative roles the Commission is obliged to work within frameworks, references, and specifications which have been laid down by – or at least have been formally approved by – the Council of Ministers. However, the extent to which the

Commission is constrained when it undertakes these roles
should not be overstated for, as both Guy Peters and Roger
Levy demonstrate in their chapters, some of the tasks associated with the roles do permit the Commission considerable room for manoeuvre. This is seen, for example, in the
potential which it has for making use of its position as the
EU's external trade negotiator, and the information and
understandings which it acquires from this position, to persuade the Council to particular points of view. It is seen
too in the exercise of its responsibilities to ensure that EU
law is applied properly in the Member States. This task of
monitoring the implementation of EU law can involve having to make delicate and politically charged judgements –
embracing such considerations as the implications for policy
development, Member State sensitivities, and the Commission's own institutional interests – on when, and by what
means, to initiate non-compliance actions. Where an activist monitoring line is taken – as, very notably, it has been
with competition policy since the mid-1980s – policy content itself can be considerably advanced, especially if the
Court of Justice is supportive of Commission actions. (On
this monitoring of law compliance task, see Mendrinou, 1996.)

It is, however, in respect of the innovative and formulative
aspects of decision-making, and in respect of 'macro' as
opposed to 'micro' decision-making, that most of the debate concerning the Commission's impact has been focused.
That the Commission is an active participant in such decision-making is not in dispute, but the extent to which it is
an independent participant, making its own distinctive contribution to policy outcomes, is sharply contested. The difference of view is centred on, as Mark Pollack puts it in Chapter
6, whether the Commission is a principal decision-making
actor or whether the Member States, and especially the larger
Member States, are the only real principals and the Commission is essentially but their agent.

The view that the Commission is essentially an agent is
associated particularly with Andrew Moravcsik who, in a series
of articles (1991, 1993, 1995) advancing an intergovernmentalist – or, as he calls it, a liberal intergovernmentalist
– view of the integration process, has argued that there is
little evidence that the Commission merits being viewed as

an independent actor significantly influencing major policy outcomes. He acknowledges that the Commission is a useful facilitator of decision-making, but not that it is a determiner of decisional content. 'While Commission involvement may sometimes expedite agreement, it has often been strikingly counterproductive and appears only rarely to have made a decisive contribution' (Moravcsik, 1995, p. 620).

Moravcsik's views have been criticised from a number of directions. Regarding his portrayal of the Commission as being confined to essentially supporting roles when major decisions are being made, the major thrust of the criticisms is that he concentrates too much on the formal decision-*taking* stage and not enough on earlier stages of decision-*making*. Moravcsik's critics readily acknowledge that at the decision-taking stage the representatives of Member States, meeting in the forums of the European Council and of the Council of Ministers, are indeed the formal decision-makers. But, they suggest, is it not the case that what happens at this stage is shaped and directed by developments at earlier decision-making stages: stages in which the Commission plays a leading role? In short, it is argued that the Commission is an important decision-making participant and influence in its own right, but this only becomes apparent if attention is directed beyond formal and final decision taking to the whole decision-making process, and in particular is directed towards the preparation of the decision-taking ground. As Daniel Wincott (1995) argues in the context of a critique of Moravcsik's repudiation of any significant role for the Commission in the launching of the 1985 SEM programme.

> the basic, innovative policy techniques required for the internal market programme had been fashioned in the daily work of the supranational institutions (essentially the Commission and the Court of Justice) long before the Member States considered these issues ... The creation of these policy techniques certainly cannot be regarded as a sufficient condition for the '1992' project ... [but] ... their creation constituted a necessary condition for the intergovernmental bargains struck in the autumn of 1985. (p. 606)

In support of his view that EU policy outcomes are not much influenced by Commission preferences, Moravcsik (1995) points to a number of examples which he believes provide evidence for his case: the CAP regime that was fashioned in the 1960s along lines which meant the Commission 'failed to achieve most of its major goals'; the process of monetary integration since 1970 in which the Commission is regarded as having been largely marginalised; and the Maastricht political union negotiations in which the Commission is seen as playing virtually no significant role – apart from when it teamed up half way through the negotiations with the Dutch Presidency to present a revised draft treaty which was quickly rejected by almost all other Member States.

A similar interpretation to that of Moravcsik of the policy impact of the Commission is provided by Mark Pollack (1995a) in his analysis of the 1988 and 1992 reforms and expansions of the structural funds. The decisional outcomes in both years are, Pollack contends, to be explained primarily in terms of intergovernmental bargaining and changing national interests. Drawing on his case study material, Pollack argues that the Commission can be a useful facilitating actor in EU decision-making, but the Member States establish the context in which the Commission functions and it is within this context that the precise roles and influence of the Commission are specified.

The examples cited by Moravcsik and Pollack are far from being the only instances of the Commission desiring, but being unable, to exercise a decisive influence over decisional outcomes. Other examples of Commission 'failure' are not difficult to find. In recent years they include matters as diverse as: the inability to persuade the governments of the Member States to give to the Commission the control over the authorisation over company mergers it has sought (see Bulmer, 1994a); the lack of progress made in the Council of Ministers with Commission proposals for a carbon energy tax (see Zito, 1995); and the failure in 1996 to persuade the European Council to transfer unspent CAP budgetary allocations to spending on transport infrastructure networks.

But evidence that the Commission's preferences do not always prevail does not mean that there are not circumstances and instances in which it does take a leading role and exercise considerable influence within EU decision-making forums. It is indisputably the case that the Commission is not a principal formal policy actor at the big, set piece, occasions when 'macro' decisions are formally taken, and it is also the case that it is not a final decision-taker on important and sensitive policy issues. However, it very often – especially in the context of the EC pillar of the TEU – has a very significant impact on what policy issues are considered by the formal decision-takers, in what terms they are considered, when they are considered, by whom they are considered, and with what receptivity they are considered. Several chapters in the book – most notably those by Liesbet Hooghe, Tom Lawton, Lee McGowan, and Desmond Dinan – bear witness to the Commission making such impacts on EU policies. A number of published case studies have borne similar witness. Amongst these case studies are:

- Sandholtz and Zysman (1989) have, like Moravcsik, examined the launching of the internal market programme in the mid-1980s and they conclude, amongst other things, that the Commission took advantage of an increasingly favourable attitudinal climate to shape the tone and direction of the debate, to provide the focus for specific policy deliberations, and to persuade key governmental and non governmental actors that nothing short of a bold and wide ranging programme of action would do: 'The international and domestic situations provided a setting in which the Commission could exercise policy entrepreneurship, mobilizing a transnational coalition in favour of the unified internal market' (p. 100).

- In a similar vein, Sandholtz (1993a) has argued that in the sphere of telecommunications policy the Commission, from the early 1980s, 'played the leading role in promoting collective action . . . The engine pulling the EC towards a common, liberal, modernized telecommunications regime has been the Commission of the European Communities . . . The Commission initiated the proposals for market opening, set the agenda for Community deliberations, and pushed for approval of specific directives. In every instance, the Commission was ahead of the member states in its objectives for EC-level reforms' (pp. 242, 254–5, and 267 respectively).

- Fuchs (1994 and 1995) has taken a similar view to Sandholtz of telecommunications developments, arguing that 'the Commission has played an essential role in the process of restructuring European telecommunications, not the least because it cleverly exploited the situation of insecurity and change dominant in this field on the national level' (1995, p. 414).

- Analysing how decisions were made about the size and content of the EU's Fourth Framework Research Programme, which was adopted in 1994, Peterson (1995) makes the point that although the decision-making process was characterised by considerable political argument and froth in the Council of Ministers about the overall size of the budget, the Commission got most of what it wanted. It was able to do this by making use of a number of resources, most particularly its detailed knowledge of ongoing and relatively uncontroversial sub-programmes and its close working relationships with key expert and user groupings via an elaborate web of policy networks. Cuttingly, he notes 'while ministers and MEPs were still bickering (in 1993) about the broad parameters of the Framework IV Program, the Commission and its advisers were effectively making many crucial decisions that would determine which proposed projects and firms benefited from EU support' (p. 402).

- In a quite different policy area, equal opportunities, Sonia Mazey (1995) has commented on the Commission's policy promotional activities, noting that its role has been crucial in creating and using policy networks and in steering and managing incrementalist policy development.

- In the sphere of energy policy, Janne Matlary (1997a) shows how the Commission has played a central role in developing policy and edging (very slowly) the EU towards what the Commission hopes will eventually be a common energy policy. In so doing, the Commission has used approaches that it has also used in several other policy areas: the mobilisation of supportive networks (with large industrial users especially important in this case); the linking of the policy to other policy developments (with the completion of the internal market and the protection of the environment being cited by the Commission as requiring a more developed energy policy); the forceful use of such policy and legal instruments as are already in its possession (with, for example, EC Treaty competition powers being tested, if necessary in the Court of Justice); and bringing forward ambitious proposals, even when it is recognised they may run into political difficulties.

There is, therefore, a considerable body of evidence indicating that the Commission exercises, in its own capacity, a considerable influence not only over routine and administrative decision-making but also over innovative and policy decision-making. The nature of this influence can vary over time and from sector to sector, with probably the most pervasive, recurring, and important influence stemming from the Commission's policy entrepreneurial activities. These activities take various forms. They can, for example, involve the Commission seeking to create opportunities for the launching of new initiatives – by, perhaps, working through transnational networks which can be used to bring pressure on governments – and by launching such initiatives when it seems appropriate to do so. Equally, they can involve the more modest, but no less crucial, task of picking up on, and exploiting, opportunities as they are presented: most notably by offering European-level solutions to problems that are concerning key policy actors.

CONCLUSIONS

The Commission is at the heart of the Union in all sorts of ways. It undertakes a large number of responsibilities, it exercises a wide variety of roles, and it is the institution which is most readily associated with what the EU does.

This position of the Commission at the heart of the Union arises in large part because of the many tasks which have been assigned to it by the treaties, by secondary legislation, and by other EU institutions. It arises partly too, however, because the Commission has actively sought, and has often taken advantage of, opportunities to strengthen its positions and to extend its roles. As Fuchs (1995) observes in the context of EU telecommunications policy 'The common element that can be detected despite all the differing, sometimes contradictory, activities of the Commission is a conscious effort to extend the prerogative of the Commission and the institutions related to it' (p. 472). Majone (1991, 1992 and 1994a) and Cram (1993, 1994, and 1995) have also commented on the Commission's desire to increase its influence and competences, with both showing how progress has been made – sometimes in seemingly unpromising circumstances and policy areas – in furthering this desire via the astute use of a variety of strategies, tactics and techniques. As Cram (1995) has observed, the Commission 'has learned to respond to opportunities for action as they present themselves, and has attempted to facilitate the emergence of these opportunities' (p. 8).

Clearly, therefore, the Commission is much more than an administrative institution, implementing, servicing, and coordinating the ideas, the needs, and the decisions of others. It is also a proactive policy-oriented institution. There are several, in practice overlapping, aspects to this, from its involvement in policy networking activities of various kinds to its willingness to generate initiatives and make proposals 'of its own' (in so far as any proposal from any quarter in such a multi-faceted and interlocking organisation as the EU can be described as being 'of its own').

The Commission is thus very much an institution which needs to be understood. The chapters which follow have been written with the purpose of helping to develop such an understanding.

Note

1. The author would like to thank Clive Archer for his comments on a draft of this chapter.

2 European Commissioners 1952–1995: National Routes to a European Elite

Andrew MacMullen

INTRODUCTION

In the study of national governmental systems the analysis of the recruitment and composition of the political personnel of the executive branch is a standard feature. This typically includes the socio-economic background of cabinet ministers, the mechanisms and patterns of their recruitment, and the identification of trends over time. While the powers and functions of the European Commission, and the staffing of its permanent bureaucracy, have received much attention, there has been no systematic study of the Commissioners as a group. This chapter makes a first step towards filling this gap.[1] It gathers data on the highest political level of the European Commission – the Commissioners themselves.[2] The focus is on the characteristics of the College of Commissioners and changes in its nature over time. At its most simple it attempts to answer the basic questions: where do Commissioners come from and what sort of people are they? The factors investigated include: patterns of appointment and tenure of service; gender and age; education and previous occupation; political experience and affiliations; and involvement in European and international organisations.

The personnel studied are the Members of the High Authority of the European Coal and Steel Community (ECSC) from 1952–67, Commissioners of the European Economic Community (EEC) and European Atomic Energy Community (Euratom) from 1958–67, and Commissioners of the merged executive of the European Communities (EC) and

Table 2.1   Commission Colleges: 1952–1995

College	Period	Duration (months)	Size	Holders (120 total)
ECSC HA1 (Monnet/Mayer)	Aug. 52–Aug. 59	85	9	12
ECSC HA2 (Malvestiti/Del Bo)	Sep. 59–Jun. 67	94	9	13
EURATOM 1 (Armand/Hirsch)	Jan. 58–Dec.61	48	5	6
EURATOM 2 (Chatenet)	Jan. 62–Jun. 67	66	5	7
EEC 1 (Hallstein I)	Jan. 58–Dec. 61	48	9	12
EEC 2 (Hallstein II)	Jan. 62–Jun. 67	66	9	10
EC 1 (Rey)	Jul. 67–Jun. 70	36	14	14
EC 2 (Malfatti)	Jul. 70–Dec. 72	30	9	10
EC 3 (Ortoli)	Jan. 73–Dec. 76	48	13	17
EC 4 (Jenkins)	Jan. 77–Dec. 80	48	13	13
EC 5 (Thorn)	Jan. 81–Dec. 84	48	14	17
EC 6 (Delors I)	Jan. 85–Dec. 88	48	14 + 3	18
EC 7 (Delors II)	Jan. 89–Dec. 92	48	17	17
EC 8 (Delors III)	Jan. 93–Dec. 94	24	17	18
EU 1 (Santer)	Jan. 95–Dec. 99	60	20	20

European Union (EU) from 1967–95. The names and chronology of the Commission Colleges are shown in Table 2.1. There have been fifteen Colleges since 1952, which have been made up of 120 individuals, half of whom have served in more than one College. In some cases major differences appeared between the periods for which particular Colleges or individuals were appointed to serve and those which actually took place. Thus, the first High Authority of the ECSC was prolonged in the aftermath of the 1958 'coal crisis' because of disagreements between the governments (especially France) over the replacement of the College. In this situation, the existing members were required to continue in office (in some cases under protest) until the eventual replacement was agreed. The same applied for its successor and the second EEC and Euratom Commissions in the aftermath of the 1965 crisis, so that the implementation of the Merger Treaty was delayed until the middle of 1967. The number of holders is, of course, normally greater than the size of any particular College of the Commission because of premature departures, either for age/health reasons or to take up some other position. At the individual level, vacancies were not always filled promptly or, in some cases, not at all before the next complete replacement of the College of Commissioners.

APPOINTMENT PROCEDURES

The basic framework for the appointment of Commissioners has always been defined in the various treaties establishing the European Communities. The constant factor has been the notion that Commissioners are chosen for their general competence, that they should be independent in the course of their duties, taking no instructions from any government or other body, and that governments should respect that principle. Individual Commissioners can only be removed before the expiry of their fixed term by the Court of Justice for incapacity or gross misconduct. No Commissioner has been removed for misconduct. One (Borschette) was retired in 1976 by the Court after suffering a stroke. Although certain broad principles – nomination of individuals by the governments of member states, with the concurrence of all the others, service for a fixed term, and the allocation of two Commissioners for 'large' countries and one for 'small' – are often viewed as having been followed from the start, there have been significant changes over time.

The ECSC in particular followed a unique scheme for the High Authority. Under Article 10 of the ECSC Treaty, eight members of the first High Authority were to be appointed by the governments by common accord. These eight were then to co-opt a ninth member, by at least five votes. After six years the members were to be appointed by a slightly different procedure, eight by the national governments, either acting unanimously or by five votes out of six, while the ninth was to be co-opted as before. Three members (chosen initially by lot) were to retire every two years, with a procedure for filling alternate vacancies by government nomination and co-option. Each government, however, also had the right to exercise a veto on each nominee (whether appointed by the national route or co-option). If a national veto was exercised more than two or four times (depending on the number of places to be filled) the question could be referred to the Court of Justice which had the power to declare the veto void. In fact the formal veto system appears never to have been used, and this rather tortuous process was never brought to a decision in the Court.

These provisions would have produced a continous rotating corporate existence for the collegiate leadership of the High Authority, with its nomination slightly insulated from direct control by national governments. This was a compromise which had resulted from the divergence between Monnet's original conception of a largely free-standing High Authority and the strongly expressed opposition in the ECSC negotiations of a number of governments (Monnet, 1978). There was no requirement that the College should include all nationalities; the only stipulations were that members should be nationals of Member States with no more than two from the same country. The Monnet High Authority in fact had two members each from France, Germany, and Belgium (including the co-opted member), and one each from Italy, Netherlands and Luxembourg. The second College started with two each for France, Germany, and Belgium (including the co-opted member), and one each for Italy, Netherlands and the Luxembourg. By 1967, following a series of retirements, cooptions, reappointments and replacements, and the non-replacement of President Del Bo who retired on health grounds, it consisted of two each from France, Germany, and Luxembourg, one each from Belgium (acting President) and the Netherlands, and no Italian.

The national grip was tightened in the provisions of the EEC and Euratom Treaties. Now all the Commissioners were to be appointed directly on the nomination of national governments acting unanimously, for a fixed term of four years. This procedure, with its shorter period of service, absence of co-option, and no restriction on the use of national vetos clearly signalled some potential reduction in the autonomy of Commissioners individually and collectively. The allocation of Commissioners between nationalities was made clearer, ensuring that there was an explicit balance. In the case of Euratom, it was clearly not possible for every nationality to be represented since there were only five Commissioners. Luxembourg lost out, but because of this the Luxembourg Government appointed a permanent representative to the Euratom Commission with a watching brief (Euratom, 1958).

In the case of the EEC, the informal national allocation formula which became conventional was clearly established from the start. This gave every country the right to one Commissioner and the three large states the right to two. It was the EEC model which was adopted when the three institutions were merged into a single EC Commission with effect from 1967 and then used through successive enlargements of the EC/EU from six to fifteen states. Consequently there were a series of incremental increases in the size of the College of Commissioners, in spite of continued criticism, most notably in the two 1979 reports on the European Institutions (Spierenburg, 1979; Committee of Three, 1979).

Reliable information on the processes by which Commissioners have been appointed is limited. The formal proceedings are private, and the important decisions are taken informally over lengthy periods within and between the various Member States. The final decision is reached at a meeting of national government representatives, normally at Foreign Minister level, but this is simply the formal conclusion of a series of intergovernmental consultations. It is clear that the general approach is not collective, and it is recognised that it is the prerogative of each government to nominate its own Commissioner(s), and there is little inclination for others

to interfere with that choice. Indeed one former Commissioner stated that 'the Council of Ministers' . . . always accepts
the nominees put forward by the national governments'
(Tugendhat, 1987, p. 159). The most obvious exceptions
relate to the higher-profile nomination of the President, where
there are collective negotiations and in some cases clear
national disagreement. In the aftermath of the 1965 crisis,
French objections to the renomination of Hallstein as President of the newly merged Commission were so strong that
his nomination was withdrawn entirely by the German government. The 1994 British veto of the Jean-Luc Dehaene and
his replacement by Jacques Santer was a dramatic illustra-
tion of the failure of informal processes in the context of
British political sensitivies dictated by domestic party considerations. The consultative process on the nomination of
ordinary members, involving from EC4 also the President-
elect, seems largely concerned with discreet jockeying for
position with regard to the distribution of portfolios amongst
the potential new Commissioners.

In this situation it is the nomination decisions of individual
governments which is crucial in determining the composition of the College. Each Commissioner is, in effect, inde-
pendently appointed, on the basis of national governmental
choices, so that the balance of the College derives from the
sum of these decisions and its cohesion is problematic. Nor
is there any other external discipline applied, as for example in the case of multi-party coalition governments where
the ministers representing different political parties must
cohere in order to maintain a working majority in the legislature. Only the recent changes introduced in the Maastricht
Treaty, applied for the first time to the Santer College, for
collective confirmation by the European Parliament may
produce a long-term structural change in this approach.

CHARACTERISTICS OF COMMISSIONERS

This study focuses on the outcome of the nationally-based
appointment process, rather than tracing the process by which
individuals have been nominated. By investigating tenure
in office and the social and political characteristics of those

Table 2.2   Age of Commissioners on Appointment 1952–1995

Age Range (inclusive)	First Appointment (N=120)	All Appointments (N=203)
35–39	3	3
40–44	14	11
45–49	17	14
50–54	24	24
55–59	22	26
60–64	13	15
65–69	7	7
	100 per cent	100 per cent

Note: All ages were counted to the nearest year integer. Where exact dates of birth were unknown, they were assumed to be 1 July for purposes of calculation.

Commissioners appointed, developments over time and national differences can be identified, and conclusions may be drawn regarding national policies on renomination of Commissioners and broader issues of autonomy from national governments.

Gender, age and tenure

One thing is clear about the personal characteristics of the 120 individuals who served as Commissioners in the period under study: as a group, Commissioners are mainly male, with 94 per cent (113 out of the 120 individuals) being men. For the first 37 years, the College of Commissioners was an exclusively male club, with the first (two) female Commissioners not being appointed until the Delors II Commission in 1989. The representation of women dropped to one in seventeen in the Delors III Commission before reaching five in twenty in the current Santer Commission.

The age range of Commissioners on appointment is shown in Table 2.2. It is very striking that nearly half first entered the College in their fifties. The 20 per cent starting at 60 or older comfortably outnumber the 17 per cent who commenced before the age of 45. The results for first appointments and all appointments are not very different. This is due to the fact that nearly half the Commissioners

Andrew MacMullen

Table 2.3   Terms Served by Commissioners 1952–1995

Country Commissioners*		No. of Terms Served (full or part)					
of origin		1	2	3	4	5	Average
Spain	3	0	1	1	1	0	3.0
Denmark	3	1	0	2	0	0	2.3
Netherlands	8	3	2	2	1	0	2.1
Belgium	8	3	2	2	1	0	2.1
Germany	16	5	7	3	0	1	2.1
Portugal	2	0	2	0	0	0	2.0
France	18	9	5	3	1	0	1.8
Italy	20	10	8	2	0	0	1.6
UK	9	5	3	1	0	0	1.6
Luxembourg	11	7	4	0	0	0	1.4
Ireland	6**	6**	1	0	0	0	1.3
Greece	4	4	0	0	0	0	1.0
ALL	108	52	35	16	4	1	1.8
% of all terms served		27	37	25	8	3	n/a

Notes:

* To avoid artificially inflating the number of single-term Commissioners, new starters in January 1995 have been excluded while those renominated to serve from that date have been credited with that term.

** In January 1981 the incumbent Irish Commissioner (Burke) was not renominated. He was replaced by O'Kennedy, who resigned in 1982, and Burke was then appointed and served through the rest of the Thorn Commission (EC5). Since Burke's two terms were interrupted by this hiatus (for reasons of partisan politics since he was a Fine Gael politician and there had been changes of government between Fine Gael and Fianna Fail), they have been treated as two single terms.

serve only one term (or less), and that these are disproportionately distributed in the higher age ranges.

The practice of governments in determining the number of terms their Commissioners should serve has varied considerably, as shown in Table 2.3. While the largest single group of Commissioners (52) are those nominated for a single term, these only account for 27 per cent of the terms served. The core of service (over 60 per cent) is provided by those Commissioners who served for two or three terms. While the figures may be subject to some distortion through retirements caused by ill health or death, particularly for the smaller countries,[3] they demonstrate the considerable variation among Commissioners as a body, and also between countries. The individual record for the number of terms is held by the German trade union official Wilhelm Haferkamp, who served through five Colleges from 1967 to 1984. But the absolute record in years belongs to the Belgian Albert Coppé, who served continuously for over twenty years from the creation of the High Authority in 1952 to the end of the Malfatti Commission in 1972. For more general purposes of comparison, the relative proportion of single-term appointments and the average number of terms served per Commissioner may be taken as significant indicators. It may be assumed, given the learning time in taking up a new post, that longer terms of service are generally associated with greater effectiveness in performance of a Commissioner's role. It might also provide more insulation from national government influences.

Service for only one term (or less) may be due to a number of causes: voluntary withdrawal to take a different post; voluntary retirement due to age; involuntary retirement through death, health or personal reasons; failure to reappoint by national government due to disagreement over policy; or redistribution of national patronage for partisan or personality reasons. In many cases of failure to renominate, it is not clear which factors are decisive, or indeed whether the publicly stated reasons are the genuine ones. With the exception of genuine health problems, the other cases may indicate limited autonomy from national government. Some appointments are clearly stop-gap nominations. Carrelli and Guazzaroni (Italy), and Bodson (Luxembourg), were all examples of nominees aged in their sixties who served very short periods to fill a gap. Malfatti (an Italian EC Commission President) and O'Kennedy (Ireland) are examples of a substantial number who served short terms in the Commission before losing interest and returning to national politics. Where Member States nominate individuals whose interest in the Commission is limited and of a lower priority than other prospective posts, this may be taken as evidence of the dominance of domestic political priorities.

The data seems to suggest that countries may be divided into groups regarding their appointment practices. Germany, the Netherlands, Belgium, and Denmark (plus Spain and Portugal on more limited evidence) have provided longer periods of service. France and Italy, very close to the EC mean, have mixed shorter and longer periods of service. Luxembourg would probably also share this group but for the unfortunate loss of members through death and ill-health. In the case of France, it is significant that most of the single terms of tenure occurred in the 1950s and 1960s, the period with the unstable political background of the Fourth Republic, the transition to the Fifth, and the distinctive views of President de Gaulle on European issues. Since then, all but one French Commissioner (Pisani) have served two or more terms. In the case of Italy, the single terms are distributed sporadically, and appear to be associated with domestic patronage requirements. There is some anecdotal evidence which suggests that most Italian politicians, in highly factionalised parties, have been reluctant to leave Rome for too long in case their domestic political position is compromised.[4] This is consistent with the evidence cited below of the marked lack of senior Italian ministerial figures. The UK has maintained a mixture of single and double terms, with only Leon Brittan achieving a third term. Ireland has allowed only one Commissioner to serve consecutive terms, while Greece has changed its Commissioner on every opportunity. The Irish and Greek examples demonstrate the effects of domestic politics through changes of party control in the national government. Alternation in power between Fianna Fail and Fine Gael, or New Democracy and PASOK, leads to straightforward exercises in partisan nomination for a single post. More consensual coalitional arrangements in Belgium, the Netherlands, Denmark and Portugal have provided more possibilities of continuity of representation even when there is only one post to be filled. Larger countries with two Commissioners can facilitate continuity since the posts can be allocated to different parties, whether coalition partners or government and opposition.

The great majority of single-term Commissioners who wished to serve longer but were denied renomination by their own governments appear to be straightforward cases of the reallocation of domestic political patronage. The incompatibility between nominating government and incumbent Commissioner indicates no particular clash on European policy, but is simply based upon party affiliation. In some cases there may have been complaints about ineffectiveness or inappropriate personal behaviour. But these are likely to be kept private, and there are some countervailing examples of notoriously inefficient Commissioners (Haferkamp being the classic example) who enjoyed renomination by their governments. There are however a limited number of exceptions, where clashes over policy are significant. After de Gaulle in the 1960s, Prime Minister Thatcher provided the most prominent case with her refusal to renominate Lord Cockfield at the end of his first term.

The mean age for each College at the start of its term is shown in Table 2.4. It appears that in the pre-merger period there was a tendency for the age to creep up with the significant levels of re-appointments. This reached its peak in the first merged Rey Commission in 1967 where a large number of 'veterans' were found places, and the average age was only kept down by the fact that three of the newcomers were relatively young. In the 1970s, as the veterans were phased out (none of the pre-merger members survived into the 1973 Ortoli Commission), the mean age came down, but then showed a significant increase again in the 1980s with Delors I showing a new peak. This was not a consequence of elderly members staying on, but of an infusion of older new blood.

The working of the appointment system has an influence on the continuity of the Colleges. The degree of overlap varies. Typically, about half the Commissioners from one College serve in the next, although they may be diluted by enlargement. But in some transitional periods, such as the Rey and Delors III Colleges, there was a particularly high level of stability, while Delors I saw a large infusion of new faces. The process of renewal also has implications for the political balance within each College.

Political affiliations

Some 81 per cent of Commissioners have possessed a public and explicit party identification, through political career or self-proclaimed membership. In terms of the major European families of political parties, 36 per cent have been Christian

Andrew MacMullen

Table 2.4   Age, Continuity and Political Balance at Appointment of
Colleges 1952–1995

College	Mean Age (Years)	Continuing Members in College	Political Score Left-Right (1–7)
ECSC HA1 (Monnet)	51.4	—	4.0
ECSC HA2 (Malvestiti)	54.0	6/9	3.6
EURATOM 1 (Armand)	50.4	—	4.2
EURATOM 2 (Chatenet)	52.0	4/5	4.6
EEC 1 (Hallstein I)	54.3	—	4.1
EEC 2 (Hallstein II)	55.2	8/9	4.4
EC 1 (Rey)	55.3	9/14	4.6
EC 2 (Malfatti)	50.3	5/9	3.9
EC 3 (Ortoli)	50.6	6/9 (13)	3.7
EC 4 (Jenkins)	51.0	6/13	3.5
EC 5 (Thorn)	54.8	8/13 (14)	4.4
EC 6 (Delors I)	56.8	4/14	3.6
EC 7 (Delors II)	53.8	8/17	3.8
EC 8 (Delors III)	56.2	10/17	4.1
EU 1 (Santer)	52.1	8/17 (20)	3.5

Democrats (including Gaullists and British Conservatives),
34 per cent Socialists and 11 per cent Liberals. The residual
19 per cent have included career diplomats and technocrats,

who might have been party members or sympathisers but have not left obvious public evidence of their party affiliation.

Mere party labels, however, are not entirely satisfactory in assessing the political complexion of the Colleges. Some parties are notably broad churches, with Christian Democrats being a good example where there may be very different business or trade union wings of the party. Liberal parties in Europe are divided into two camps, with a distinction between centrist social liberal parties and those on the right which are vigorously laisser-faire. The distinction between Christian Democracy and Liberalism in continental Europe is partly based on a confessional–secular divide which is largely irrelevant to the policy agenda of the Commission.

It is more helpful to place individual Commissioners on a left–right scale based upon economic and social policy, making divisions within parties where appropriate, and imputing positions to non party politicians where the evidence is available. On this principle, in Table 2.4, 94 per cent of Commissioners have been allocated scores, on a 7 point left–right scale from 1 (state intervention/collective provision) to 7 (laisser-faire/individualism). The 3.9 mean score for Commissioners lies almost exactly at the centre, on the intersection of social liberalism and the more centrist current in political catholicism. Long term, there has been a slight trend from right to left, with an average score of just over 4.1 in the Colleges of pre-merger period, just under 4.1 for the first five merged Commissions, and 3.8 from Delors I to Santer. In the first twenty years, there was an overall preponderance of Christian Democrats and business orientated Liberals, some of them technocrats rather than regular party politicians. Since then, the Commission has been increasingly politicised (as discussed below), and there has been an increasing proportion of Socialist, Social Democrat and Labour politicians. A dramatic example is the Santer Commission in which 10 of the 20 members of the College are Social Democrats.

Education

The great majority of Commissioners have enjoyed the benefits of university education.[5] Figures on numbers and subjects

Table 2.5   University Graduates

First Appointment	% Graduates	Degree Disciplines				
		Arts	Law	Econ	SocSc	SciTech
Pre-merger (HA1–EEC2) (N = 41)	78	0	50	19	0	31
EC1–5 (N = 36)	89	13	44	28	6	9
EC6–EU1 84 (N = 43)	3	50	25	11	1	1
All (N = 120)	83	5	48	24	6	17

Note. Where individuals possess more than one degree, the higher degree is normally taken. 'Econ' includes business studies. 'SocSc' includes sociology, political science, and public administration. 'SciTech' includes medicine.

studied are given in Table 2.5. The overall total of 83 per cent of Commissioners who are graduates could be further increased by including those who enjoyed further professional training which might possibly be considered of equivalent status.[6] Six of the non-graduates entered public life from a trade union/socialist politics background. Three of the remainder had their university education disrupted by war and political exile. Four others entered family businesses as their first employment experience.

There appears to have been little significant change in the overall level of education. The main interest is in the division between disciplines. Half the graduates have been educated in Law, the discipline considered most appropriate for senior public officials in much of continental Europe. Economics is next with a quarter of the graduates. Although science and technology appears to have a strong presence, this has declined significantly over time. Ten of the seventeen natural science graduates were appointed to the pre-merger Commissions. Nine of these were to the ECSC and to Euratom, and only one to the EEC. This pattern has been carried through into the merged Commissions, with a total of only four individuals with natural science degrees being appointed to the Delors and Santer Commissions. The

Table 2.6   Occupational Experience of European Commissioners on First Appointment

OCCUPATION	HA1–EEC2 N=41 %N	EC1–5 N=36 %N	EC6–EU1 N=43 %N	All N=120 %N
Private Business	39	6	26	24
Public Business	7	6	9	8
TU Official	7	3	7	6
Law	15	17	26	19
Education	17	14	28	20
Journalism	10	11	7	9
Other Professions	2	11	7	7
Official (Domestic)	39	31	16	28
Official (Foreign)	29	31	14	24

Note. Individuals are entered for all significant occupations in their career prior to first appointment to Commission, with the exception of political offices which are shown in Table 2.7. Percentages do not total 100 since many individuals have multiple entries.

educational background has increasingly been that of the generalist administrator in the public services or higher managers in the private sector. Education in the higher levels of the natural sciences and technology has become the exception.

Occupational background

The previous occupations of Commissioners are shown in Table 2.6. Over 50 per cent have served as permanent officials, in central civil service, sub-national government, and public sector agencies. These are fairly evenly divided between those with purely domestic posts, and those with a strong international aspect in foreign and diplomatic services and international trade institutions. There does appear to have been a decline in the number of officials in the most recent cohort, which is related to the increasing politicisation of the College. Commissioners with business experience are the second largest significant group. This declined in size in the 1970s, but has shown a resurgence from the 1980s. They have always out-numbered the continuing small group of trade union officials. There has been

Andrew MacMullen

Table 2.7   Political Experience of Commissioners on First
Appointment

POSITION	HA1–EEC2 N=41 %N	EC1–5 N=36 %N	EC6–EU1 N=43 %N	All N=120 %N
National Parliament	44	72	72	62
Directly elected EP	0	0	30	11
Government Minister	24	42	53	42
Foreign	0	24	22	18
Finance	10	24	43	30
Econ/Trade/Ind	70	47	48	52
Agriculture	20	29	26	26
Other	30	11	35	36
Junior Minister	5	14	16	12
None	49	28	14	30

Note. National Parliament includes UK House of Lords and other Upper Houses whether directly or indirectly elected.
Of the 13 directly elected MEPs, 7 were also national parliamentarians. Individuals may be entered under more than one ministerial portfolio category, but only once per portfolio and only once as a Government Minister. Percentages of portfolios do not total to 100 because of multiple entries.
Individuals are entered as Junior Ministers only if they have never served in a full ministerial position.

a growing representation of lawyers (in addition to the many legally qualified civil servants) and a significant element of intellectuals from education (mostly university staff but with some school teachers), and journalism. Commissioners with a substantial practical farming background are rare, but not those experienced in agricultural administration and politics. The overall impression is of domination by upper administrative and managerial occupations, with a leavening of other professional and intellectual groups. However, in many cases these occupations are quite remote, since more recent activities have been almost exclusively in the political sphere. There are a few cases where a professional political career started so early, usually via student politics, that other outside experience is minimal.

National political experience

Table 2.7 shows that, overall, more than two-thirds of Commissioners have previously held a clearly political office, such as membership of the national or the European Parliament (EP), or service as a government minister (senior or junior). The total figures of 62 per cent with parliamentary and 54 per cent with ministerial background should be considered in the context of a long term trend towards the politicisation of the College membership. In the pre-merger Colleges, only half of those appointed had any type of public political background, while in the more recent period the proportion has risen to 85 per cent. There has been a substantial increase in those with a national parliamentary background, from under a half to nearly three quarters of those entering in the more recent periods. Significantly these are being supplemented by those with elected experience in the EP.

Ministerial experience has increased even more dramatically, from 29 per cent to nearly 70 percent between the appointments in the first period and those of the Delors I–III and Santer Colleges. The nature of the ministerial portfolios has also changed. Former Agriculture Ministers, not surprisingly given the key role of the Common Agricultural Policy (CAP), have always been present. But while the Economics/Trade/Industry group has maintained its absolute representation, its relative share has decreased. The big change has been the arrival of Foreign and Finance Ministers. Indeed, the Delors II College contained four former national Ministers of Finance. Since Foreign and Finance Ministers are traditionally among the most important posts in national governments, their arrival in the Commission may mark an increase in political weight for the institution. It also appears to demonstrate a move away from the more narrowly technically based roles characteristic of many Commissioners in the past towards a broader and more political approach. Thus, the Santer Commission includes two former Prime Ministers (Luxembourg and France), with three former Foreign Ministers (Spain, the Netherlands, and Portugal) and one former Finance Minister (Finland.) In this development towards the participation of former top level government ministers, there are some national differences. In general, it is clear that smaller countries are more likely to send ministerial 'heavyweights' than the larger ones. Italy has been conspicuous in its failure to send any top ranking political figures to the Commission.

European and international experience

The EC was only one part of a much wider network of European and global organisations which were created and expanded in the decade after the end of World War II (Archer, 1994). Many of those concerned with the establishment of the EC were also involved in other international organisations. Table 2.8 demonstrates that two-thirds of Commissioners had previous experience of active participation in some of these other organisations. In the early period, it is clear that the Organization for European Economic Co-operation (OEEC later OECD) and the Council of Europe were important sources of experience, along with the United Nations and its agencies. It is not surprising that people who worked in one international organisation often went on to work in others, including the European Community. It is also clear that in many cases personal links were created which may have been important in facilitating securing other positions.

Another striking aspect is the fact that the recruitment to the College of Commissioners has partly fed off the creation and existence of the EC institutions themselves. Three quarters of the pre-merger appointed Commissioners, from Monnet and Hallstein onwards, had played major parts in the initiatives and intergovernmental negotiations which actually created these institutions. It has also been a common pattern for many of the Commissioners from acceding States to have participated in the negotiating team which brought their country into membership. Thus Erkki Liikanen moved directly from being the head of the Finnish Mission to the European Union to being the first Finnish Commissioner. Some Commissioners (such as Ortoli, Deniau, Narjes, and de Silguy) had previously worked on the staff of the Commission, either as permanent officials or in the *cabinets* of Commissioners. Another trend has been experience as

Table 2.8   Experience of European and International Organizations on First Appointment

ORGANIZATION	HA1–EEC2 N=41 %N	EC1–5 N=36 %N	EC6–EU1 N=43 %N	All N=120 %N
European Community	29	50	49	43
Formation	75	56	24	47
Commission	0	17	5	8
Eur. Parl.	25	28	62	41
Other	0	11	24	6
European–Atlantic	32	28	21	27
OEEC/OECD	46	40	11	34
NATO/WEU	23	40	56	38
Co. of Eur.	31	30	78	44
Other	8	20	0	9
United Nations	20	19	2	13
European Movement	10	14	7	10
None Identified	37	28	37	34

Note: European Community: the 'formation' of the EC includes intergovernmental negotiations, drafting of reports and treaties, and accession negotiations between candidate state and EC. 'Commission' includes officials and *cabinet.* 'European Parliament' includes both nominated and directly elected members. 'Others' include Economic & Social Committee, the European Investment Bank, and Committee of Permanent Representatives.
European–Atlantic: includes work on creation of these organisations, service on their secretariats and membership of parliamentary assemblies. 'Others' includes Benelux and various specialist agencies.
United Nations includes General Assembly, and specialised agencies.
European Movement includes active participation or office holding in such organisations as the European Union of Federalists, Action Committee for the United States of Europe, etc. It does not include passive membership of all-party European groups in national parliaments.

members of the EP, either the original nominated body or the directly elected institution. The growth of European institutions has multiplied the career opportunities for those relatively highly skilled, motivated, and mobile individuals who can exploit these potential connecting paths.

A fairly small number of Commissioners appear to have played active parts in the various pro-integration political promotional groups which constitute the various branches of the European Movement. While this particular data may well be somewhat inadequate, it does suggest that involvement through intergovernmental and international career routes rather than a strong value-based disposition to promote European integration is the key element. It should also be noted that over half of the Commissioners for whom no previous specific involvement in European organisations can be identified, had occupational backgrounds in public service as national Ministers or senior civil servants. There, as a matter of course in an increasingly global system, they will have been involved in international and intergovernmental contacts. At the distinctly European level, practically every national Minister whose country is a member of the EU, will have attended meetings of the Council of Ministers in Brussels.

CONCLUSIONS

Commissioners show some common characteristics which cut across their national origins, although their prospects of service are heavily dependent upon national factors. In spite of significant differences based upon national peculiarities and variations in educational systems, composition of the civil service, and career patterns of politicians, they can be fitted into broad gender, age, educational, occupational, and political categories. The College has been predominantly male and late middle aged. The majority have been university educated, mostly with qualifications in law or economics. The dominant occupational experiences have been as State officials, managers in private or public business, and lawyers. Political affiliations have been largely centrist and increasingly within the partisan boundaries of the main national governing parties. A national political career at the parliamentary and ministerial level is becoming almost the norm. Active experience in European and international organisations is a very frequent characteristic.

The profile of characteristics to be found among Commissioners has implications for the functioning of the Commission. In age, education, and professional background they match the pattern typical of higher political and administrative personnel in national governmental systems. In their management functions they tend to be well qualified, with a high level of general administrative experience. In many cases they also bring particular specialist expertise to their policy portfolios. Most have been subject to those constraints and disciplines imposed in political or official careers which are also required for participation in the collective responsibilities of the College. Only a minority have experience of private sector industry, commerce, and finance. But most will have wide experience in negotiating with companies, trade unions, and interest groups in their previous careers. While each College has a variety of political affiliations in its membership, the spread of opinion is no greater than is routinely accommodated within government coalitions in European countries which operate within a centrist tradition, leaning either to the right or left. Many of the Commissioners have personal understanding of coalition compromises from their ministerial and parliamentary experiences. The increasing political experience of more recent Colleges reduces the danger of a technocratic approach which might neglect public opinion.

The growing ministerial background of Commissioners is likely to aid them in their work with the Council of Ministers. It increases their own political weight and prestige, and also furnishes them with contacts with their national counterparts. It also enhances the practice of Commissioners acting as an informal communications channel to their countries of origin (Middlemas, 1995). Combined with the system of appointment and the patterns of limited tenure, the picture which emerges is of a complex relationship between European Commission autonomy and national linkages. It combines national and European roles rather than distinguishes clearly between them. A modified and politicised concept of *engrenage* or intermeshing (Coombes, 1970) may be considered as encapsulating a system in which the political nature and significance of the Commission role has been recognised with the increasing seniority of the appointments.

It is clear that many Commissioners work within the political institutions and agenda of what has been described as the society of Europeans (Grosser, 1980). They tend to be connected to a broad web of international political, diplomatic, administrative and economic networks. In an increasingly transnational environment, the role of European Commissioner frequently appears as a logical progression through a coherent pattern of activity.

Notes

1. This chapter has benefitted from discussion of previous papers presented to the Research Seminars in Politics at the University of Durham, and to the ECPR Workshop on 'National Political Elites and European Integration' in Madrid April 1994.
2. The data relating to the Commissioners, including their biographical details and periods of office, and the rotation of colleges has been gathered almost exclusively from publicly published sources. These include standard reference works (of the *Who's Who* type), EC/EU official publications and press releases, and government organization manuals. In a few cases these have been supplemented by information supplied by embassy officials in London.
3. Two out of twelve Luxembourg Commissioners suffered this fate.
4. I owe this point to Professor M. Cotta at the 1994 Madrid ECPR research sessions.
5. This includes the Grandes Ecoles of France.
6. Such as military officer training at St Cyr and Sandhurst, Diploma in agriculture, Chartered Accountant status, and graduation from teacher training college.

3 Identities in the European Commission
Maryon McDonald

INTRODUCTION

The material for this chapter draws on an anthropological study of life inside two of the institutions self-consciously active in the construction of Europe. The study began in 1991 and has involved full-time fieldwork inside the European Parliament (EP) and then the European Commission, lasting over three years in all.[1] The focus here is on aspects of life inside the Commission.

Anthropological fieldwork means living and working daily in the milieu being studied. It is premised on the notion that it is peoples' own perceptions of the world that determine their behaviour, and that if you want to understand why people do what they do then you need, in priority, to understand their own ideas, observe their ideas in action, and do so in their own context The methodology is, of course, both more complex and self-consciously problematic than any bald statement of this kind could allow, but in practice it can mean – and has meant – anything from drinking coffee and 'chatting' to sitting in on formal meetings at all levels, and anything from active participation in the seminar of an entire Directorate General (DG) to donning boots at the weekend for a walk with a straggle of keen Commission ramblers. This is not the methodology of questionnaires and formal interviews, although these activities are not excluded either where those being studied expect them.

In research of this kind, where the aim is to grasp people's own perceptions, the anthropologist is always guided by the priorities and preoccupations of those being studied. One issue that arises in this context is that of identity. Questions of identity, especially national and ethnic identity, have become important in the post-1960s world generally, and strongly so within Europe (see Macdonald, 1993). More specifically, the structure of EU governance and the internal structure of its institutions mean that questions of identity carry a moral and political load inside organisations such as the Commission that they might not carry elsewhere. This chapter offers a brief outline of some of the axes around which identities in the Commission can crystallise.

IN THE SERVICES

An important differentiation inside the Commission is that between the *cabinets* and the 'services'. (See Chapter 1 for an explanation of the nature of this differentiation). Identity is always relational, and the *cabinets* pose one point of reference in relation to which the 'services' define themselves as such.

The *cabinets* are sometimes given the English-language title of 'cabinets'. Although some officials of British background prefer 'private office', the terms 'cabinet' (Engl.) and *cabinet* have been operating as linguistic equivalents in some quarters in internal Commission sociolanguage. Similarly, there are some British officials who insist on 'Departments' rather than 'services' , and the Commission's translators will gleefully cross out 'services' and insert 'Departments' if they can get their hands on the text, but it is 'services' that have dominant currency in day-to-day discussion. More important, however, than the sociolinguistic alignments that even talking of such a distinction can create is the distinction itself: for better or for worse, everyone knows that life in the *cabinets* and life in the services are not the same.

Those in the services have to know their place. No matter how high their category and grade, there are matters from which officials in the services are, to their resentment, excluded. Even in some noted cases where it is felt that the services do all the work, the *cabinets* are the ones, it is said, with the power and prestige They are the ones who have the final say in co-ordination, and who can variously champion, appropriate, change, dump or simply disavow texts from their services. Those working in the *cabinets* may be of lower educational achievement, and have less administrative and EU experience, but they can still seek to tell a well-established and devoted category 'A' official what to do. Or they can simply ignore him. The services, for their part, can try to by-pass the *cabinet* of their Commissioner or they can spill valuable beans to other *cabinets*. The relationship bristles with ambivalence.

The *cabinets* are, in different contexts, admired and condemned. The *cabinets*, in the Commission mythology of services and *cabinets* alike, are the devoted and hard-working sites of long, caffeine-soaked nights; they are said to require special stamina and special people; but they are also bounded by tales of tears and stress. They are metaphorically and actually elevated offices to which some officials from the services might aspire if they are bright and politically astute enough and from which they will be welcomed back into the services (usually at a higher level) with admiration. But the *cabinets* are also the site of national affiliations and interests and a source of structural contradiction. They readily recruit people directly from national contexts, by-passing the services, and they have regular contacts with national administrations, national lobbyists and the permanent representations. They also notoriously 'parachute' their chosen national recruits directly into key service jobs, over the heads of well-qualified and experienced officials in the services. We shall come back to aspects of this.

Within the services, the DGs offer important units of identification. Whether or not a DG has a strong identity depends on a number of factors, including the size of its budget, its degree of legislative competence, the 'security of its European vocation' (meaning generally the political support it commands, the clarity of its competence in the treaties, and its capacity to fight for and win turf inside the Commission), plus the frequency of its relations with other DGs. In 1992, when I first began research inside the Commission, DGIII (Internal Market and Industrial Affairs) was undoubtedly a DG with a strong identity and a confident self-image. Commission officials might look puzzled occasionally when asked what other DGs did (and often just confessed total ignorance and indifference the nearer one got to DG twenty-something) but no-one could not know about DGIII.

DGIII has felt itself to be in some sense the 'real' Europe, there from the beginning and in every sense close to the coalface. In the perception of its own officials, it was DGIII that had produced the Single European Market (SEM) on which so much else depended. 'What *is* Europe if not a market?' Moreover: 'This is new wine in old bottles. We are the Common Market. That's what Europe is: the Common Market.' The boundaries of a self-conscious rationality were often drawn in relation to other DGs. DGI (External Affairs) was the 'nobility' it was admitted, but DGIII had its feet on the ground: '*on est du terroir, nous*' a new recruit from DGI was told in his first DGIII meeting. Moreover, the boundaries of legislative over-enthusiasm in DGIII's internal meetings were often drawn by reference to the 'mad market' further down the *rue de la Loi* (where most of the Commission's offices were then located). 'You ought to be in DGVI!' it would be said, to suggest to anyone that they had overstepped the mark, or 'are you going to discuss the shape of cucumbers next ?!'

The clearest identity is in conceptual opposition, and DGVI (Agriculture) was a regular cipher in this way in DGIII's internal construction of its own image and proprieties. Other DGs with little or no legislative competence, including DGX (Audiovisual, Information, Communication and Culture) or those whose position seemed relatively fragile, such as DGV (Employment, Industrial Relations and Social Affairs), were also called upon in DGIII and elsewhere to assert a DG's own proprieties.

For those who wished to claim order, realism and rationality for themselves, DGV was not an uncommon point of reference, and was often required to represent idealism and disorder. A congruence of epistemology and political priorities has meant that areas dealing with the 'cultural' or the 'social', whilst seen to give a 'human face', have to battle for their credibility. This is inevitable within a structure of ideas, common within Europe and beyond, in which economics/culture, or economics/the social, and facts/values, biology/culture, reason/emotions, material/ideal, reality/ideas, and more, are all still credible and self-evoking dualities (cf. McDonald, 1989, 1996). Gender imagery has also played a role in shaping perceptions and portrayals of DGV, for it contains the Equal Opportunities Unit, a unit unique in the Commission in that it is staffed almost entirely by women. Moreover, DGV as a whole has had, at times, almost twice the number of women in 'A' category posts as, for example, DGIII. This relative attraction of men and women between the two DGs is perhaps, within that same complex of dualities, hardly surprising. It is also the case very generally that a male definition of the world in which women are perceived to be the point of entry of disorder is something which anthropologists have found in many parts of the world. For a variety of reasons, therefore, it is perhaps not surprising that DGV has represented disorder to other people, and this same status has, in the past, proffered its own empirical confirmation by encouraging a relatively high turnover of staff.

New staff at the higher levels and new legislative confidence have nevertheless helped to bolster DGV's image, internally and externally. The passing of the '1992' deadline, meanwhile, and the hiving off of the 'Internal Market' to a new DGXV in 1993, brought a transitional crisis of confidence in a DGIII formally left with 'Industrial Affairs': 'Industrial policy ? *Is* there one?'. In such a context, DGV began to appeal to DGIII officials ('At least there is something there to get passionate about!') and even the far-flung reaches of a purportedly fun-loving DGVIII (Development) seemed suddenly to offer serious clarity of action 'with the Lomé Convention, and so on' to gather around. However, this crisis of confidence was not sufficient, interestingly enough, to re-cast DGVI (Agriculture) in a newly attractive light for DGIII officials. DGVI remained one place you could cite as a way of counting your blessings for what you had, however confused your own domain might have become.

Other images and self-comparisons and contrasts are common between DGs in the Commission, and these symbolic boundaries are taken by some to be indicative of the distance between DGs, with the DGs in general perceived to be 'like fiefdoms' and co-ordination between them a perpetual problem. DGXVI (Regional Policy) and DGVIII (Development) are sometimes seen as doing much the same thing as each other, dispensing the means of equality, but with the one doing it inside the EU and the other outside

it and with different notions of efficacy. DGXVI sometimes
feels hounded by DGIV (Competition) and has contact with
other DGs for the general revisions of the structural funds.
But DGVIII is felt, and feels itself, to lead a very different
life from other DGs, to the point that DGIII and DGVIII
are said to be 'almost different planets!' Although it might
seem that all these different perceptions and images of the
DGs must represent some internal homogeneity, they do
not. The coherence of an image constructed relationally, in
external relation to another DG, says nothing of the internal coherence of the DG in question, and DG identification
is always able to give way contextually to other, cross-cutting
loyalties or identifications – along the lines of religion and
political party, for example, or language and nationality. We
shall return to these last two factors in a moment. It should
be noted, moreover, that inside any DG there are other structural cleavages which can sometimes produce very real problems of identification and communication. In DGIII, for
example, the majority of 'A' category officials are lawyers,
economists, and from a natural science background. Angry
scientists commented to me on several occasions that it was
often in that order that officials were tacitly ranked, that
they themselves were in danger of being invisible for key
promotions, and that they were rarely informed of the broader
political scheme of things in which they were meant to be
working. In more general terms, it was common to find, in
this and in other DGs, perceived differences between 'horizontal' and 'vertical' directorates or units, sometimes said
to be congruent with notions of 'thinkers' and 'doers', but
always felt to be congruent with upper and lower echelons
of the Commission's structure or 'hierarchy'. The 'horizontal' sections are often resented.

LANGUAGE

In the 1950s and early 1960s, when the Commission was being
established – in the form both of the High Authority of the
European Coal and Steel Community and as the Commission of the European Communities – it was still possible to
feel confident that going beyond nationalism was a self-evi-

dently correct and righteous path to take. However, this confidence was later seriously shaken by events. Attitudes to language are tied in with these events, as are concerns outside and inside EU institutions about legitimacy.

There have been two principal periods during which questions of legitimacy have been raised. First of all, concerns were voiced in the late 1960s – a period when it was first noticed that the original, self-evident legitimacy of the Community, defined against a past of war, was losing relevance to a new generation. Amidst demographic changes, increased studentification, and the re-invention of the category of 'youth', a new 'generation' was self-consciously establishing itself in contra-distinction from its parents. Old certainties such as modernisation, progress, reason and positivism, many of which had informed the EC project, were put in question. This was a time when cultural diversity was invented, a time of civil rights marches in the US, a time of decolonisation and counter-cultures, a time when the alternative worlds of regionalism, particularism and relativism appealed, and when new nationalisms and new identities, ethnic and national, began to crowd the map in Europe and beyond.

The response of the EC at this time was to try to draw young people, against the prevailing current, back into the 'European' fold through youth programmes, largely exchange schemes, and then much later on through the active 'conscientisation' programmes of the 'People's Europe' project. The structural funds also developed, partly in response to the economism of the EC.

The second period which launched new worries about legitimacy has come about since the launch of the SEM. This unprecedented flurry of perceived 'interference' from Brussels (whatever the original intention), with more directives in a shorter time than ever before, was bolstered and coloured by two other sets of events. On the one hand, the Berlin Wall fell, and many old certainties fell afresh with it. On the other hand, the Maastricht Treaty was negotiated and seemed to threaten national identities in a context in which, with the SEM, Brussels 'interference' already appeared as established fact. Going beyond nationalism had once seemed morally right, in the years after the Second World War, but now this was widely perceived as a moral and political threat. Not surprisingly, referenda results sent many of the old certainties still surviving in Brussels diving for cover.

In Europe and beyond, the old nationalism package, made up of people–history–language–culture–territory, was revivified in the new post-1960s regional, ethnic and national identities, and spread widely. A measure of its continuing appeal is that it can feel quite 'natural' for 'a people' to wish to express themselves and their 'culture' in 'their own language'. In very general terms, the Commission has ostensibly maintained a model in which linguistic expression goes beyond nationalism: internally, the main working languages are usually French and English, and externally there is rarely made available, in consultative committees for instance, the full quota of interpreting booths for all the EU languages. The EP, on the other hand, as the self-conscious *vox populi* in Europe, tends to insist on the revitalised linguistic diversity model. The Commission has regularly argued for 'rationalisation' and the Parliament has come back with notions of the importance of every MEP speaking his or her own language. The two different models sometimes come into open conflict when a Commission representative addresses an EP Committee in English or French, the language of his or her briefing notes, only to be chided by an angry MEP of the same nationality for not speaking his or her mother-tongue.

Although French and English may be said to be the main working languages of the Commission, in practice the way in which officials speak to each other involves a speech which outsiders might find mixed or wrong. It would constantly be possible, although not actually done in normal daily speech, to pick out the syntax or semantics of one language in another. The perception of a language as 'mixed' derives its force, of course, from linguistic models of national languages. The development of a discipline of linguistics and the invention of national units were coincident in the eighteenth and nineteenth centuries. National units and the boundaries of language were often created together. Languages and nations found their 'origins' in philology, and grammars provided models of bounded correctness.

Within the Commission, a German speaking French to a Dutchman about a text in English does not cause surprise. This is a world which has self-consciously moved 'beyond nationalism', and movement across linguistically defined boundaries is an everyday affair. An outsider's surprise or admiration can bring a chuckle and a response to the effect that 'we don't think about it'. However, there are definitely contexts in which a consciousness of national linguistic boundaries does occur. For example, if any text, the above-mentioned English text for example, has to go outside the DG or outside the Commission, a consciousness of national languages then emerges, but not always in a way that an outsider might expect. Formally or informally, a *visa linguistique* is required for the text. Formal translation, through the Translation Services, takes too long; someone whose mother tongue is English is called on within the relevant unit to take a look at the text. This is not always a simple matter. The multilingual and mobile childhood of some officials in the Commission makes the 'mother tongue' neither easy to define nor necessarily of any close relationship to the language spoken daily in the respective national context. However, time presses, and anyone with a reasonably good knowledge of English may feel confident to give the go-ahead. The resultant text is not always 'English' as someone born, brought up and still living in England might understand it.

Written texts destined to move beyond the DG obviously bring evocations of the world outside the DG and outside the Commission. National models of correctness then reassert themselves over the daily sociolanguage of internal communication. Written texts have in any case been the prime emphasis of many education systems and national-language grammars. It is not surprising that it should be there that the frontiers re-emerge most readily.

Whilst the spoken language in the Commission services is relatively free of such constraints much of the time, there are moments when the boundaries do re-emerge in the domain of spoken language also. Firstly, for example, they re-emerge as conscious strategy sometimes, especially for those whose mother tongue is neither English nor French. A high-ranking Portuguese official explained to me that he deliberately chose, in any formal discussion, to speak English if his interlocuters' dominant language was French, and vice versa. Secondly, informal communication channels pass predominantly through those of the same nationality and those known to speak the same language. Thirdly, inter-service meetings sometimes begin with the explicit offer of a choice of languages. This can also happen in the special circumstances of inter-unit level meetings, across directorates. Usually, the choice is between English and French – and responses calling for another language are both meant and taken as a joke. In general, it will effectively be up to the Chair of the meeting to decide, and no-one usually objects. Moreover, if the Chair speaks English and people reply in French, this is taken as normal. Fourthly, a particular linguistic consciousness emerges where French is concerned. It is overwhelmingly the case that French has dominated in the Commission, or is seen to dominate. There are pockets where English dominates, in specific units or sectors (usually where the 'client' group prefers English), and where French may not be heard at all. These, however, are sufficiently exceptional to be noticeable.

'The language of the Commission is French' has been a common self-commentary in the services. Some feel that this is in part due to living in a city where French is in daily use. It is noticed, however, that the dominant form of French used in the Commission is 'dictated by the French Academy not by Brussels'. This can be explicitly underlined for officials occasionally: for instance, at one inter-unit meeting, where several units were getting together for the first time, the German Chair initiated discussion in English and then stopped to ask if that was OK for everyone. Amidst the ritual shrugging of shoulders that generally greets self-consciously diplomatic, inter-service chairing of this kind, a single voice proclaimed: '*Vous pouvez parler anglais si vous voulez. Je le comprends, mais je refuse de le parler . . . Il faut bien défendre la langue française*'. This was said with a smile, and the meeting then continued in the usual way.

Such open linguistic statements may be relatively rare but there is a pervasive awareness that 'the French stick up for their language'. It is important to bear in mind here that the French language has been historically required to bear a moral and political load unique in the everyday languages of European nation-states. The French language and French national identity have been quite explicitly implicated the one in the other through two hundred years of self-conscious, national fragility. What to a French person can seem perfectly normal, and perhaps necessary, can to others seem pathological. Histories of the Commission are told in which French officials, at the moment of the 1973 enlargement, became very worried about the future of their language: 'The Germans had spoken more German previously, but they did not seem to mind. Only the French were worried. They became neurotic about what was going to happen to French'. English-speakers, it is said, will apologise for using English sometimes – but 'the French just stick to their guns'.

To different notions of what constitutes language, we need to add the different moral, political and historical evocations that any single language can produce. In this sense, French easily appears to be 'the more ideologically sound', as one official put it, of the daily working languages. It was also the language of the long-serving President Delors and his *cabinet*, and was the language of the previous, long-serving Secretary General, Emile Noël. All this has helped to create a situation in which some anglophones on detachment from national administrations claim that they soon realise that, when working alongside permanent officials, 'if you don't speak French, they make you feel even more that you are not one of them'. There are stories of non-French officials of the same nationality speaking French to each other in the corridors, even if they are sometimes struggling, and prominent British officials have been known to prefer to speak only or mainly French. One poignant instance of this involved one such British official who self-consciously spoke only French daily in order to be properly European; however, he sometimes used expressions that had no such clarity of linguistic definition for others. For instance, in response to proposals, he might say '*Je ne sais pas si c'est une bonne idée*'. In his adamant and well-intentioned French, he unwittingly required others to know English so that he could be properly understood. Only accomplished anglophones around him grasped that here he was saying 'no', and some confusion inevitably resulted.

Personnel changes at the topmost levels of the Commission, coupled with the accession to the EU in 1995 of three new

Member States, have caused some officials to talk of a shift in the language used in the Commission services, and certainly there are now more new recruits speaking English than there were previously. There has also been increased external pressure to try to introduce more German (a point which some German officials have found both embarrassing and 'unrealistic'). For some French officials, the future of French in the Commission is a serious cause for concern. This concern easily appears to others to be simple 'hysteria'. It is nevertheless a concern which has the capacity to recruit other officials contextually, through the implication of French in the definition not of France but of Europe. Some see in the French language a bulwark against the cultural might of an English-speaking United States.

INCONGRUENCE AND STEREOTYPES

Unity and difference

The following paragraphs look at the question of stereotypes. The idea of 'stereotypes' as currently understood was invented in the 1920s, after the First World War. In the circumstances at that time, discussion of 'stereotypes' began and thrived as a discussion about 'prejudice', and how to go beyond this. Stereotypes meant, above all, *national* stereotypes.

What do stereotypes have to do with the European Commission? Given the circumstances, both historical and historiographical, of the creation of 'Europe' in the period after the Second World War, it is perhaps not surprising that there is a strong feeling amongst many officials in the Commission that stereotypes are something that European civil servants have gone beyond. 'We don't think in terms of national difference'. There is an *'esprit européen'* and a European identity. If there are differences, they are 'personality differences'. If there are cultural differences, then that is part of Europe's 'richness'. And so on.

There is an immensely positive discourse to be heard along these lines, generally in contexts of obvious displays of commitment, in some contexts of negotiation, and especially from those newly arrived. It is also likely to be the response to any unknown outsider naive enough to pose a direct question on the issue, and it thereby constructs the boundaries of the Commission and its cultural proprieties. 'Personality differences' and 'cultural richness' are statements perceived by some to be political and moral correctness, and seem to leave the idea of a European unity intact. Such statements are matched by the tolerance in the language sphere of linguistic usages which elsewhere would be considered 'mixed' or simply wrong.

However, national identifications and stereotypes *do* occur in the Commission. One reason for this is that the way in which 'Europe' itself is defined means effectively that it can conceptually require the existence of the nation. Amongst lower level officials, giving positive content to 'Europe' can be difficult. This is partly due to perceived problems of information, but there is also a conceptual problem. Quite commonly, Europe is contextually defined by what it is not: temporally, it is not the past, it is not war; spatially, it is not the US or not Japan, and it is not roots, national attachments or prejudices. 'I only have to go home to feel European', one official explained. 'Europe' and the national/home identification can conceptually require each other. At the same time, national identification continually threatens to intrude and divide the Europe so created.

There are two main reasons for this. Firstly, there is the obvious reason that, for 200 years, the nation and national identification have posed as inalienable objects, and have been important means of identification for the self and other, a means of asserting or describing difference. Secondly, the Commission is both fed by and reproduces this traditional mode of identification and difference. For better or worse, national identity is seen to be encouraged in the Commission not only by external pressures, but also by some features of the modes of recruitment and promotion, by the *cabinets* system, the national officials on secondment, and *parachutage*. These aspects structure important contradictions into the heart of the organisation.

There is much bitterness about the aspects just mentioned. The conceptual opposition of Europe and national identification can contextually become contradiction, and a moral and political opposition. People who came in through the *concours* (examination) system, who have been in the Commission for years, who feel they have struggled to build something called Europe, can suddenly find themselves passed over for promotion – ostensibly on national lines. It is often claimed that promotion comes about through the support of the national context of the candidate, through the *cabinets*, the national politicians and the permanent representations, rather than through merit or any 'European' propriety. Moments of anger and disillusionment are rife on these points – to the extent that one senior official explained : 'One certain way to failure here is to be European'.

A meeting of incongruent systems

We come back then to the question of national identity, and the question now of stereotypes.

To appreciate this question properly, it is important to bear in mind the following general points. When different conceptual and behavioural systems meet, then there is often an apprehension of incongruence. The systems do not match, do not 'fit', giving a sense of disorder; there is commonly both a perception of, and empirical confirmation of, disorder in the other. These apprehensions are often made sense of in national terms – it is there that difference is most commonly noticed and in those terms that it is readily understood. Definition and self-definition are always relational and contextual; cultures are not homogenous wholes but relationally constructed; and nations do not consist of essences or given national characters. Rather, nations provide the boundaries by which difference is most easily constructed and recognised. At the same time, difference is also widely understood in terms of the ideas which came with nineteenth-century nationalisms and which we generally know, for short, as the ideas of positivism and romanticism. These points are not meant to imply any stage-by-stage process of thought but a simultaneity of definition and experience, a unity of theory and observation.

Put more simply, we often make sense of difference unthinkingly in terms of a dichotomy such as rationality/irrationality ('we' are rational, 'they' are irrational), or reason/ emotions, realism/ idealism, practicality/ impracticality, work/

leisure, work/family – and many other similar dualities which
were noted above and which, in daily life, can easily and
contextually evoke each other. It is in terms of such dualities that differences between the sexes have also been understood, and even the two sides of the human brain (there is
said by some to be a part for 'reason', another for 'emotions') and much else besides. In various and ever-chang-
ing forms, such dualities and their recensions are pervasive.

These are dualities in terms of which differences between
northern and southern Europe have often been asserted or
described, and in other contexts they can describe differences between different countries – Britain and France, for
instance. These differences operate at the level of everyday
life in the Commission. For instance, differences of gender,
nationality, and language (including pitch and use of the
body) between an English boss and a French woman working for him resulted – for both – in apparent empirical
confirmation of French emotionality on the one hand and
British coldness and rationality on the other. When the French
woman had problems at home, her problems brought no
sympathy : 'She seems to get so emotional about everything
anyway'. Irritation and mutual misunderstanding were then
further encouraged when the English boss asked the French
woman to stop calling him 'Monsieur' and to call him 'Jim'.
This seemed at once contradictory and singularly inappropriate to a woman accustomed to the proprieties of hierarchical deference: 'I don't understand'.

There are several examples of this kind, some flagrant,
some trivial, and some of which can go right into the heart
of marital attraction and marriage break-up. As one Spanish official commented of her Belgian ex-husband, also working in the Commission: 'He was crazy about everything
Spanish – and seemed to expect me to be so passionate
and sexy all the time'.

On the point of first names amongst the British: I was
repeatedly told, by British officials, that this derives from a
self-consciously British tradition in the civil service wherein
everyone is ideally part of a team, sharing information, collegial, all on the same side. Sometimes, when the British
come to the Commission, and especially those with a British civil service background, it can feel like 'anarchy'. The

systems do not match – to the point that there can appear to be 'no rules at all'. But then the British always knew the Continent was like that. All emotion and no rationality. 'All ideas and no practicality'.

The British, Danes and others know, of course, about the 'hierarchy' in the Commission. They spend some time trying to change or subvert it. For them, the hierarchy is not structure: 'It seems to be something to do with personal rank and honour, but precious little to do with management'. At the same time, their own behaviour, as we shall see again in a moment, can seem to others to lack clarity or to encourage the view that they are variously 'difficult', 'disloyal' and even 'anarchical'. There is, then, a mutual perception of anarchy involved when different systems meet, and each perception can feel empirically true.

A north/south division is frequently apparent. The attribution of 'north/south' changes contextually, but the countries generally in the north are Britain, Ireland, Netherlands, Denmark, Germany, Luxembourg, sometimes Belgium (and since their accession Sweden, Finland and Austria); those in the south are France, Spain, Italy, Greece, Portugal and, on certain points, Belgium. France's metaphorical inclusion in the 'south' is owed, in part, to the unusually long tenure of President Delors. However, France is itself divided in some contexts into north/south differences, as are many other countries, and countries of the north or those of the south can become metaphorically opposed among themselves through the same imagery. The Spanish are sometimes said to be the northern rationality of the south, and distinguished from Italians, just as the Irish sometimes become the festive soul of the north. All such divisions can be used not as simple national or geographical divisions but as metaphorical statements in which moral and political perceptions and preoccupations both take up, and are distributed in various ways across, geographical and ethnological space. Some do not talk of north or south, but of '*nordiques*' and '*latins*', for example, or of '*nordiques*' and '*méridionaux*'. The prospect of new northern countries becoming part of the EU, together with an impending change of President and Presidential style, were among the factors which, during my research, injected a special north/south salience into any perception of national difference.

Among those from the north, there seems to be a greater, or perhaps louder, sense of unease. This is partly because the idiom of a rational, ideal-type bureaucracy is theirs and it is this discourse which can most easily define 'problems' with public credence or legitimacy. In the meeting of different systems in the Commission, there is an incongruence, at once conceptual and practical, of the frontiers between: administration/politics, public/private, public/personal. Seemingly political, private or personal matters appear where, for those from the north (and especially for the British and Danes), they should not. This intrusion or mismatch is inherent to perceptions of disorder, a sense of unease. There is a feeling of 'contradictory forces', of 'unpredictability', a lack of trust. There can seem to be no coherence in time (including no obvious, shared filing system or erratic minutes) and no coherence in space (no co-ordination, no collegiality, no readily shared information). There can seem to be only idealism ('look at their *notes!*') and competition, sabotage and power. Everything seems linked to the person (sensitivity, honour, arcane personal networks, *hommes clés*, or – particularly under Delors – the President).

It is important to interject here that there are many officials for whom, whatever their background, there *are* some modes of co-ordination, which are also essential systems of control; for whom there *is* structure, and simple ways of getting information: 'Make friends'. 'Be sole master of your *dossiers*'. 'There is lots of autonomy'. 'There is plenty of space in which to do creative and exciting things'. 'It is "democratic"'. 'If there's a problem, send it up the hierarchy; it's not difficult'.

For many from the north, however, it *is* difficult and there *is* a problem. There are no job descriptions. The hierarchy is there only to check up on you or to be used to get rid of problems, or to spoon-feed you. 'You are treated like a child'. 'A hierarchy has to check even your simplest letters'. 'You cannot take responsibility'. 'There are no clear rules'. 'It is like trying to re-create your job everyday'. 'It is continual self-starting. Where are the frontiers?' 'How far can you go?' 'It's a cruel place. You could lose your dossier – or your job – any day. Nothing is clear'.

· Within all this, the ideals of the relative impartiality of an administrative system, a system ideally independent of

politics and the personal, encounter systems in which the
political and the personal play an important role. There is
pressure from both or all sides.

Rules and the personal

To summarise part of the problem of perceived national
difference, it is necessary to be rather crude and general.
Parts of northern Europe have been fertile ground for three
sets of ideas: (i) an impersonal, rule-governed market; (ii)
an impersonal, rational bureaucracy; and (iii) abstract virtue,
encouraging the notion that, independent of social context,
there is something called 'loyalty', 'honesty' and so on. In
parts of southern Europe, on the other hand, virtues and
loyalties might more readily be linked to particular social
contexts, often kin-based, with honour and decency attaching
to persons and obligations, often of a familial or patron-
client kind; and markets and state structures can become
very much a part of, and work through, these relations. (For
some elaboration of these points, see Delamont, 1995; Dilley,
1992; Hart, 1992.)

An important point here is that there is no easily neutral
language in which to discuss such differences, and that ex-
pressing one system in the terms of the other can all too
easily give rise to accusations of 'corruption' in the south
by northern Europeans and accusations of disloyalty, dis-
honesty and perfidy in the north by southern Europeans.
On this last point, for example, a Spanish official complained
to me of bad behaviour by a northern official to whom he
had, within his own idea of hierarchical clarity and propriety, regularly passed information and from whom he expected a strict return; the northern official in question,
however, had certain managerial notions of 'information flow'
which meant he communicated information to others. He
was not to be trusted.

In southern Europe, patronage systems of various kinds
operate as an important, if not the only, moral system. There
is not space to give details here, or to distinguish as one
should between the different proprieties involved in and within
Spain, Italy and Greece, for example. (There are many anthropological studies of the various systems in operation[2].)

In the Commission, as outside it, patronage systems have a self-evident importance for those who operate them: indebtedness can be created as a matter of pride and honour, and similarly debts repaid with loyalty and support. It would, from within such systems, be naive to imagine that life works differently. Honour and manliness are among the rewards of knowing how to work this system, and shame, naivety and stupidity are among the sanctions on ignorance.

There are internal criticisms of the patronage systems from those who actively participate in them, but these tend to be criticisms which sustain them. For example: 'He's *our* Commissioner and he's done nothing for my husband!' It is a common feature of many patronage systems and of the way they are sustained that each party seeks more honour or more help and favours. At the same time, there is awareness amongst all parties that this is not the only available moral system, both in their own terms and in the context of living and working alongside people from other backgrounds. Moving between the moralities available is quite common. When someone else gets the job, task, help or promotion and you don't, then you can openly condemn the *piston, magouille, imbroglio* or *enchufe* at work; as to your own success, however, well this happens *'par hasard'* or *'par accident'*.

At the same time, perceptions from the north can place moral stress on those from the south, with the latter feeling that their every move can bring accusations of corruption and even fraud. There is inevitably resentment about this. Some of the actions of those from southern Europe do not always, they know, have the formal sanction of official rules and official approval, whether at home or in the Commission. They do, however, have an informal sanction: their own pride, virtue and morality which cannot easily be given expression in the idiom of the ideal model of an impartial and rational administration favoured by many from the north.

Wherever one set of proprieties does not match another, there is ample space for misunderstanding to work both ways. There is space for southern Europeans to accuse northerners of a naive idealism and to claim an honourable realism, practicality or cunning for themselves. Moreover, where southern discourses have fully a space for honourable loyalties and alliances, for their own precedence, reciprocities and

proprieties, northern discourses can appear to southerners
to have nothing. There appears to be a gap, a silence. Into
this silence is read a whole world of suspect behaviour, a
world of corruption all the more insidious because it is not
talked about or practised openly. Two Danes were seen lunch-
ing together: '*Mais les voilà!*' One was left to assume the
rest. Or two northern officials talked to a lobbyist, whose
cause turned out to be successful: 'They're taking money,
believe me', an Italian official insisted. It would need only
one such case to be discovered, on either side, for cries of
'typical!' to be heard and for a whole world of discursive
truth to appear to be empirically confirmed.

Many examples could be given of perceived north/south
or national differences as outlined here. Some examples can
seem trivial but they are part of the general misunderstandings involved in the encounter of different conceptual systems, which cannot be lightly dismissed for those who live
them daily. This encounter of difference, and the ways in
which it is understood, poses some problems for the Commission. For example, definitions of 'corruption' can be a
source of controversy, and reporting procedures are themselves inevitably embedded in the differences already described. 'Management' can also be a problem area in general.
Another problem is that the meeting of what we can, in
anthropological shorthand, call different and incongruent
systems is compounded by the difficulties for officials of
thinking through and talking about such issues in an easily
available language and without, moreover, seeming un-
European, or 'prejudiced', or ignorant or simply derogatory.

The issues involved sometimes become entangled, too, with
other sources of tension and instability, including the demands posed by the regular changes of Commissioners, the
sometimes competing demands or agendas of Commissioners or their *cabinets,* or of *cabinets* and services, as well as
other differences already referred to within the services themselves. Such issues, along with related questions such as
perceived time pressures, bring discussion and complaints
of stress, of 'burn out', exhaustion, anxiety, depression,
marriage break-down, and sometimes alcoholism. Many of
these conditions are self-perceived or defined by colleagues.
They do not always reach the doctor. Nevertheless, within

the Commission, they account for almost 40 per cent of officially recognised 'invalidity' claims.

CONCLUSION

Many of the points made in the above paragraphs suggest that any analytical view of the Commission as a unitary entity is problematic. They also suggest that it is unhelpful to try to view the Commission through the lens of any formal organisational model without first examining the cultural assumptions built into that model. The priorities and perceptions, the relations and the understandings, and the misunderstandings, whether problematic or constructive, through which the Commission works are complex and changing. There is, moreover, little advance to be made in trying any 'institutional' analysis on the one hand and a focus on 'personalities', say, on the other, with all the evocations this would offer of the dualities or dichotomies already mentioned, and with all the reifications that either of these categories would entail. What we have in the Commission are different – sometimes competing, sometimes enriching, sometimes contradictory – ideas of what the organisation is and does, and how it does or should work, and similarly different constructions of the 'person' and of the proper place of the 'personal'.

A good deal more could be said here about the perceived national differences involved, and much of what has been said inevitably needs qualification to fit the full complexity of daily life. It is undoubtedly easier, within the Commission, to be of certain nationalities than others for linguistic, moral, political or historical reasons (see Abélès *et al.*, 1993). It is often easier, for example, to be Irish than to be German. Particular caution may be needed, however, on some of the paragraphs of the previous section of this chapter. Cultural caution is needed, for instance, about 'invalidity' definitions, and about any of the other related definitions – 'alcoholism' included (see McDonald 1994). All such categorisations are inevitably cultural, and can be fraught with difficulty. No-one should begin naively to imagine from the above paragraphs that the Commission is somehow inherently 'sick' or that officials drink more than anyone in any other institution. Such conclusions would be serious misrepresentations. Also, the comments I have cited are obviously uttered in particular contexts. Mention has been made of some of the factors which can make questions of difference salient. And, an interested researcher can appear to offer a willing ear for grievances which, in the Commission, cannot easily find another forum for expression.

I should stress that the Commission is contextually perceived, all the while, to be an exciting and enriching place to work by many of its officials. What we can say, nevertheless, is that the celebration of post-1960s cultural diversity and richness, which we are all now supposed to enjoy, is not easy to live daily in a world such as the Commission in which European unity is such a vital ambition. In this context, local versions of the conceptual mismatch that diversity might carry elsewhere are constantly in danger of appearing more serious than they might in other contexts and of erupting into the world outside with a life of their own. The Commission is required to face and to negotiate daily the structural contradictions and the complex moral and political baggage, the tensions and the compromises, of Europe and nation and of unity and difference that stand prominently at the heart of the EU, and which pervade any discussion of its history and its future, its shape and its 'added value', and its very *raison d'être*.

Notes

1. The research on which this chapter draws was financed by the Economic and Social Research Council, the European Commission and the Wenner–Gren Foundation A large part of the work in the Commission was carried out as a member of a team consisting of myself and two French anthropologists, Marc Abélès and Irène Bellier.
2. Examples of the best-known studies include: Blok (1981); Boulay (1974); Campbell (1964); Davis (1977); Gellner (1977); Gellner and Waterbury (1977). Gilmore (1987); Giovanni (1981); Herzfeld (1980 and 1985); Loizos (1975); Peristiany (1965); Pitt-Rivers (1954 and 1977); Wikan (1981).

4 Administrative Culture in the European Commission: The Cases of Competition and Environment

Michelle Cini

INTRODUCTION

The study of the cultural aspects of the European Commission is a relatively new area of interest for students of the European Union (EU). Yet increasingly the application of anthropological insights into the functioning of the European institutions has helped to add a new dimension to the old institutionalism, opening up new avenues for research on topics once considered well-worn (Abélès *et al.*, 1993). This chapter builds on work already undertaken on the Commission's administrative culture, to consider the Directorate General (DG) as the most appropriate level of analysis for research into the Commission's cultural components (Cini, 1995). The primary objective of the chapter is to consider the relationship between policy content, policy process, and administrative culture.

ADMINISTRATIVE CULTURE AND THE COMMISSION

The application of a cultural approach to the study of organisational and institutional politics is not well established, although there is a substantial literature on organisational culture in the business administration and industrial sociology fields. Some might argue that the use of any notion of *culture* to explore institutional contexts is bound to be vague and unsatisfactory, and as a result should best be avoided. It is certainly true that there are other, perhaps more easily definable, concepts that can be used in its place. But the fact that there is no accepted definition is not an insurmountable problem, as long as certain pitfalls are avoided. Part of the difficulty has been that the word culture has tended to be used in a rather woolly manner, with little definition at all.[1] This is a rather strange phenomenon given that respectable political scientists usually thrive on defining their terms. Nevertheless, culture, undefined, supposedly speaks for itself.

In this chapter, the notion of a culture rests upon an assumption that it is culture that gives meaning to human actions. From this standpoint, culture derives from a 'system of ideas and signs and associations and ways of behaving and communicating' (Gellner, 1983, p. 7), that amounts to a 'shared set of normative understandings of the world (Rengger, 1992, p. 97). As Allaire and Firsirotu (1982) observe:

> [A] cultural system embodies the organization's expressive and affective dimensions in a system of shared and meaningful symbols manifested in myths, ideology and values and in multiple cultural artifacts (rites, rituals and customs; metaphors, glossaries, acronyms, lexicon and slogans; sagas, stories, legends and organizational lore; logos, design, architecture). This cultural system is shaped by ambient society, the history of the organization and the particular contingency factors impinging upon it; it changes and evolves under the influence of contemporary dominant actors and the dynamic interplay between cultural and structural elements. (p. 213)

As a result, an appropriate methodology for examining the culture of organisations demands investigation into their belief systems, shared values and institutional ideology, alongside an assessment of the myths, symbols and norms that pervade the organisation (Cini, 1995). Organisations are 'at once, social creations and creators of social meaning' (Allaire and Firsirotu, 1982, p. 216) and it is in both of these senses that we must seek to understand administrative culture within the European Commission.

The context in which this chapter has been written is a broad one. It rests upon a desire not only to understand (or at least interpret) the Commission, but also to clarify its role within the European policy process. Administrative culture is, of course, only one of many conceptual lenses through which one can understand the workings of the Commission. Although there is no assumption here that this lens will offer a complete and comprehensive explanation of how the institution functions, it is nevertheless a starting-point for developing an awareness of how individuals, collectively, give meaning to what they are, where they are, and what they do. The context within which these actors (Commission officials in our case) exist, is an institutional one. It is therefore crucial that our conception and definition of culture is located clearly within the framework of the Commission.

The approach of the 'new institutionalists' is helpful here, in that it focuses attention upon the institution, and makes suggestions as to how the institution might affect policy content and policy outcomes.[2] In rejecting the descriptive institutionalism of the past, the new institutionalists seek to redress what they consider to be a behaviouralist imbalance in institutional studies. Institutions are seen as being more than instrumental organisations or sets of organisations. Their role goes beyond that of being simply tools of political players and, as such, they are deserving of more attention.

However, the new institutionalists seem to see administrative culture as only one of many institutional variables. For example, Bulmer (1994b) quotes March and Olsen (1989) in stating that embedded within institutional settings are beliefs, paradigms, codes, cultures and knowledge (p. 425). Yet administrative culture is much more than just one item in a list of variables. It is what underpins all activity within institutions, creating a foundation of shared meaning, interpretation and values upon which all institutional activity rests.

COMPETITION POLICY, ENVIRONMENT POLICY, AND ADMINISTRATIVE CULTURE: SOME EMPIRICAL CONSIDERATIONS

The level of analysis

As far back as 1970, the Commission had been labelled a 'porous organization in which different styles of administration

and different normative approaches compete[d] for domination' (Coombes, 1970, p. 291). It was even noted that at
the top of the Commission hierarchy 'the preservation of
collegiality ha[d] come to involve reconciling different norms
by a process of internal politics' (ibid, p. 254). This theme
of fragmentation or compartmentalisation has subsequently
become well-established in the literature on the European
Commission. There is, of course, nothing new in claiming
that sections, divisions, or directorates within institutions
develop their own independent identities within broader
institutional frameworks. As part of a considerable literature on this subject, Peters (1992) suggests ways in which
actors of this sort are able to pursue their own (purposive)
policy or (reflexive) institutional objectives through the policy
process (pp. 115–16). Following Peters, it is assumed in this
chapter that the identity of the Commission's main sub-units,
the DGs, is closely allied to their functional responsibilities.
Certainly, the policy administered within individual DGs is
important in determining what Cram (1994), amongst others,
has called the 'policy style' or 'administrative style' of the
DG (p. 201). Mazey and Richardson (1993b), and Donnelly
(1993) also use these terms to make distinctions between
different parts of the Commission. As Donnelly puts it, '[t]he
wide range of executive, supervisory and legislative functions
carried out by the different services inevitably lead to differing administrative styles' (p. 77).

Since it is now increasingly common to consider the Commission from an administrative style perspective, it comes
as no surprise to learn that DGs within the Commission have
their own approach to policy, their own ways of working,
and their own political and organisational objectives. In asserting their distinctiveness, DGs tend to be protective of
what they consider to be their own sphere of policy influence, in some cases even seeking to 'steal' policy competences
from elsewhere in the Commission. Demarcation disputes
are not uncommon.

If we are looking for a level of analysis at which to explore the administrative culture of the Commission, it would
seem to make sense to look specifically within the DGs. This
level of analysis raises a difficult issue, however, for it is not
altogether clear whether we should be looking for a specific

Commission or *DG* culture, or, more generally, for a variety of cultures that exist *within* the Commission and the DGs. The distinction is not merely semantic. It gets to the heart of whether there is indeed an administrative (Commission or DG) culture, or whether what we should really be talking about is the effect of cultures brought into an institutional setting from elsewhere.

In looking for evidence of the existence of a common cultural identity across the Commission, the questions to address would certainly have to include the following: is there any indication of there being a European vocation amongst officials?; is there a commitment within the institution to a distinctive vision of European integration?; is there a European public service (however defined) that might serve to bind together Commission staff?; is there a collective vision of the role to be performed by the Commission as it seeks to consolidate its position within the system of European governance?; and is there leadership within the Commission dominant enough to forge consensus as well as compliance throughout the institution?

There have certainly been times in the history of the EC/EU when the answer to these questions would have been in the affirmative. However, in the mid-to-late 1990s there is less evidence of a strong, common, and cohesive Commission-wide culture. Insofar as there can be said to be such a culture at all, it is a rather weak one. It has been unable to combat the centrifugal forces that have persistently given the DG enough institutional autonomy to maintain a distinctiveness and a degree of separation within the Commission system. It is hypothesised here, therefore, that although the Commission has certain features that may well define it as an institution, culturally it has very little cohesion.

It is undoubtedly true that political, national, religious, professional, linguistic and administrative divisions within the Commission are important. Bellier (1995) sees both tension and opportunities arising out of the juxtaposition of an embryonic European identity and national cultures. This, she believes, is a potential barrier to further European integration. Her focus is therefore primarily on the influence of national, linguistic, administrative and political cultures *upon* the Commission. Bellier is closest to the

perspective taken in this chapter when she focuses upon
the autonomy and identity of DGs (pp. 54–5). Her position
is that DG identity rests upon the substance of DG activity,
the personality of its leaders, and professional relations within
the policy area concerned. This identity can be uncovered,
therefore, by focusing upon differences that exist between DGs.

The remainder of this chapter looks at two Directorates
General: DGIV, which administers the Commission's competition and state aid policies; and DGXI, which oversees
the Commission's policies on the environment.[3] In each case,
three perspectives shed light on the DGs' distinctiveness.
The first perspective, on path dependencies and policy characteristics, links institutional identity to policy evolution and
organisational history. The second addresses the question
of institutional autonomy, relating this to the discretionary
capacity of DG officials. The third perspective looks beyond
the boundaries of the Commission to consider the external
constraints and opportunities facing the DGs. From each of
these three perspectives, empirically-based interpretations of
the two DGs emerge. These interpretations lead to conclusions about the underlying cultures of the DGs and the
importance of cultural distinctiveness in determining their
policy prerogatives and outputs.

Path dependencies and policy characteristics

Competition policy
At its most preventative, competition policy exists to stop
firms behaving in a manner harmful to competition. Control of restrictive practices, abusive monopolies, and anti-
competitive mergers usually lie at its heart.

Competition policy was the first common policy of the
European Community (EC), but by the late 1970s it had
the appearance of a policy that had become sidelined. In
spite of extensive competition policy powers given to DGIV
staff and to the College of Commissioners between 1957 and
1962, advocates of a strong competition policy seemed to
be swimming against an ideological tide, even though legislative and judicial activity in the restrictive practices field
was considerable. During the 1970s, DGIV staff consistently
found themselves at odds with the nationally-orientated

interventionist spirit of the times. In consequence, DGIV was not thought of as being a prestigious DG and the competition policy portfolio was not seen as being especially attractive for ambitious Commissioners.

Over the course of the 1980s, the policy was revitalised as the process of completing the internal market helped the Commission to make much more use of its extensive competition powers. Revitalisation was also assisted by the recruitment of staff – especially lawyers – from national competition authorities, which confirmed DGIV's legitimacy based on an acknowledged expertise in the antitrust field.

The work undertaken by the staff of DGIV is largely shaped by the nature of the policy it administers. However, this does not imply that DGIV's policy objectives are clear-cut. An initial question to address might be whether DGIV's primary policy goal is the promotion of competition, or whether market integration or pro-competitiveness goals tend to supercede the competition criteria. Although DGIV staff have been keen to stress the compatibility between a strong competition policy and the creation of a single European market, there are times when a solely negative (deregulatory) approach to integration does not suffice. So, although there may be a potential compatibility between market-building, political integration, and competition policy, in practice the application of interventionist common policies frequently provides a virulent source of conflict between policy means and policy ends. However, EU competition policy itself involves much more than just market-creation, as policies do not stand isolated from each another. Indeed, policy-makers and administrators dealing with competition policy have often had to face a great deal of political pressure from national governments and industrial lobbies, raising important and sensitive questions about the impact of a politicised policy on industrial structure, behaviour, and performance.

It could be said, therefore, that the tensions inherent in the application of a European-level competition policy, together with a collective awareness of the organisational history of DGIV, shapes many of the basic assumptions under which officials work. The most obvious example of this is that there has long existed within DGIV an underlying assumption that competition is a good thing. This may seem fairly innocuous, but behind this are other assumptions about the predilections of firms (and states) when faced with a potentially harsh competitive environment. So while competition as such is generally viewed positively by DGIV staff, industrial actors and national governments tend to be viewed with an underlying suspicion. This, no doubt, shapes judgements when DGIV exercises its policy competition role, and when it acts as prosecutor, judge and jury during the process of bringing competition cases to completion.

Environment policy

Involving in essence the creation of a regulatory regime, European environment policy has rested since its emergence in the early 1970s on a two-pronged approach. on the one hand, overseeing the application of multi-annual environmental action programmes that act as frameworks for policy priorities and statements of principle; on the other hand, pursuing a legislative programme, usually involving the drafting of new directives or the updating and consolidation of more long-standing ones. As a result of this legislative approach, policy emphasis has been placed on standard-setting, a process that implies the replacement of national regulations or national 'voids' with European-level rules. This raises important questions about whether what the policy aims to do is really the 'upgrading of a common interest' or simply the pursuit of the 'lowest common denominator'.

Like DGIV, DGXI's internal dynamics and its relationship with other Commission and EU actors has in part been conditioned by its functional responsibilities and its organisational past. A key feature of this organisational past in respect of DGXI is recruitment policy. When a new DG is created, recruitment normally takes place from existing DGs and from other European institutions. But when DGXI was set up in the late 1960s environmentalists rather than European officials were appointed. One senior DGXI official has remarked that from the very start this gave the DG a reputation for being dominated by what he called 'ecological freaks'.

A sense of difference and commitment was therefore instilled in DGXI staff from the outset. Environment officials often exacerbated this sense of difference by giving the impression that they were working in a political vacuum.

The drafting of legislation seemed to take place behind closed doors without, apparently, much regard for policy being made elsewhere in the Commission. Even Non-Governmental Organisations (NGOs) seemed excluded from the process. As a result, in a very short space of time DGXI officials produced a huge amount of legislation – over 12,000 pages of it by 1993, according to one DGXI official. With those who would have to implement the legislation rarely involved at the formulation stage, the Commission's environment policies were often considered unrealistic, unworkable, and even utopian by those whose job it was to apply them at the grassroots level.

The politics of the environment evidently shapes the work done by DGXI staff. But a commitment to environmental principles has made it extremely difficult, if not impossible, for the DG to achieve its ultimate aim, which is to have a positive impact on environmental outcomes. In the Fifth Environmental Action Programme (OJ C 138/1993) which was drawn up in 1992 to cover European environmental strategy over the 1990s, a number of themes, not all of them new, were expanded upon to form the basis of a new way of working in DGXI.

The theme of shared responsibility became a first principle. It focuses on the relationship between the many different levels of government involved in the development and application of policy. Within the European institutions generally, and most notably in the Commission, this principle has manifested itself concretely in the establishment of a number of networks and institutional forums that it is hoped will assist in the translation of environmental strategy into environmental practice. As part of this development, attention has shifted from legislative outputs to policy implementation.

Integration is the second crucial theme that has come to dominate the formulation of environment policy and its ground-level implementation. In this case, integration is taken to imply the inclusion of environmental concerns into other sectoral policy domains so that, for example, the process of distributing research grants by DGXII (Research) now includes serious consideration of potential environmental impacts. Such environmental considerations are fast becoming part-and-parcel of the criteria upon which all Commission

decisions are assessed. Likewise, DGXI staff are now expected
to consider very carefully the practical feasibility of their
proposals. This might involve, for example, the application
of certain agreed operational principles, such as the principle of BATNEEC – that is, best available technology not
entailing excessive cost. It must also imply a change in
mentality amongst DG staff, so that henceforth they see themselves as more 'mainstream' Commission officials. Clearly,
this approach raises crucial questions about policy aims and
objectives, questions about which there remains a fair degree of uncertainty. For example, what exactly does 'mainstream' imply in this context? Does it mean that environmental
principles are considered merely as contributors to the single market goal, or that all other policies must henceforth
take into consideration the environmental implications of
their planned actions?

Institutional autonomy and administrative discretion

Competition policy
Since the mid-1980s, the autonomy that comes from wielding administrative discretion has highlighted DGIV's distinctiveness. This does not simply apply to an image of the DG
presented externally, but it also reflects the self-perception
of DGIV officials. That is to say, it relates to the identity of
the DG, and stems at least in part from a confidence endowed by its extensive set of legal powers. DGIV has a range
of policy-making powers of different strengths in different
spheres of competition policy. Its powers of investigation,
especially those which have been popularly characterised as
'dawn raids' because they allow for unannounced on-the-
spot investigations, are much covetted by other Commission
DGs, not least by DGXI which would itself like to possess
stronger enforcement capabilities.

But the uniqueness of DGIV's powers lies most particularly in the barrier it is able to construct between itself and
the Council of Ministers. Other than for a few broad Council regulations issued to exempt certain classes of agreement
from the competition rules, DGIV has little need to take
part in the consensus-building, log-rolling politics of the
Council. This does not mean that competition policy is in

any sense de-politicised. Rather, the arena within which politics is played out in the competition policy domain is shifted from the Council to the Commission services and, inevitably, also to the College of Commissioners. Where there is scrutiny over the policy, it comes from the Court of Justice (ECJ) rather than from the Council or, indeed, the European Parliament (EP). Moreover, resource constraints mean that DGIV increasingly seeks to find enforcement shortcuts. An ever-growing use of informal settlements in competition cases (in the form of administrative letters known as 'comfort letters') is crucial, given that the ECJ has a limited right of review over them. The flexibility of the DG in applying its own priorities, and the scope for political interference in the application of the policy is enhanced as a result.

Much is made of the iconoclasm and missionary zeal of DGIV officials, though this is perhaps not quite as strong in the mid-to-late 1990s as it was at the end of the 1980s. The DG's legal powers and scope for discretion provide much of the explanation for its policy outlook and its tendancy to assume high moral and ideological ground.

Environment policy
DGXI is generally considered to be a weak DG within the Commission. Its inability to win arguments or to have its priorities translated into EU priorities provides ample evidence of its marginal character. This is partly the result of its late arrival on the political scene. More importantly perhaps, it reflects the perception that its policies seem far removed from mainstream Commission priorities.[4]

So while DGIV is characterised by procedural autonomy and discretion, it is more appropriate when looking at DGXI to consider the constraints to which it is subject. These constraints are not simply legal, though the DG certainly does not have the enforcement capacity of DGIV. Rather, the constraints facing DGXI are primarily ideological, in the sense that its officials often have been promoting a vision of ecologism which neighbouring DGs have tended to consider unattainable. In addition, its particularly technical focus and what seems to be a disregard for the political dimension of policy does not help to raise the profile of the DG from that of a minor league player.

DGXI's powers are conventional to the extent that they rely on the Council and the EP (as well as the Commission itself) for support. Although a traditional regulatory approach continues to dominate, since the end of the 1980s efforts have been made to introduce new and more innovative means of tackling environmental problems such as market instruments. These have not been wholly successful, and in some cases (most notably in the case of the carbon/energy tax) have failed to gain the support of the Council.

It would, however, be misleading to claim that DGXI officials have no administrative discretion when formulating policy on the environment. But such discretion is only really noteworthy if outcomes are affected. The watering-down of standards in both the Commission and the Council, the influence of the industrial lobby in countering ecologically motivated agendas, and the variability in implementation rates when policy finally comes to be applied, means that the policy initially advocated by DGXI is often far removed from eventual outcomes, and that the DG's policy process is characterised more by policy contraints than by institutional autonomy.

Beliefs that the DG has not been very effective have led to a conscious attempt by elites within the Commission to alter DGXI's underlying culture. Leadership is clearly important in this respect and this has been forthcoming in recent years, both at Commissioner level (especially when the outspoken Carlo Ripa de Meana was Environment Commissioner between 1989 and June 1994) and at official level. This emergence of stronger leadership is important as it has led to a top-down exercise in altering the underlying assumptions, belief systems and ethos of DGXI officials. One senior official, who transferred into DGXI from a more industry-orientated DG, has gone as far as to say that there has been a concerted effort to change the culture of the DG. What this amounts to is an attempt to go beyond structural and procedural change (although these too were important elements within the Fifth Action Programme) to change the underlying rationale of, and justification for, environmental policy. This attempt at change is centred on a concerted effort to turn environmental constraints into environmental opportunities.

External constraints and opportunities

Competition policy
In spite of the reassertion of a more interventionist ethos in Western Europe since the early 1990s, the persistence of neo-liberal thinking, taken together with the (at least partial) establishment of a European single market, has consolidated the Commission and the Member State governments commitment to competition controls. DGIV has benefited from this evolution in the climate of opinion. What is more difficult to ascertain is the extent to which DGIV itself has influenced the spread of a neo-liberal ethos, or has simply reacted to events outside its control (Cini, 1994). The relationship is a difficult one to untangle. It is clear that if DGIV is to have any impact upon its external environment, it has to use its capacity to influence relevant agendas and attitudes. However, with only 200 or so 'A' grade (policy-level) staff, DGIV is limited in its capacity. It is simply unable to react to every European-level abuse of competition. Its work, therefore, is as much about defining how firms and governments ought to behave – that is, establishing the 'rules of the game' – as it is about chasing up and prioritising breaches of those rules. Ultimately, therefore, a large part of DGIV's policy concerns the shaping, administering and indeed the creation of markets, through a mixture of deterrence, coercion, and encouragement.

It is necessary to be careful in assessing the impact of the application of neo-liberal logic within DGIV since the mid-1980s, as there is an identifiable gap between rhetoric and reality. While there is no doubt that the rhetoric remains of a purist neo-liberal type, competition policy is not always so pure in content when applied to real cases. Exceptions to the pro-competition ethos take the form both of legal exemptions and are also written into some of the policy statements of DGIV. It is clear that the promotion of competitiveness, alongside the promotion of competition, forms part of the policy agenda of the DG, even if the rhetoric often belies this feature of the policy.

Neo-liberalism as a rhetorical device should not, however, be underestimated. For DGIV staff it underpins a shared view of the world which almost goes as far as delineating good from evil and right from wrong. The language used to define interventionist or anti-competitive acts is almost biblical in the sense that images of *evil* firms or *good* governments simplify an extremely complex process of analysis. The biblical imagery can also be applied to the 'missionary' zeal with which DGIV staff pursue their cases. There exists amongst officials a shared commitment to the spread of DGIV values, not only within the EU but also globally (Cini, 1994).

DGIV staff thus tend to take as their starting-point a 'big picture'. It is a picture which is determined as much by ideological predilections as by industrial realities, although the two are more or less merged by those applying the competition rules to specific cases. The relationship between the world view held by DGIV staff and the policy approaches, ideologies, and economic arguments which are in the ascendant outside the DG are thus extremely important. The climate of opinion in the EU has altered dramatically since the mid 1980s, not necessarily forging a complete ideological consensus, but changing the centre-ground enough to enable the work of DGIV to be considered for the first time as a pivotal aspect of the work of the Union and, more specifically, of the Commission. The single market programme, itself partly driven by this ideological shift, has further propagated the shift, feeding into the same process and facilitating the work of DGIV.

This does not all mean that DGIV's policy is now applied without constraint. Neo-liberal thinking has come under attack in the 1990s. Moreover, specific competition questions and, more pointedly often, specific competition cases, can provoke strong feelings and can give rise to sharp national and sectoral antagonisms. This can result in strict competition criteria being set aside, especially if the College of Commissioners decides that political sensitivities must guide decisions. Nonetheless, the underlying legitimacy of DGIV seems now to be firmly entrenched.

Environment policy
The neo-liberal thinking that continues to carry weight within the Commission has, on the surface at least, not been conducive to the emergence of a strong, prioritised environment policy. While DGIV was both influenced by, and

influential in, the rising ascendency of neo-liberal thinking from the mid-1980s, DGXI staff were facing a serious challenge to their underlying assumptions about ecology and industry, founded largely on notions of sustainability. As a result, what Weale (1992), amongst others, has identified as 'ecological modernisation' was introduced gradually into DGXI thinking, subsequently consolidated by a new wave of thinking that emerged after the 1992 Rio summit.

In the EU, this new thinking has focused particularly on the notion that, in future, those with the highest environmental standards should set the level of 'product acceptability'. The implications of the adoption of such a system of beliefs for DGXI and its policy is clear. It implies the need for the completion of the process of integration of environmental concerns into other policy areas; it requires much more of a precautionary approach to policy formulation; and it means that a more sophisticated understanding of the relationship between a range of public policy objectives must be developed.

However, it is all very well identifying an 'ideology' of ecological modernisation within the official documentation. What is not so visible is the extent to which elites have really succeeded in replacing what appeared to be a rather simplistic set of morally founded ecological beliefs with a much more complex belief system. Certainly, if interviews are an acceptable source of reference, DGXI staff seem to have accepted the new regime.[5] It is interesting to note that, by contrast, attitudes towards and expectations of DGXI from *outside* the DG have not altered so speedily. As one DGVII (Transport) official commented: 'What DGXI write on paper has very little to do with the real world. They are not living in the real world. They simplify issues and are optimistic'. It would certainly take time for this official to be convinced of any deep-seated change in the basic assumptions and beliefs prevalent within DGXI.

ADMINISTRATIVE CULTURE IN DGIV AND DGXI

In this chapter, administrative culture has been interpreted as a shared understanding of the world within an institutional arena, deriving from a collective system of ideas, beliefs, symbols and behavioural characteristics. On this basis, it is clear that the cultures of DGIV and DGXI are very different. While DGIV officials share a belief in the virtues of the competitive industrial environment, they also see themselves as situated on the moral high-ground, endowed with a mission to establish norms and to encourage working practices that promote competition. DGXI's culture is, by contrast, more difficult to pin down. It is currently going through a process of transition, as leaders seek to forge a new underlying ideological consensus and identity. Thus, whilst in the past DGXI culture was ecological in a purist sense, a more tempered industry-receptive, market-oriented view of environmental problem-solving has been advocated by new elites, and seems gradually to be gaining acceptance amongst officials.

The fact that a top-down and conscious attempt is being made to alter a DG culture suggests that there is an awareness that cultural differences between DGs are a source not only of institutional friction within the Commission, but can also result in policy inconsistency and policy failure. More generally, it is recognised that when inter-service disputes enter the public domain the Commission's reputation suffers enormously, and its ability to play an assertive role in the European policy process is weakened.

Of course, not all of the bureaucratic politics played out within the Commission stems from cultural differences. But cultural differences do make for durable inter-service cleavages. As long as there is no cohesive all-inclusive Commission culture, cultural differences between the DGs will continue to hamper efforts to turn the Commission into a more unified and a more effective policy-making body.

Differences of various sorts between DGs will doubtless persist. But the Commission is perhaps most damaged when differences take the form of DGs developing their own conflicting visions of the world, of the values of officials being shared only by their DG colleagues, and of institutional identification being with the DG rather than with the Commission as a whole.

CONCLUSIONS

This chapter has examined the individual characteristics and distinctiveness of two of the Commission's DGs. It has been argued that questions of administrative culture must be explored at this level of analysis as well as at the level of the Commission as a whole if a complete picture of the operation and motivation of the Commission is to be drawn. However, it has been possible here only to touch upon certain elements of DG activity, attitudes and influence. There is clearly a lot more to be said – about, for example, organisational norms inside the DGs, day-to-day working practices, and differing modes of communication and behaviour. What should be clear, even so, is that aspects of institutional life such as ideology, belief systems, values, myths and symbols, must be taken into consideration when studying the Commission.

The precise nature of links between administrative culture, policy processes, and policy outcomes are complex. That such links do exist, however, is widely recognised. Sabatier (1987), for example, has implicitly suggested a causal link between culture and policy, arguing that before altering policy approaches it is necessary first to alter basic values. Weale (1992) has also concurred that it is impossible to understand developments in public policy without uncovering the belief systems that lie at the heart of the policy process. Weale is, however, right to point out that caution must be exercised in assuming any direct and simplistic causal relationship between belief systems and policy outcomes. It is all too easy to make facile 'leaps of faith' when seeking to explain matters of policy.

The conclusions to be drawn from this chapter about the relationships between Commission culture, organisation and policy are, therefore, tentative. The main conclusion is that cultural insights help us to interpret the Commission. They help us to consider the Commission from an institutional perspective – as a political and a policy actor in its own right, and not simply as an arena in which politics occurs. Administrative culture alone does not explain policy formulation, policy content or indeed policy outcomes; neither does it explain all aspects of institutional life. But it does help us to understand more fully why and how the Commission does the things it does. It opens a window on the institutional subconscious.

Notes

1. Allaire and Firsirotu (1982) have pointed out that one commentator, writing in 1952, managed to identify 164 definitions of culture!
2. The work of March and Olsen (1989), amongst others, is very useful in this context, for it deals with cultural issues in a political context under the heading of new or historical institutionalism.
3. Fieldwork, in the form of interviews, was conducted in these DGs between 1993 and 1995.
4. Delors certainly showed little interest in environmental policies for most of his three terms of office.
5. This has had a knock-on effect on attitudes to DG XI elsewhere. One interest group representative commented that DG XI had been 'infiltrated'.

5 A House with Differing Views: The European Commission and Cohesion Policy

Liesbet Hooghe

This chapter explores the role of the Commission in institutional change in the EU. Building upon a case study of the Commission's central role in cohesion policy since the mid-1980s, I examine theoretical implications for understanding how the rules of the game may be altered.

The reform of the structural funds in 1988 was a bold attempt to transform a system of financial reimbursements into a policy where decisions and resources are shared among European, national and subnational actors. But the outcome has been more modest than anticipated by the designers. To explain this gap between original purpose and actual outcome, many studies have focused on the interests and relative power of national and subnational actors. However, such external explanations ignore the relative autonomy of Commission actors to shape outcomes. As is shown in section one of this chapter, the reform of the structural funds has been heavily contested in the ranks of the Commission, and those favouring a flexible implementation of the rules have gained the upperhand.

The politics of contestation in the Commission challenges our conventional understanding of institutional change in the EU, as is highlighted in section two. Section three moves beyond cohesion policy to propose an alternative approach to institutional change. It is argued that it is necessary to make a clear distinction between purposeful actors and political rules. A central concept in structuring the interplay between actors and rules is the role perception of actors. I focus on Commission officials, and show that the complex institutional EU environment sends out a variety of incentives which form a 'menu' of possible interests or ideas for officials to emphasise. Commission officials set their goals by *selectively* taking cues from this setting – they are not 'pre-programmed'. A better knowledge of the range of roles Commission actors may select is the first step to a better understanding of how their actions may alter the rules.

COHESION POLICY AND SUBNATIONAL EMPOWERMENT: HIGH EXPECTATIONS AND MIXED RESULTS

The Commission became subject to great change when Jacques Delors became its President (Hooghe, 1996b). Having been instrumental in bringing about the internal market programme in 1985, Delors launched the cohesion concept in 1986 as the social complement to the internal market. Under the banner of cohesion policy, he obtained a quadrupling of the budget for structural policy for the period 1987–99. Moreover, he pushed through an overhaul of the structural funds in 1988 and steered the policy through a major review in 1993 despite a critical mood among the Member States.

'Cohesion' was the deliberately vague label for an ambitious policy with a double purpose. On the one hand, it summarised a novel policy rationale for economic development in the poorer regions of the EU (then EC). On the other hand, it held a political promise to involve subnational actors more openly in European decision-making. The target groups of Delors' approach were *les forces vives*, a variety of organised public and private actors with a stake in the local economy and society. Amongst these actors, subnational authorities figured prominently. The reform was to empower subnational authorities in the European arena, especially in those Member States where they were weak. By specifying how this empowerment should be organised, it was hoped that a more uniform pattern of subnational involvement could be achieved (Smyrl, 1996).

The central instrument of cohesion policy consists of multi-annual structural programmes for indigenous regional and local development. The programmes – which are based on three structural funds (dealing with regional, social, and agricultural issues) – are designed, run and monitored by the Commission in concordance with national and subnational authorities. 'Partnership' among Commission, national and subnational authorities is the chief institutional innovation underpinning an emerging system of multi-level governance. In practical terms, partnership is taken care of through a cascaded structure of committees where the three partners flesh out consecutive stages of the programming. This is a radical departure from earlier practice, where interactions were restricted to two partners – the Commission and national authorities – and were kept at arms' length (Tömmel, 1992).

The first round of programming was concluded in 1993, and the second generation of the reformed structural programming is scheduled to end in 1999. The major impact in terms of decision-making has been that central state executives have been forced to share powers with subnational governments and the Commission. In the area of cohesion policy, state-centric governance has thus been challenged by multi-level governance. Expectations for political influence have been raised among subnational actors in countries where they are presently weak, such as in Greece or Ireland, and where they are politically entrenched, as in France, Spain, Belgium and Germany. Where the allocation of competencies is contested, as in Spain, Britain or Belgium, cohesion policy has fed into that conflict. Multi-level partnership is thus a reality, and there is ample evidence that it has shaken up territorial relations. However, the results have fallen short of the high expectations of the policy drafters and many subnational actors that the policy would encourage more uniform subnational involvement. European cohesion policy has promoted more, not less, variation in subnational mobilisation (Hooghe and Keating, 1994; Marks, 1996; Smyrl, 1996). For the longer run, then, cohesion policy may tilt territorial relations in the direction of subnational governments, but in the short term it has tended to exacerbate contention about resources and competencies (Marks, 1996).

Most analysts have focused on national or subnational actors to explain the gap between original purpose and actual outcome. One line of reasoning is that the Member States have used their dominant position in the EU framework to rectify the pro-regional bias in the original policy. Central governments are reluctant to lose sovereignty in this area, and they have the power to claw back control. So state-centric governance returned with a vengeance (Pollack, 1995a). Other analysts find the source for the muddled outcome in the existing structure of territorial relations. They argue that a 'Europe of the Regions' was destined to fail because the divergences among regions and local governments in resources, competencies and interests made collective action extremely complicated (Hooghe and Keating, 1994; Smyrl, 1996; Anderson, 1996). The logics of national government interests and subnational divergence provide compellingly simple explanations for the mismatch between original purpose and outcome in EU cohesion policy. Factors *outside* the Commission forced the latter to yield to a more modest policy. This explanation rests, however, on two debatable assumptions. First, it assumes that the Commission is an actor with a given agenda: to maximise subnational empowerment through cohesion policy. In reality, cohesion policy has been highly contested in the Commission since 1988. The original blueprint laid down in the 1988 structural funds reform was largely the work of a small committed group around Commission President Jacques Delors. Several units in DGs which were affected by the reform resented being forced to change their priorities and practices. The Commission is not a unitary actor.

Secondly, it assumes that the Commission was overruled by more powerful actors with different preferences. There is, however, little evidence of such a 'forced' retreat. It would be misleading to attribute the dilution of the original purpose to Member State pressure; it was Commission-driven. From the early days of the 1988 reform, the implementation of partnership had been a major issue among the Commission services involved in structural programming. On the one hand, DGXXII (Co-ordination of Structural Policies), which had been set up by the committed group around Delors, which had masterminded the reform, and which subsequently took responsibility for the coordination between the three funds, defended a strict application of partnership. It wanted to maximise subnational input in structural programming and, in the long run, to encourage a European-wide system of territorial relations where subnational authorities from Germany to Greece were assured an influential role. On the other hand, the funding agencies and particularly DGXVI (Regional Policies) wanted a more flexible approach: the Commission would promote subnational involvement, but this should not necessarily happen at the same speed and in the same way throughout the Union. By the end of 1992, the latter line had prevailed, and DGXXII was abolished. Hence the coalition of Commission actors favouring an integrationist conception of cohesion policy lost out to a coalition championing a more flexible, decentralised cohesion policy. So by the start of the negotiations for the 1993 review in the Council of Ministers, the new policy was already consolidated. In the Council – the privileged arena for Member State interests – Commission officials successfully resisted attempts to weaken the Commission's new policy position. When some Member States tried to further erode partnership and to weaken the Commission's role, the Commission negotiators mobilised support in the European Parliament, among a dissenting minority in the Council of Ministers (Portuguese, Irish, and Belgian governments), and among subnational governments. This enabled the Commission to largely deflect Member State pressure for further dilution of the reform (Marks, 1996).

Whether one focuses on the tug of war in the Commission or in the Council, Commission officials emerge as actors with access to a variety of power resources. These enabled them to contend for policy adjustments that best suited their interests and ideas.

SHIFTING STARTING POINTS

The political activity and contestation around cohesion policy raises a number of issues that challenge our conventional understanding of change in the EU. The following four propositions can be made:

1. European policies are shaped by actors who cannot simply be equated with institutions such as the Council and the

Commission, or with the Member States. Divisions about policy exist *within* EU institutions and *within* Member States, as well as *between* them. Cohesion policy was not so much shaped by power relations between the Council and the Commission, with Member States seeking maximum benefit and minimal loss of sovereignty and wielding Council powers to reign in an integrationist Commission. Rather, divisions inside these institutions had a profound impact on the policy. First of all, the Council was not a unitary actor. In 1993, three governments backed the Commission for reasons of policy or political calculation, proving that some state executives are sometimes quite prepared to give up state control over a major policy in return for other ends (Marks, 1996). Inside the Commission, purpose and direction of cohesion policy were contested, as shown above. And inside several Member States, different options were hotly debated, as is demonstrated by Jeffrey Anderson (1996) in an analysis of the German position on the 1993 review. New and old Länder held divergent positions, as did different services within the Federal Government – in particular the Ministry for Finance and the Ministry of Economics. At decisive moments, these different actors forged alliances with like-minded actors outside the German domestic context. For example, the new Länder talked to the Objective 1 regions (underdeveloped regions) from the cohesion countries (Spain, Greece, Portugal and Ireland) to dissuade them from vetoing the recognition of the new Länder as Objective 1 regions. Also, parts of the Commission (particularly the Commissioner Bruce Millan and his services in DGXVI) and the new Länder governments formed an alliance against the German Federal Government during the negotiations of the 1994–99 programmes.

The question thus arises when is it still useful to conceive of the Council, the Commission or the Member States as unitary *actors*? It may be better to view them as arenas – as sets of political rules which provide the context for a variety of political actors to pursue competing agendas.

2. Individuals or small groups of people matter. 'The structural funds were developed by three people. The opposition was total: Member States, the Funds . . .' (official of the former DGXXII, interviewed by the author in October 1993).

The preferences or motivations of Commission officials matter, though officials do not work in an anarchic world but within a set of institutional rules. Rules constrain purposeful actors, but actors can also change rules. Specifically, they can use existing rules to institute new ones that place them in a more strategic position to pursue what they want. By using presidential authority and the President's influence in administrative organisation and personnel policy, Jacques Delors and his *cabinet* shielded the task force for the 1988 reform from sources of opposition, in particular from the fund managers in the three affected DGs and from national bureaucracies. When the package went to the Council, they made sure that reliable officials would defend the 'Commission position' before the Member States. They upgraded the task force to a Directorate General (DGXXII), won the battle inside the Commission for making DGXXII the spokesman for the Commission, and parachuted one of the central drafters into the DG and just in time to lead the negotiations. Thereafter, the existing political rules in the Commission turned against the original drafters. The most powerful (and most affected) Directorate General, DGXVI, regained the initiative, by exploiting its hold on the purse, by relying on contacts with national and regional authorities, and by using its relative autonomy in policy direction, administrative organisation and personnel policy to restructure on its own terms.

The challenge for analysts is thus to specify the institutional levers which purposeful actors can pull to achieve their goals. More generally, the question is how this *interplay between purposeful actors and institutions or rules* works.

3. Motivations are complex and enduring. One official described the contestation between the DGs over cohesion policy as 'a brutal battle', but emphasised immediately that underlying fierce power politics was a deeply rooted conflict of ideas and ideologies. Actors were often motivated by a number of issues: more or less supranational control, more or less Europe of the Regions, the prevalence of one DG over another, the need for a mobilising idea for the Commission versus running things efficiently, public intervention versus free market, and career concerns. Their stances often reflected

enduring beliefs and motivations, or role perceptions, which they tended to carry from one issue to another, or from one post to another. Several core drafters of the reform moved on to chase other policy-initiating jobs; several reluctant officials were and remained predominantly efficiency-oriented managers, in or outside cohesion policy. Motivations proved to be very complex in the ideological domain. Most actors believed firmly that the EU had to be more than an economic market, but they supported cohesion policy for different reasons and assigned subnational partnership different priorities. Many believed that markets work more efficiently if public actors provide a stimulating setting of collective goods, especially in backward areas; partnership was useful as a potential venue for affected interests to combine forces. For others, the EU had an obligation to solidarity, that is, to provide benefits to those who stood to lose in a single market; partnership might give weaker subnational actors a stronger voice to demand solidarity. A third group believed that the most important challenge was to democratise decision-making by involving a wide array of societal and public actors in the European arena; partnership was a crucial vehicle for democratisation. In an address to the Objective 2 regions (regions suffering from the decline of traditional industries) in 1991, Jacques Delors skilfully blended this message of efficiency, solidarity and democracy: ' . . . we want you to be in a position to mobilise all vital forces in your region. In the age that democracy is spreading, it is magnificent to know that you have often successfully brought together public and private actors, business, trade unions, agricultural organisations, and associations. We want to support this partnership for a simple reason: we believe that nowadays development is more a matter for local agents than a matter for the central level . . .' (Delors, 1991, translation by the author). The 1988 reform was strongly inspired by concerns about democracy and solidarity, but, over the years, those who emphasised enhancing market efficiency and solidarity took the lead. This changed the character of partnership from an objective as and of itself to a means to achieve other goals.

The question for analysts is how to capture these motivations, which often present themselves *as a complex mixture of*

*ideas and interests, and how to relate them to the institutional
constraints under which actors work.*

4. European integration is politics, not the outcome of functional or rational-bureaucratic processes. The divisions on
cohesion policy echo a deeper struggle in the EU. The pro-
tagonists of cohesion policy, for all their internal differences,
strongly feel that they are defending a particular societal
model: ' . . . This battle is well worth the effort . . . because
we are defending a cultural model, neither the Japanese
model nor the American model . . . but the social market
economy . . . the Rhine model. And that idea is shared from
the south of Spain to the north of Sweden' (senior official
in a 'cohesion' service interviewed by the author, July 1995).
They share this ideal with actors in the Council, the Parliament and in society at large. However, it is contested by
other actors, including colleagues in the Commission: ' . . .I
have combatted public interventionism, protectionism and
overregulation – that has been my mission to date, that has
been my ambition' (senior official outside the 'cohesion'
services interviewed by the author, December 1995).

The question for analysts is how prominent these *broader
'projects'* are in the European Union. To what extent has
this politics permeated the Commission, inducing Commission
officials to take *political* stances?

These observations undermine the assumption that the
Commission is a unitary actor with fixed preferences. Different units or individuals promote different goals; there are
cracks in the 'monolith'. This forces us to re-define the issues at stake in European integration. The gist of European
politics is not only about the locus of control – a supranational
interest in expansion versus greater central state control. It
is a much richer complex, consisting of both narrower matters like career concerns, political calculation, better policy
results, administrative expediency . . . and more profound
issues like the balance between political regulation and the
market, solidarity and opportunity, efficiency and democracy.
It is necessary also to re-define the political actors who make
European politics. Political change in the EU is not so much
the outcome of the interplay between the 'Council' or the

'Commission'. The European arena is much more crowded; change results from purposeful actors exploiting these institutions as arenas to tilt the course of events in their direction.

There are three ways to proceed from here.

1. The complexities which have been noted above could be regarded as background noise and there could be an opting for parsimonious explanatory models. The state-centric model is the best known instance of a parsimonious model. However, it argues its parsimony at the expense of three simplifications. It assumes that European policy outcomes can be explained by interests and power – which minimises the role of ideas, ideology or persuasion; it argues that what really drives EU politics are national interests as formulated by state executives – which erases supranational institutions or subnational actors from the picture; and it conceives of states as unitary actors, or at the very least effective aggregators of domestic interests – which simplifies European politics to interstate negotiations in a rather perfect two-level game. This approach has produced some excellent work on European integration, both in a traditional institutionalist or historical mould (Moravcsik, 1991, 1993; Milward, 1992) and through the use of a rational choice framework (Pollack, 1995b; Garrett 1992, 1995). However, bearing cohesion policy in mind, validity is sometimes sacrificed in the name of parsimony. A predominant focus on interstate negotiations fails to capture that EU policies have become increasingly contested among a wide set of actors.

2. Generalisations could be eschewed. Many case studies of particular policy areas, issues or decisions show a seductive fascination with the unique features of a case: the determination of certain individuals, the presence or absence of 'a rapport' among key players, a brilliant idea, an unexpected crisis, external intervention, drama, luck and fate, and an unusual confluence of circumstances. Case studies sometimes offer rich insights into power and political dynamics. However, explanations of particular outcomes are almost always overdetermined. As the account of cohesion policy shows,

it may just be possible to capture the essence in simpler causal processes which can travel across cases.

3. There could be a search for a structure underlying the multiple issues, the actor crowdedness, the multi-level coalitions, and the variety of strategies (from interstate bargaining to transnational mobilisation) that characterise EU politics. How might such a structure, especially as it relates to the Commission, be uncovered? I suggest proceeding in three steps:

— People live and work in a world of rules. In conducting their affairs, Commission officials, for example, are constrained by the way in which authority is allocated in the EU. More directly, they are constrained by the rules of the game in the Commission, and most immediately by the rules of their own Directorate General or subdivision. Furthermore, Commission officials are EU citizens, who in their particular way are influenced by the increasing interdependence of political, social and economic life in Europe. A sharp distinction should be drawn between political actors and political rules (institutions).

— People do not live in institutional cages. They bring their own interests and ideas with them. Moreover, actors are often keenly aware that they are able to set their goals by selectively taking cues from the institutional setting. Political actors are seldom puppets on a string. They are purposeful actors, and the purposes they seek are partly moulded by the political rules, but they are also partly driven by personal preferences acquired autonomously from political rules. These preferences need to be identified.

— Roles are the place where rules and reasons meet (Scaring, 1991, 1994). Roles refer to a relatively permanent set of expectations – a structure of motivations, beliefs and attitudes about the part one seeks and thinks to play. They grow out of reflections on one's location in the institutional setting and one's personal preferences. If we have, for example, a perception of how Commission officials view their role in the EU, we may understand why some might push for a change in cohesion policy that others would resist. Roles vary from actor to actor, but it is possible to demarcate a limited number of distinct types of role perceptions – a typology in other words – varying according to a few underlying dimensions. So by identifying and categorizing the roles actors play, we can give structure to the complex world of European politics.

There are at least three uses for such a typology. First, it could explain why people choose particular roles in the EU: the *typology as a dependent variable*. The theoretical questions centre around the interplay (and relative weight) between rules and reasons, and between interests and ideas. Substantively, insight in the causal dynamics underlying the typology sheds light on what drives European integration. For example, if role definitions vary systematically with the nationality of the respondents, then this would suggest a significant impact of national background.

Secondly, the typology is a 'thoughtful' way to catalogue personal stories and case studies. So the limited number of ideal-typical roles constitute a reservoir for a more refined understanding of the EU: the *typology as an interpretative framework*. For example, the types contain expectations about the role of ideology or democratic values in the Commission and in EU governance: the salience of these factors, the substance, and the different opinions on them.

Finally, these particular motivational types would make it possible to predict coherent patterns of attitudes and behaviour and help to explain particular outcomes – the *typology as an independent variable*.

Understanding the political roles actors play, and how they have come to hold them, thus requires knowledge of the institutional setting in which they are located and of the cues actors have actually taken (rules); the personal ideas and interests they have, and which of those they bring to their activity (reasons); and the interplay between rules and reasons. Understanding political change requires one thing more: a grasp on the institutional levers that purposeful actors, playing a particular role, could pull to push forward their stance.

THE ROLES COMMISSION OFFICIALS COULD PLAY

Commission officials are central actors in the game of European politics. In the case of EU cohesion policy, we found that divergent agendas from different corners in the Commission prominently shaped rule change. Understanding the roles Commission officials play seems, therefore, a good place to start the study of political change in the EU.[1]

Officials live in a multi-layered institutional setting, which provides them with a variety of often incompatible incentives. They are not 'pre-programmed' to consistently promote European interests or to enhance the Commission's control over EU policy. Rather than a uniform role prescription, a 'menu' of possible motivations, beliefs and attitudes emerges from a multi-layered structure of political rules. The world they live in contains at least three distinct settings of political rules: they participate in EU governance; they are employees of a European institution, the Commission; and they are citizens of the EU. I will look at each institutional setting in turn to show how a menu of possible motivations emerges for Commission officials in search of a role.

Participants in EU governance

EU governance is multi-layered, ambiguous and open-ended compared to governance systems in national states. This context sends out particular signals to all political actors in the European arena, and that includes Commission officials. It induces them to choose between political orientations and administrative orientations, but is clearly skewed towards politics. And it also encourages them to choose between a 'European' administrative and political style of inclusiveness, persuasion and interlocking, or the maintenance of particular national administrative styles. Here, the political rules of EU governance are more equivocal, though national styles that are exclusive and hierarchical do not sit well with EU governance.

The Commission's hybrid role as a bureaucracy and political player on the European stage stands out. As and of itself, this mixture of political and administrative roles is common in modern administrations (Aberbach *et al.*, 1981; Suleiman, 1984; Suleiman and Mendras, 1995; for a theoretical argument in the American context, see Wood and Waterman, 1993; on the historical interplay between political authority and administration at national level, see Page

1985). Senior civil servants usually work in two worlds simultaneously. They make and take orders for routine actions
in the hierarchical world of bureaucracy, on the basis of
written rules or rational analysis; and they mobilise support
for contentious actions in the non-hierarchical world of
politics, through persuasion or arm-twisting. But several features of the EU framework combine to tilt the balance for
the Commission towards politics, and at the same time to
blur distinctions between bureaucratic and political roles.
These features are :

Open-ended objectives
The EU does not have a political executive that can claim direct political legitimacy, nor a body that gives political direction. The Commission itself, as Neill Nugent explains in
Chapter 1, is neither a conventional political master in its
own right nor does it have its hands tied wholly by one. The
absence of common purpose and the lack of political accountability leave many Commission officials permanently vulnerable
to political criticism. They may react in two ways: they may
choose to tread cautiously or, alternatively, they may set their
own agenda and go out to mobilize other actors. Either way,
Commission officials are pulled into the political world.

Ambiguity of the Commission's status
Commission officials are career civil servants, but they are
given the unique power to initiate and draft legislation, and
they have the duty to be the engine of integration (Article
155, EC). Different from their national counterparts,
Commission officials have a constitutional obligation to play
a prominent 'political' role that is not simply a by-product
of their technical expertise or tenure. This power is jealously guarded by Commission officials, though it puts them
at odds with their lack of political accountability. So Commission officials are expected to 'shake up' things. The price
for the right to be partisan is a loss of bureaucratic integ-
rity. Matters that could be bureaucratic in less ambiguous
institutional contexts may easily become politicised in the
EU. To a much greater degree than in national environ-
ments, the bureaucratic and political worlds are blurred.

Multi-layered structure of authority

EU governance is a system where authority is fragmented over different institutions and different territorial levels. The EU is not a Westphalian state (Caporaso, 1996): there is no single, hierarchically concentrated, exclusive core of authority where demands are prioritised. It is true that the fifteen central state executives still constitute the single most powerful nodes of authority, but they are increasingly locked in mutual dependencies of competencies and resources with actors at supranational and subnational levels (Marks *et al.*, 1997; Sbragia, 1993). Commission officials have to deal with a multiplicity of competencies (mostly shared with other actors), principals to serve (most notably the Council, the EP, individual Member States, and the public), demands, and resources (many on loan, others severely limited).

The complexity of EU governance compels actors to simplify decision-making. That may logically take them in two directions. There are strong incentives to 'harmonise' decision styles into a European-wide style, which travels across policy sectors and European territory. Rather than insisting on unilateral action, actors make policies jointly, and rather than trying to impose tasks, they coax affected parties to collaborate. In other words, actors are compelled to play a 'game' of mobilising and nurturing support (Mazey and Richardson, 1993a; for a lively account of the experience of British civil servants in the Commission, see Christoph, 1993). As one senior Commission official put it: 'This is a Japanese House, you have to convince ... It is a House where nobody can take the luxury of not answering a good argument and nobody gives orders and nobody takes orders. You have to convince, so you have to know your task' (interview with the author, July 1995). However, there are also temptations to carve up the work in national pockets, where actors, principals, and demands tend to be fewer and more familiar and the allocation of resources is clearer. Rather than substituting an overarching European decision style for a variety of national political and administrative styles, officials may pursue a national style tailored to each national pocket (for a theoretical argument of the EU as a consociational system, see Taylor, 1991). Maintaining national styles sounds attractive when national nodes of authority are relatively intact and when state actors are prepared to give Commission officials access to the resources they need. But in other cases, one would expect Commission officials to prefer to pursue a European policy-making style.

Viewed on the bases of these three features, Commission officials hardly emerge as passive servants exercising a role etched in EU governance rules. Instead, they receive varied and partially conflicting incentives, which invites them to select from the menu what suits best their personal preferences. In Douglass North's terms (1990), they are purposeful actors in a relatively rule-free environment, seeking alliances with others to form various 'groups bound by some common purpose'.

My reading of EU governance strongly suggests that Commission officials take political stances on many occasions. This raises a major question of substance: what political goals might they seek to advance?

Employees of the Commission

As employees, Commission officials may be constrained differently depending on their location in the services. The second step in understanding variation in role definitions is thus to approach the Commission as an institution. If the rules were unambiguous and uniform, the motivations of Commission officials would reflect the Commission's institutional position. That is, they would be more or less preprogrammed to strive for maximum integration and for stronger supranational decision-making. In reality, the weight of the institution is far from perfect.

In the first place, Commission officials work in units with different task descriptions, and these may send signals at odds with the institutional interest of the Commission. Directorate Generals are often portrayed as worlds on their own. This has induced some authors to explore systematic differences in administrative cultures (see for example, Michelle Cini in Chapter 4; Wilks, 1992b; Bellier, 1994). Location in the services may have an impact on role definition in various ways. Officials in implementation or management units could be expected to have different views on their role than those in services emphasising policy initiation. Other significant distinctions may be found between DGs with broad horizontal mandates versus those with specialist task descriptions; DGs with a strong treaty base or money to spend versus those without these resources; DGs responsible for free market policies versus DGs responsible for social regulation.

Secondly, even in their immediate work environment Commission officials are less rule-bound than is often assumed. The rules are not always clearcut. In a young, evolving institutional setting like the Commission it is hazardous for purposeful organisations, and even more so for individuals, to 'specialise' in particular tasks. The organisation and task descriptions of the various services change at a high rate. Hence DGs send ambivalent signals to Commission officials. Rather than being served dishes that are pre-prepared for particular places in the Commission organigram, officials are offered a flexible menu with options which are available irrespective of where they sit: more policy initiation or more management; a generalist or specialist approach; more emphasis on competence prerogatives or more on networking; a focus on the market or on a social dimension? This leaves, once more, Commission officials considerable space to select from the more detailed menu the options that suit best their personal preferences.

However, in the context of EU governance, some options have been shifted upwards to more prominent places on the menu. In a politicised environment, and particularly one where the Commission is expected to be the engine of European integration, senior Commission officials in particular have traditionally been encouraged to emphasise policy initiation, take a generalist approach, and to explore forms of joint efforts beyond economic market integration. It has usually taken a little more personal determination to be a manager, a specialist, or a free marketeer.[2]

Citizens of the Union

We have thus far considered how political rules of the EU governance system and of the Commission environment may constrain Commission officials. We have found them imperfectly rule-bound. There is a third set of institutional constraints, often overlooked by analysts, which may give some structure to the remaining indeterminacy. Commission officials are not only participants in governing Europe and employees of the Commission, they are also citizens of an emerging European polity.

This needs some explanation. Many studies on European integration rely on a particular understanding of the conflicts structuring European politics. For most analysts, European integration has evolved around particular disagreements on purpose and method. Is it meant to produce economic benefits through cooperation or is the goal political union? And should the method of integration be intergovernmentalism or supranationalism? These may no longer be the major fault lines in the post-SEA era (Hooghe and Marks, 1996). The type and scope of salient issues has broadened considerably, a wide range of subnational interests has been mobilised directly in the European arena, and authoritative governance has been dispersed from central states to supranational and subnational actors. European integration has gone beyond a process of market deepening to the making of a polity. The EU is best conceived as a comprehensive framework of political rules which regulate how political actors may debate political options for the European society and make binding decisions on matters of public interest. The debate has shifted from 'whether a European polity is desirable' to 'how to design this European polity'. The gist of European politics is a struggle between contending projects or designs on the European political economy and on due political process. This encompasses a range of issues such as state and society, political regulation and the market, equity and liberty, efficiency and democratic accountability, and identity.

Much of the contention tends to crystallise around two dimensions: territorial identity and ideology. The latter pits proponents of a 'European societal model', as epitomised in the social market economy, against market liberals who argue for more space for market forces. The near-debacle of Maastricht has made salient the former dimension: territorial identity. This issue is not so much whether European or national identity should prevail – for most EU citizens,

Europe remains a much weaker pole of identity than the national state, though a minority has a greater attachment to Europe. The more interesting question is whether territorial identities ought to be exclusive or could be nested – a majority of European citizens recognise significant European and national or regional identities at the same time, though a minority holds exclusive attachments. (On the territorial aspects of public opinion see the twice-yearly *Eurobarometer* surveys).

Territorial identity and ideology become foci for contestation as European citizens are affected by the changing rules of political, social and economic life in European society(ies). As these dimensions become salient, they induce political actors to take positions. Commission officials, as citizens of an emerging European society, have great incentives to import these issues into the Commission. There are signs that these debates are being conducted in the Commission itself, with officials taking opposite sides.

However, there are limits to how far a Commission official can go in pushing particular ideological options or exclusive identities. Indeed, the rules of EU governance and of the Commission environment conspire against polarisation. To participate in EU governance and to be an effective Commission employee, it usually pays off to seek grand coalitions and avoid manifest partisanship. Hence, Commission officials define their roles at the intersection of three contexts: EU governance, Commission, and European citizenship.

CONCLUSION

Commission officials are central political players in the EU. Understanding how they seek to play their part holds great promise for the study of EU political change. They are influenced by several sets of rules, including those defining EU governance, the Commission environment, and European civil society. These produce a varied 'menu' of interests or ideas which Commission officials may want to pursue. The choice of dishes is not random. Firstly, recommended options are printed in bold, whilst alternatives are in regular font: Commission officials are encouraged to select political above administrative dishes, creative above routine food, and to avoid strong partisan seasoning. Secondly, many dishes on the Commission's menu also appear on the menus of other EU political actors, making the choices facing Commission officials more and more like those of other actors in the EU. As voters, political parties, interest groups, and governments increasingly debate the impact of European integration on identity, quality of life and work, Commission officials are compelled to take these issues on their plate, and to pronounce themselves on the proper seasoning. Nevertheless, Commission officials retain, in the end, remarkable space to shape their role in ways that fit their personal preferences. In the multi-layered setting of the European Union, the menu of role options is varied and sophisticated.

Notes

1. The seminal classics on the Commission bureaucracy are the sociological studies of Coombes (1970) and Michelmann (1978). More recently, one could add the more anthropologically oriented studies of Ross (1994) and Abélès *et al.* (1993).
2. The current Commission under Jacques Santer wants to give priority in promotions to officials with management experience. This is a reaction to the legacy of 'disorganisation' left by the Jacques Delors Commission, which had put great emphasis on policy creation and innovation (Ludlow, 1991; Grant, 1994; Ross, 1995).

6 The Commission as an Agent
Mark A. Pollack[1]

INTRODUCTION

Nearly four decades into its existence, the precise causal role of the European Commission in the processes of European policy-making and European integration remains theoretically contested and empirically unmapped. The standard theoretical approaches are well known, and require little elaboration here. On the one side, intergovernmentalists such as Moravcsik and Garrett have generally depicted the Commission (and other EU institutions) as essentially passive agents of the EU Member States, facilitating cooperation and lowering transactions and monitoring costs, but unable to exert any independent causal influence on the process of European integration. Supranational institutions like the Commission do not run amuck and shape the integration process, they argue, but obediently attend to the preferences of the Union's most powerful Member States (Moravcsik, 1993; Garrett, 1992). On the other side, neofunctionalists, students of the Commission, and students of multi-level governance have often bristled at the idea of the Commission as a 'mere agent' of the member governments, asserting that the Commission possesses considerable autonomy or independence from the member governments and often deals directly with interest groups and subnational governments within the Member States (see, for example, Haas, 1958; Marks, 1993; Nugent, 1995).

In the course of this debate, which is itself nearly three decades old, the precise causal role of the Commission has remained in dispute, and the very notion of the Commission as an agent has become a semantic bone of contention between the two bodies of theory. In this chapter, I suggest that principal–agent analysis, far from prejudging the question of Commission autonomy and influence, in fact offers us a valuable set of tools with which to problematise, hypothesise, and test propositions about the independent causal role of the Commission in the processes of policy-making and integration. More specifically, I suggest that principal–agent analysis, if used with care and discrimination, can allow us to pinpoint the factors which explain variation in both the autonomy of the Commission from the Member States and in its influence on policy outcomes in the EU.

I begin by sketching a simple principal-agent model of the relationship between the member governments as a collective principal, and the Commission as their executive agent, and discuss the conditions under which we might expect the Commission to enjoy some autonomy from its Member State principals, and the difficulties of testing such hypotheses empirically. Next, in the second section, I examine one of the most important powers of the Commission, its formal right of initiative, in the light of rational choice theories of formal agenda-setting. I suggest that the Commission's right of initiative does indeed confer genuine agenda-setting powers for the Commission when the Council votes by qualified majority, but that these powers depend upon a number of other factors specified by rational choice theories, and that our empirical understanding of the agenda-setting process is underdeveloped. Third, I discuss the theoretical and empirical debate on the Commission's supposed powers of informal agenda-setting, or political entrepreneurship, arguing that Commission entrepreneurship is real and important, but that the Commission's leadership potential is limited in ways which should be acknowledged in the literature. In the final section, I conclude by reaffirming the utility of the principal–agent model for the study of the Commission, acknowledge some of the weaknesses of the principal–agent approach, and suggest a few methodological cautions for future research.

Two broad arguments, one theoretical and one methodological, run throughout the analysis. In theoretical terms, I suggest that the Commission's independence, and its success or failure in formally and informally setting the agenda of the Member States, is a function of three primary variables: the distribution of information among the Commission and the Member States; the distribution and intensity of Commission and Member State preferences; and the decision rules governing EU policy-making. In methodological terms, I suggest that hypotheses about the Commission's causal role are exceedingly difficult to test empirically; that we should therefore beware of drawing broad conclusions about a Commission influence that may often be more apparent than real; and that empirical testing of such hypotheses therefore calls for considerable methodological caution by empirical researchers.

THE COMMISSION AS AN EXECUTIVE AGENT

In the standard principal–agent model of delegation, a group of collective *principals*, such as the EU member governments in the Council, may under certain conditions choose to delegate authority for certain functions to a supranational *agent,* such as the Commission, in order to minimise the costs, and maximise the gains, from mutual cooperation (Moe, 1984, 1987, 1990; Weingast and Moran, 1983; Kiewiet and McCubbins, 1991; Pollack, 1997). This act of delegation, however, immediately raises a problem, in that the agent may have preferences systematically distinct from those of its principals, and it may use its delegated powers to pursue its own preferences at the expense of the preferences of the principals – to 'shirk'. As Terry Moe argues, an agent such as the Commission might enjoy both the incentives, and the capability, of shirking in this way:

> A new public agency is literally a new actor on the political scene. It has its own interests, which may diverge from those of its creators, and it typically has resources – expertise, delegated authority – to strike out on its own should the opportunities arise. (Moe, 1990, p. 121)

Furthermore, in addition to its delegated powers, the agent may enjoy privileged or asymmetrical information regarding its performance, its budgetary needs, the technical requirements of a given policy proposal, and so on. Without some means of acquiring the necessary information to evaluate the agent's performance, therefore, the principal seems to be at a permanent disadvantage, and the likelihood of agency losses seems large.

Principals, however, are not helpless in the face of these agency advantages. Rather, when delegating authority to an agent, principals can also adopt various *oversight mechanisms* which can mitigate, if not eliminate, the informational asymmetries in favour of the agent, and limit the amount of agency shirking. The essence of oversight procedures is that they allow for (a) *monitoring* of the activity of the agent, to determine the extent of agency losses, and (b) *sanctioning* of the agent in light of the information thus provided. The first part of this definition refers to the (partial) correction of informational asymmetries in favour of the agent, while the second allows for the principals to apply positive or negative sanctions against the agent so as to reward appropriate behaviour and punish shirking. In the case of EU institutions, however, both monitoring and sanctioning activities are difficult and costly to the member governments, and these difficulties can create a certain discretion, or slack, to supranational agents like the Commission – even though, in the EU political system, Member State principals remain the dominant actors. Let us consider the difficulties of monitoring and sanctioning, very briefly, in turn.

Imperfect information, and the difficulty of monitoring

In the principal–agent literature, monitoring the activities of an agent can take several forms. 'Police-patrol' oversight, for example, involves the active monitoring by the principals of agency behaviour, as in the case of Congressional oversight committees, and is the most obvious and effective method of oversight. Such police patrols, however, are costly and time-consuming to the principals, and are in any event likely to capture only a cross-section of agency activities. For this reason, McCubbins and Schwartz (1984) suggest, principals may rely on 'fire-alarm' oversight, whereby third parties (citizens, organised interest groups) monitor agency activity and, if necessary, seek redress through appeal to the agent, to the principals, or through judicial review. Such fire-alarm oversight mechanisms, they concede, are likely to produce patterns of oversight biased in favour of alert and well-organized groups, but from the perspective of the principals they have the double advantage of focusing on violations of importance to their political constituency, and of externalising the costs of monitoring to third parties. Finally, principals may employ 'institutional checks', whereby one agent, such as a comptroller's office, may be created with a mandate to monitor the behaviour of another agent, and raise a fire alarm in the event of agency shirking.

Within the EU, Member States rely quite heavily on police-patrol oversight, most obviously via the complex system of oversight committees adopted under the rubric of comitology which exist in a number of areas of EU policy. Such committees, although complex and unwieldy, generally allow member governments to monitor Commission activity rather closely, providing them with an accurate picture of the Commission's behaviour. In addition, the Union also provides for fire-alarm oversight through the use of Article 173, which allows any member government or any directly affected individual to request judicial review of Commission actions before the European Court of Justice. Other EU institutions, such as the European Parliament (EP) and the Court of Auditors, also provide the member governments with additional information about the Commission's activities, thereby substantially mitigating, if not eliminating, the inherent informational asymmetries in favour of the Commission. In short, the Commission is closely watched in its duties, by the member governments, by individual plaintiffs, and by other EU institutions.

Member State preferences, decision rules, and the difficulty of sanctioning

In order to influence agency behaviour, however, Member States must not only be able to monitor agency activities, but also to apply sanctions when they discover agency shirking. The nature of such sanctions, widely discussed in the principal-agent literature, include, *inter alia*, the threat of budget cuts, of legislative overruling by the principals themselves, and, most drastically, of a revision or cutting-back of the powers of the agent in response to shirking. Using such sanctions, much of the literature argues, legislative principals such as Congressional oversight committees or Member State 'comitology' committees may credibly threaten agents with sanctions for shirking, and thereby control the behaviour of their agents.

The application of sanctions against an agent like the Commission, however, is not automatic, but generally requires a positive decision by the principals to impose such sanctions. The ability of the Member States to do so is a function of two factors emphasised in the principal–agent literature: the distribution and intensity of Member State preferences, and the decision rules governing the application of sanctions. With regard to Member State preferences, McCubbins *et al.* (1989) suggest that an agent like the Commission can *exploit conflicting preferences* among its principals to escape sanctions and pursue its own preferences, within limited bounds. That is to say, if a decision to sanction an agent like the Commission requires a majority (or a unanimous vote) among the Member State principals, then the Commission may drift considerably from the Council's collective ideal point, as long as it does not call forth the requisite majority (or unanimity) among the Member States required for the imposition of sanctions. Thus, insofar as the Commission can avoid alienating the requisite majority of Member States, principal-agent models suggest that the Commission may enjoy considerable discretion in its actions, without the fear of sanctions being applied.

With regard to decision rules, Scharpf's (1988) analysis of institutional change suggests the difficulty of sanctioning an agent is a function of two decision rules, namely the voting rules for the application of sanctions, and the 'default condition' in the absence of such a decision. *Ceteris paribus*, the application of sanctions is most difficult where the voting rule is unanimity, granting any single actor veto power over such sanctions. Less demanding decision rules, such as a simple or qualified majority of the principals, by contrast, make sanctioning correspondingly easier, and thus restrict the autonomy of the agent. In the EU's comitology system of oversight committees, for example, the Council majority required to overrule Commission decisions varies from one type of committee to another, with advisory committees unable to overturn Commission decisions, management committees able to refer decisions to the Council by a qualified majority, and regulatory committees able to refer decisions by only a blocking minority. As a result, the Commission should enjoy considerable discretion under the advisory committee procedure (typically used for competition policy), somewhat less discretion under the management committee procedure (often used in agriculture), and the least discretion under the regulatory committee procedure (used for particularly sensitive issues) (Gerus, 1991; Docksey and Williams, 1994).

Second, and equally important, Scharpf argues that a *status-quo* default condition makes institutional reform – and, by extension, revision of the agent's mandate – more difficult, by privileging the existing delegation of authority to the agent. Take, for example, the threat of treaty revision, in which the member governments might agree to revise the mandate, and reduce the powers, of an agent like the Commission or the Court of Justice. Such a treaty revision is, in some ways, the ultimate threat, but the institutional barriers to carrying out such a threat are high. Not only would such a revision require a unanimous vote of the member governments, and ratification by national parliaments and some national electorates, but the default condition for treaty provisions is the status quo, meaning that in the absence of a unanimous agreement on treaty revision the powers of the Commission or the Court stand.

Some of the Commission's powers, however, are established not by treaty provisions but by Council regulations with a fixed expiration date, as with the structural fund regulations or the regulations governing the Framework R&D programme. In these cases, the relevant regulations require periodic revision and readoption in the Council, meaning that the default condition is not the status quo, but the expiration of the programme, and with it the Commission's executive powers. The practical upshot of this need for Council revision, then, is that disgruntled Member States are periodically given the opportunity to 'clip the Commission's wings' if it acts in a way that diverges from their interests.

Empirical implications, and the challenge of empirical analysis

In sum, the autonomy of an agent such as the Commission is a function of several factors, including the distribution of information between the agent and its principals; the distribution of preferences among the principals; and the voting rules and default condition governing the application of sanctions against the agent. If these hypotheses are correct, the implications for the autonomy of EU institutions are two-fold. First, differences in the monitoring and sanctioning mechanisms for the Commission and the Court of Justice would lead us to expect, and allow us to explain, the apparent autonomy of the Court in influencing the course of European integration, since the Court enjoys greater informational advantages vis-à-vis member governments and is subject to fewer mechanisms of Member State sanctioning, leaving only the somewhat remote threat of treaty revision. The Commission, by contrast, is subject to a multiplicity of Member State control mechanisms, including most notably the comitology procedure, and its autonomy is accordingly more constrained. Second, with regard to the Commission in particular, the precise mix of these control mechanisms, and their credibility, varies from one Commission function to another and over time; this in turn implies that Commission autonomy also varies over time and across issue-areas, as a function of these varying control mechanisms. The question of supranational autonomy, therefore, is not a binary question of obedient servant or runaway Eurocracy, but one of specifying the conditions of an autonomy that varies across agents and issue-areas, and over time.

Unfortunately, testing such hypotheses empirically is far more difficult than it might appear at first blush, and the principal-agent literature is replete with methodological warnings about the difficulties of distinguishing between obedient servants and runaway bureaucracies. In essence, the problem is that agents such as the Commission may *rationally anticipate* the reactions of their principals, as well as the possibility of sanctions, and adjust their behaviour in order to avoid the costly imposition of sanctions. If this is so, then agency behaviour which at first glance seems autonomous may in fact be subtly influenced by the preferences of the principals, *even in the absence of any overt sanctions by the principals.* Indeed, as Weingast and Moran (1983) point out, the more effective the control mechanisms employed by the principal, the less overt sanctioning we should see, since agents rationally anticipate the preferences of the principals and incorporate these preferences into their behaviour. In this view, sanctions should take place only rarely, when an agent such as the Commission miscalculates the likely reactions of its principals, or the likelihood of sanctions in response to its actions.

The relevance of these observations becomes clear when we examine the record of Member State sanctions under the EU's comitology system of oversight committees. According to Gerus, for example, the management and regulatory committees for agriculture issued some 1894 opinions on Commission actions during 1990 – not a single one of which was negative (Gerus, 1991, Table 2)! At first glance, the remarkably low rate of committee referrals to the Council would seem to suggest that committee oversight is perfunctory, and the Commission largely independent in its actions. However, as Gerus points out, rational anticipation of committee action by the Commission may mean that the Commission is effectively controlled by the Member States, despite the startling rarity of sanctions against it. As one Commission official explained to me, having one's proposal referred from a committee to the Council can cast a long shadow over the career prospects of a young *fonctionnaire* – a powerful incentive to rationally anticipate a proposal's reception in the relevant committee (interview, March 1995).

My point here is not to suggest that the Commission enjoys no discretion in carrying out its executive functions. The point, rather, is to suggest that even with a clear set of hypotheses such as the ones generated above, it is exceedingly difficult to demonstrate Commission independence in empirical research. Commission *activity,* I would argue, cannot be adduced as evidence of Commission *autonomy* without clear and careful case studies which focus not only on the Commission's activities, but also on the policy preferences of both the Commission and the Member States, the possibilities for sanctioning and control of the Commission

by the Member States, and on the formal and informal interactions between the Commission and the Member States
in a range of policy areas such as external trade policy,
competition policy, agriculture, and the management of the
structural funds. Such a comprehensive study remains, alas,
far beyond the scope of this chapter, but it is the clear next
step in any research agenda focusing on Commission agency
and autonomy.

THE COMMISSION AS A FORMAL AGENDA-SETTER

In addition to its executive powers of implementation, the
Commission also enjoys important legislative powers, most
notably the sole 'right of initiative' for Community (EC
Treaty) legislation. In the language of rational choice theory,
this sole right of initiative provides an actor like the Commission with formal agenda-setting power, allowing it to
influence policy outputs even when the power to take the
final decision lies elsewhere (in the Council, or the Council and the EP, in the EU case). The agenda-setting power
of a policy initiator in such models depends on several key
variables, including: the institutional rules governing who
may propose an initiative; the institutional rules governing
both voting on a proposal and amendments to it; and the
distribution of actor preferences. Let us consider each of
these variables briefly.

The first and most important prerequisite for formal agenda-
setting power is the exclusive right to propose legislation,
which the Commission possesses in most areas under the
EC pillar of the European Union. By itself, however, the
right to propose is not sufficient to assure agenda-setting
power. As Tsebelis (1994) points out in his study of 'conditional agenda-setting' by the European Parliament, the influence of an agenda-setter will, *ceteris paribus*, be greatest
where the voting rule is some form of majority vote, and
where the amendment rule makes the agenda-setter's proposal difficult or impossible to amend – in other words, where
it is easier to adopt the agenda-setter's proposal than to
amend it. Applied to the Commission, this analysis of agenda
power with different voting rules and amendment rules yields

varying results depending on the voting and amendment rules governing a given piece of Community legislation.

Until the Single European Act (SEA) came into force in 1987, there was only one legislative procedure – the *consultation procedure*. Under the procedure, the voting rules in the Council were a mixture of unanimity and qualified majority, whilst the amendment rule was unanimity in all cases. However, notwithstanding these treaty provisions, the *de facto* situation for twenty or so years after the 1966 Luxembourg Compromise was that the unanimity rule was used for most votes. This meant that although it was difficult to amend the Commission's proposal, it was equally difficult to adopt the proposal, and any Member State could veto a proposal with which it is unhappy. In most areas, therefore, the Commission's formal agenda-setting power was minimal or nonexistent prior to the adoption of the SEA.

In the mid-1980s the Luxembourg Compromise began to lose much of its force. This coincided with the creation of the *cooperation procedure* by the SEA. The procedure seems to confer precisely the sort of agenda power that rational choice theorists assign to Congressional committees and other agenda-setters: the voting rule is qualified majority, meaning that the Commission need only put forward a proposal capable of garnering the support of a qualified majority of the Member States; while the amendment rule is unanimity, making it quite difficult to amend a Commission proposal. In addition, the cooperation procedure also provides some limited agenda-setting power to the European Parliament, which may propose amendments to the Council's draft legislation (Tsebelis, 1994). These amendments, *if accepted by the Commission*, then become part of the Commission's amended proposal, and can accordingly be adopted by qualified majority, but amended only by a unanimous vote. In other words, the EP gains some agenda-setting power under the cooperation procedure, but the Commission remains the middle-man in the procedure, without whose cooperation EP amendments enjoy no special status.

The *co-decision procedure* established by the Maastricht Treaty establishes a similar agenda-setting power for both the Commission and the Parliament, with one important difference: in its second reading, the Parliament may, by an absolute majority of its members, re-insert amendments to the Commission's revised draft. Those amendments may then be adopted in the Council by a qualified majority vote where the Commission accepts the amendments, and by unanimous vote if the Commission does not accept them, as in the cooperation procedure. Under the co-decision procedure, however, if the Council does not accept all of the Parliament's amendments, it must then convene a 'conciliation committee' bringing together delegations from both the Council and the Parliament to reconcile their differences in a final draft, which then returns to the two bodies for final approval. The net effect of this complex conciliation process (which, according to Earnshaw and Judge (1995), took place in 14 of the first 32 co-decision procedures) is to remove the Commission as the middle-man between the Council and the Parliament, allowing for direct bargaining between the two bodies, providing the Parliament with a possible veto of the final product – and removing the formal agenda-setting power of the Commission in the process (for details, see Earnshaw and Judge, 1995; Garrett and Tsebelis, 1996).

Finally, it should be noted that the Commission's agenda-setting power also depends in every case on the preferences of the Member States, and in particular on the Commission's ability to exploit conflicting Member State preferences. Under the cooperation and co-decision procedures, for example, there may be a large number of alternative policy proposals on a given issue capable of garnering a qualified majority among the Member States without being amended by unanimity. On an environmental directive, for example, we might imagine two possible qualified majorities in the Council, with one composed of the least environmentally advanced Member States, and the other of the most advanced. Put simply, the Commission's agenda-setting power consists in choosing which of the possible winning proposals to put up for a vote in the Council, and thus which qualified majority will be able to adopt its preferred directive. The Commission, therefore, *cannot* push through its ideal proposal without regard to the Member States' preferences, but it *can* operate creatively within the constraints of those preferences to shape the composition of the qualified majority and the content of the decision ultimately taken by the Council.

Anecdotal evidence from my own previous work indicates that the Commission has indeed used its agenda-setting power to push through far-reaching proposals in areas such as social policy, copyright harmonisation, television broadcasting, and automobile emissions (Pollack, 1995b). To my knowledge, however, no systematic studies exist of formal Commission agenda-setting under qualified majority voting, in the absence of which Commission agenda-setting – like the conditional agenda-setting posited for the European Parliament by Tsebelis – remains better theorised than documented.

THE COMMISSION AS A POLITICAL ENTREPRENEUR

Perhaps the most common and far-reaching claim of Commission influence, however, relies not on its formal agenda-setting powers – which in any event do not extend to the second and third pillars, or to revision of the Treaties – but rather on its ability to behave as a 'leader', a 'political entrepreneur' or an 'informal agenda-setter', influencing and advancing the integration process by tabling new and innovative proposals which command the assent of the member governments and nudge the Union in a more integrative direction (for general discussions, see Sandholtz, 1992a; Peters, 1994a; and Nugent, 1995). Claims of this sort are legion in the literature on the Single European Act (Sandholtz and Zysman, 1989), Economic and Monetary Union (Ross, 1995), structural policy (Marks, 1993), technology policy (Sandholtz, 1992a; Peterson, 1992), telecommunications policy (Sandholtz, 1993a), and nearly every other policy pursued by the Union, and as such merit special attention here. I refer to such claims as theories of informal or substantive agenda-setting, to distinguish them from the Commission's formal agenda-setting powers discussed above.

In the basic or standard model of informal agenda-setting, the member governments of the EU are confronted with a collective dilemma, in which Member States would benefit from common action but are faced with the transactions costs of identifying and negotiating collective action to deal with their common policy problems. In this situation, the Commission may step in as a leader or political entrepreneur, taking the lead in proposing innovating new policy ideas to 'upgrade the common interest', building coalitions within and among Member States, and brokering agreements among the member governments in the Council of Ministers, thereby facilitating mutually beneficial cooperation among the Member States, and possibly influencing the nature and content of their cooperation in a more integrative direction (Kingdon, 1984, p. 188; Sandholtz, 1993a, p. 250).

In a recent article, Moravcsik provides a compelling criticism of models of Commission leadership, arguing that such leadership is neither a necessary nor a sufficient condition for international cooperation in the EU. As he points out,

> the claim that the Commission is an effective informal agenda-setter in international negotiations rests in turn on a deeper claim, namely that the Commission is a privileged, perhaps monopolistic provider of some unspecified 'public goods', informational in nature, which increase the efficiency or bias the outcomes of negotiations. (1995, p. 615)

Yet, Moravcsik argues, the Commission can scarcely be a monopolistic provider of such goods, because it is not a monopolistic possessor of them. To take only three examples, Moravcsik points out that the Commission enjoys no monopoly right of initiative in the areas of treaty revision or in the second and third pillars, where the lead is often taken by the Member States, and in particular by the Franco-German alliance; it enjoys no monopoly of information, since member governments and private groups both enjoy access to policy-relevant information, and may provide such information and ideas in the policy process; and it enjoys no monopoly in its ability to broker compromises among the Member States, a function that is often performed by the EU Presidency or the Council Secretariat. In this view, the argument that the Commission is uniquely placed to set the EU agenda flies in the face of evidence that the resources and the functions typically attributed to an informal agenda setter are possessed by member governments and by some private interests as well as by the Commission.

Furthermore, Moravcsik suggests that just as executive agency may be more apparent than real due to rational anticipation of Member State preferences, so informal agenda-setting may represent rational anticipation by the Commission of the sorts of proposals most likely to be approved by the member governments. For this reason, Moravcsik argues, observing the Commission making a proposal, and the Member States adopting it, is not sufficient to demonstrate Commission influence over the outcome. In order to establish that the Commission is actually able to influence the substantive agenda of the Member States, Moravcsik argues, 'we must pose a counterfactual question: Would similar policy ideas have been advanced even in the absence of the Commission or other supranational officials?' (p. 615). In most cases, Moravcsik argues, similar ideas were, or would likely have been, introduced by either member governments or private actors. Focusing on a number of the major decisions in EU history, Moravcsik argues that his case studies do not support the notion that Commission entrepreneurship is a necessary condition for integration, nor that the Commission is a monopolistic provider of public goods:

> On the contrary, the transactions costs and informational requirements of preparing initiatives and mediating compromises appear to be comfortably within the means of even smaller national governments, assisted by a handful of national or Council officials. While Commission involvement may sometimes expedite agreement, it has often been strikingly counterproductive and appears only rarely to have made a decisive contribution ... (p. 620)

Moravcsik's challenge merits careful attention, laying out as it does the important and empirically verifiable claim that Commission entrepreneurship is not a necessary condition for international cooperation in the EU. The Commission may act as a political entrepreneur setting the substantive agenda for the Member States, but it may just as easily overreach and fail in its ability to do so; and we should be cautious in assigning the Commission an independent leadership role which may be more apparent than real.

Despite the force of Moravcsik's critique, one might nevertheless respond by pointing out that very few students of the Commission actually make the argument which Moravcsik refutes, namely that the Commission is a monopoly provider of leadership and therefore a necessary or sufficient condition for integration. Rather, most analysts of the Commission's role argue simply that the Commission *may*, under certain circumstances, perform the various functions of leadership, and thereby influence the outcome of decisions taken by the Member States in the Council of Ministers or the European Council.

The success of the Commission, or indeed of any political entrepreneur, in setting the agenda for the Member States depends on a number of factors, emphasised to different degrees by different authors. Many authors, for example, emphasise the personal and/or the organisational characteristics of a political entrepreneur – such as expertise, persistence, and leadership skills – as important factors underlying the success or failure of entrepreneurs in influencing policy outcomes (see, for example, Kingdon, 1984; Sandholtz, 1993a; Nugent, 1995). In addition to these characteristics of the Commission itself, however, the entrepreneurial success or failure of the Commission also depends on a number of contextual or relational factors, including most notably the distribution of information among the Commission and the Member States, the distribution and intensity of preferences among the Member States, and the ability of the Commission to strike up transnational coalitions to support and lobby for its policy proposals.

First, with regard to the distribution of information, Sandholtz (1992a, 1993a) and others suggest that the Commission's influence is greatest in those areas where it possesses the greatest policy expertise, and where the Member States face imperfect information or uncertainty, or are searching for new policy alternatives. In such cases, Member States are most likely to converge on the Commission's proposals as a 'constructed focal point' (Garrett and Weingast, 1993) around which the uncertain expectations of the Member States may converge.

Second, the distribution and intensity of preferences among the Member States is absolutely central. As in the case of formal agenda-setting, the Commission cannot simply propose its own ideal points without regard to the preferences of the Member States, particularly when those preferences are clear and intense, since such proposals are almost certainly doomed to fail, especially where decision-making takes place by unanimous vote. On the other hand, by analysing carefully and accurately the preferences of the Member States, an entrepreneur such as the Commission can increase the likelihood that its proposals will be taken as the basis of a consensual agreement among the Member States.

Third and finally, a number of authors have suggested that a central element in successful entrepreneurship is the construction of transnational coalitions of *policy networks* which may lobby the member governments to accept the Commission's proposals. Such networks may help shape Commission proposals, but they may also indirectly shape and modify Member State preferences on a given issue through a coordinated lobbying campaign within each of the Member States (Green, 1993; Peterson, 1996).

The empirical evidence on Commission entrepreneurship seems to support the standard model's claim that the Commission can shape policy outcomes under certain conditions, although it also suggests that the Commission's success in doing so has varied greatly, primarily as a function of the three factors just mentioned. Thus, for example, in the cases of the 1982 ESPRIT programme, the 1985 Single European Market (SEM) programme, and the 1988 reforms of the structural funds, the Commission appears to have exploited its own expertise and clear preferences, as well as well-developed policy networks of private actors in the Member States, to set the agenda for member governments with imperfect information and unclear preferences, who therefore converged around the Commission's proposals as a constructed focal point (Garrett and Weingast, 1993; on the empirical cases, see Sandholtz, 1992a; Peterson, 1992; Sandholtz and Zysman, 1989; Marks, 1993; and Smyrl, 1995).

However, if these cases illustrate the Commission's successes in setting the agenda for major decisions by the Member States, these and other instances also illustrate the limits of Commission entrepreneurship when confronted with member governments possessing complete information and clear and intense preferences. Take, for example, the most famous cases of Commission agenda-setting, namely the

Commission roles in the 1985 and 1991 Intergovernmental Conferences (IGCs). In the former case, I would argue that the two key Commissioners, Jacques Delors and Lord Cockfield, enjoyed a clear success in setting the agenda for the 1992 SEM programme, and for the SEA more generally. Yet Delors selected the SEM initiative, rather than an initiative in social or monetary policy, because he knew – he *rationally anticipated* – that it was most likely to garner favour with the member governments who would have to take the final decision. In the end, Delors calculated correctly that the member governments would adopt the Commission's SEM programme with very few amendments, and that the SEM would in turn relaunch the project of European integration; but in the process the Christian Socialist Delors contributed to the creation of a Europe in which the monetary and social policies which he favoured have lagged considerably behind the liberal, laissez-faire policies of the 1992 programme.

Similarly, as Desmond Dinan shows in Chapter 13, while Delors arguably played a key role in setting the agenda for the 1991 IGC on Economic and Monetary Union, the Commission played a less central role in defining the terms of the second intergovernmental conference on political union, where the Member States had much clearer and stronger preferences, and where the lead entrepreneurial role was in fact taken by the French and German governments. Delors, moreover, was widely perceived to have overreached in his political union proposals, leading the Member States to discard the Commission proposals as the basis of negotiation. Jean-Charles Leygues, a member of Delors' *cabinet*, aptly summarised the Commission's respective positions in the 1985 and 1991 IGCs:

> . . . Before we could count on being ahead of other people strategically. We knew what we wanted and they were less clear, partly because they didn't believe that anything much would follow from the decisions we asked them to make. Now they know that we mean business and they look for all the implications of our proposals. There are huge numbers of new things on the table and it will be much tougher going from now on. (quoted in Ross, 1995, p. 137)

Summing up, the Commission may, along with a number of other actors, attempt to set the substantive agenda for Member State decision-making, but it may overshoot and fail as well as succeed in these efforts; and its likelihood of success depends not only upon the characteristics of the Commission, but also on the distribution of information between the Commission and the Member States, the nature and distribution of Member State preferences, and the ability of the Commission to strike up transnational coalitions with private-sector actors.

CONCLUSIONS

In this chapter, I have argued that principal–agent analysis, and related theories of agenda-setting, provide us with a parsimonious and powerful means of problematising and theorising about the independence and causal role of the European Commission in the processes of EU policy-making and European integration. Across the three domains of executive agency, formal agenda-setting, and informal agenda-setting, I have suggested that similar factors – information, preferences, and decision rules – can be used to explain and predict variations in the Commission's independence from the Member States and in its ability to set the agenda for them. At the same time, however, I have suggested that the problem of measuring the Commission's autonomy or its influence in agenda-setting is complicated by the phenomenon of rational anticipation, and I have proposed the use of special research methods (case studies, historical process-tracing, counterfactual reasoning) to establish the precise causal contribution of the Commission to any decision taken by the Member States.

In the end, both the strengths and weaknesses of the models sketched here lie in their parsimony. Principal–agent models, like the related models of agenda-setting reviewed above, problematise and generate testable hypotheses about one particular dyadic relationship, namely that between the Commission and the Member States. In doing so, however, these models tend to de-emphasise (but not ignore) other inter-institutional relationships, as well as the informal policy networks emphasised by Marks (1993), Peterson (1996) and others. Perhaps most importantly, principal–agent models, in their focus on the dyadic principal–agent relationship, tend to adopt simple assumptions about the Commission as a competence-maximising rational actor, seeking to increase both the Union's and its own competences (Peters, 1992; Cram, 1993; Majone, 1994b). Such assumptions can be quite helpful in understanding the Commission's central role as the 'engine' of the integration process, but they fail to emphasize the very real importance of the Commission's *internal* structure and organisation. As Cram has pointed out, the Commission is in fact not a 'monolith' but rather a 'multi-organisation', composed of Commissioners, *cabinets*, and Directorates General, each with distinct preferences and distinct policy networks forming around them (Cram, 1994; Ross, 1995; Peterson, 1996). The models sketched here do not deny the importance of the Commission's internal organisation or the leadership qualities of a President such as Delors; but they nevertheless focus on the relational factors which explain the conditions under which a single Commission, like the Delors Commission, may sometimes succeed, and sometimes fail, in its efforts to advance the cause of European integration.

Note

1. The author would like to express his thanks to Neill Nugent for comments on an earlier draft of this paper, and to the World Affairs and Global Economy (WAGE) Initiative of the University of Wisconsin for research support.

7 Uniting European Industrial Policy: A Commission Agenda for Integration

Thomas C. Lawton[1]

INTRODUCTION

European Community (EC)[2] industrial policy was first explicitly identified in a 1990 Commission communication to Council and Parliament. Its legal base followed shortly thereafter, with its inclusion in the 1992 Treaty on European Union (TEU)[3]. Member States are now obliged to consult each other and co-ordinate their actions in many industry-related policy spheres. The industrial policy competence of the European Community thus needs to be understood as part of the European integration process.

This chapter recounts the story of how the Commission has achieved, by stealth, industrial policy integration. In doing so, several key questions are addressed, such as why and when the Commission started to promote industrial policy, what methods and policy instruments it has used, what sectors it has focused on and why, and which intra-Commission actors have had the greatest influence on the nature and direction of the integrationist industrial policy agenda.

INTEGRATION BY STEALTH

Several commentators have suggested that the Commission's primary organisational goals are to expand the scope of Community competence to new areas, and to increase its own competence and influence within the policy process (see, for example, Majone, 1991; Peters, 1992; Cram, 1993; Pollack,

1994). In the sphere of industrial policy, the Commission has pursued these goals via the use of a number of tactics, of which stealth has been amongst the most important. Recognising that some national governments have no wish to see a vigorous European industrial policy, or a significant role for the Commission in this policy sphere, the Commission has at times resorted to covert methods designed to bypass this intransigence. Tactics of 'covertness' or 'stealth' were used particularly during the decade of high activism which began in the early 1980s, when the Commission refrained from explicitly charting its growing power in industrial policy. Rather, it incrementally evolved its authority through developing and converging its influence in research and development (R&D) activities, trade policy, competition rules, and so forth. The support (or at least acquiescence) of national governments was achieved through the development of a Commission-led advocacy coalition, centred on a partnership between the Commission and big business, aimed at market liberalisation and competitive enhancement. To the background of the failure of national champion policies, and with the hope that collective action in Europe would restore competitiveness relative to East Asia and United States rivals, governments were persuaded that it was in the best interest of national economies to support Commission activism in many areas of business-related policy. The Single European Market (SEM) initiative was the most visible and ambitious outcome of this Commission policy activism, acting as a major catalyst to further European industrial integration.

Thus, a European industrial policy evolved piece-by-piece during the 1980s, despite the prevailing global 'policy fashion' premised upon the dismantling of national industrial policies. The Commission amassed many discredited instruments of national industrial policy, without the Council becoming aware of the full significance of their cumulative nature. In this way, the Commission expanded its competence and gradually made progress with its goal of European industrial integration.

Traditional neofunctionalist theory can help to explain the development of EU industrial policy, George (1991) and others have drawn on this theory to suggest that once the benefits of a particular European-wide policy become evident, pressure builds within other sectors of the economy for a similar approach. This is a difficult hypothesis to prove conclusively. However, if we consider it against the backdrop of the ongoing globalisation of market forces and corporate actors, the task may be more feasible. The information technology revolution has transformed the nature of modern capitalism – most obviously by increasing the levels of international trade and investment and by liberalising financial flows – and this has led to a greater integration of national economies. Global competitive pressures have, to an extent, acted as an external catalyst for integration, forcing EU countries to investigate the potential benefits to be had from pooling their resources. This has been the case for industrial policy and, indeed, also for related policy areas in that the relative success of EC industrial policy in dealing with global competitive pressures too great for the nation-state could be interpreted as a factor in the 'Europeanisation' of other policy areas under siege from the forces of globalisation such as social and environmental policies.

The neofunctionalist notion of 'political spillover' interprets the Commission as having a proactive role to play in the integration process. A shift in political authority from the national to the EU level is purposefully and actively sought by the Commission. This concurs with George's view of 'Commission leadership' being a key component of neofunctionalism. The leadership capacity of the Commission has been discussed by several commentators in recent years with, for example, Nugent arguing that the leadership capacity of the Commission has indeed increased over time (1995, p. 603). Whilst not exercising a monopoly on power, the Commission has significantly expanded its authority in many spheres of EU activity and has exercised effective leadership.

As part of its proactivism, a strategy that has been pursued by the Commission is seeking to establish certain policy areas as legitimate goals for EU-level action, achieving this, and then incorporating these policy areas into the Treaties. Nugent (1995) cites environmental policy as one such area. This chapter illustrates that industrial policy has been another. Ludlow (1991) argues that this simply concurs with the Commission's function as policy *animateur* and its role as the 'catalyst of integration' (Ludlow, 1991, p. 97). The ultimate objective, on the part of the Commission, is to fulfil its 'mission' of fostering the integration process (Nugent, 1995, p. 609).

Pollack argues that the Commission's entrepreneurship has been a major factor in greater policy power moving to Brussels in both regulatory (predominantly competition) policy and R&D policy (1994, pp. 96–7). These areas constitute two pillars of EC industrial policy as this chapter will define it. The third pillar is trade activities. It is argued that a loss of competitiveness rationale allowed the Commission to seize the leadership opportunity offered by national governments and business interests in the sphere of industrial policy at the end of the 1970s. EC industrial policy has thus evolved largely as a result of the Commission acting as a policy entrepreneur. The subsequent political spillover is due to the Commission's creation – in partnership with big business – of an advocacy coalition for many industrial policy issues.[4] The ultimate aim has been to extend the power of the Commission and to further the process of European integration.

It is this approach, combining the policy analysis-based new institutionalist theory[5] with a new interpretation of neo-functionalist thought, and centred on the Commission as a 'policy entrepreneur' or 'purposeful opportunist' (Cram, 1993), which best explains the relationship between industrial policy and the European integration process.

INDUSTRIAL INTEGRATION THROUGH COLLABORATIVE R&D

In the early days, the Community's research activities were confined to coal, steel, and nuclear energy. However, since the mid-1970s, they have gradually been extended to other fields. Little by little, a Community research and technology policy began to evolve, through a process of spillover, with the Commission acting as a policy entrepreneur (George, 1995, p. 4). During the late 1970s, large European firms, attempting to adjust to the new global competitive framework, began to perceive a need for co-operation and public policy involvement at an EC, as well as or instead of, at a national level. The EC Commission, through the person of

Vice President Davignon, saw an increased role for it vis-à-vis large European firms. As George argues, research and technological development (R&TD) policy is a good example of an issue placed upon the EC agenda by external developments (global competitiveness pressures), which was seized upon by the Commission to establish a common policy (1995, p. 5). During the 1980s co-ordination of R&TD became the central pillar of EC industrial policy, with knowledge creation and dissemination coming to be seen as central to innovation.

A symbolic starting point for large scale EC 'high tech industrial policy' activity is Davignon's 1979 meetings with the leaders of Europe's 'big twelve' electronics firms. As Sharp has argued, 'under Davignon's guidance, the Commission began to develop a more strategic approach to the IT sector' (1989, p. 202). The creation of a 'round table', comprising both EC officials and industrialists,[6] was intended to jointly devise ways in which the Community could help restructure Europe's high technology industries through research. Sandholtz and Zysman argue that the European Strategic Programme for Research and Development in Information Technology (ESPRIT) was designed by this group and then sold by the firms to their respective governments (1992, pp. 89–90). This round table heralded the beginning of the Europeanisation of the information technology sector and the development of a European 'policy style' for the industry. It was the product of two merging strands of neofunctionalism – political spillover and Commission leadership. There was a partial shift in corporate interest groups attention from the national to the European level (Mazey and Richardson, 1993b, pp. 249–52), accompanied by the Commission acting as a 'purposeful opportunist' (Cram, 1993) in a bid to further develop its agenda for integration. In effect, for high tech R&D collaboration, 'the Commission advanced concrete proposals, and industry lent essential support' (Sandholtz and Zysman, 1992, p. 90). So, from the early 1980s, there was a significant transformation in the nature of European industrial policies. As Sharp (1989) argues: 'While the 1960s and 1970s could well be called the Age of the National Champion, the 1980s may earn the title the Age of Collaboration' (p. 202).

In other words, a new 'policy fashion' (Richardson, 1996) emerged in western Europe, wherein the emphasis was on collective competition. Spurred on by the competitive challenge posed by the USA, Japan, and other East Asian economies, EC states sought refuge in collective action rather than stand-alone policies. This 'common external threat' inevitably served to deepen the spirit of unity amongst most of the EC's political and business partners. The early 1980s thus proved a period of policy transition in the EC which involved, amongst other things, an expanded role for Community institutions – primarily the Commission. Such a role was sometimes in tandem with, and was often at the expense of, national governments – depending on the industrial sector in question. The power shift was most obvious within information technology industries – where the requirement for global competitiveness and greater economies of scale was most evident and where also there was a need for an extension and redirection of research activities from traditional industries such as coal and steel into the new knowledge-intensive industries. Thus, driven by the necessity of expanding their economies of scale and sharing R&D costs, EC Member States ceded considerable policy authority in information technology to Brussels. Business supported this power shift, seeing benefits to be had in a larger 'home' market, greater trans-European co-operative linkages, and more sources of governmental R&D support. As Mazey and Richardson (1993b) argue: 'increasingly, groups themselves have recognised the logic and momentum of greater Europeanization of solutions' (p. 252). Crucially, the Commission actively sought this new policy competency, arguing that competitiveness could best be achieved if policy was implemented at a European level (Cram, 1994; Pollack, 1994; George, 1995).

From the early 1980s, the Commission's participation in R&D had two separate and distinct manifestations: firstly, through its financial involvement in pan-European Eureka[7] projects; and secondly, through EC Framework Programmes which it played a central role in developing and managing (there have been four Framework Programmes since 1984 – the Fourth Framework Programme covers the years 1994– 8). Within this two-pronged technology policy, the Commission placed considerable industrial policy emphasis on knowledge creation and dissemination. The special 'strategic' role accorded in the 1980s to science and technology in general, and information technology in particular, was described in the following terms by Commission Vice-President, Karl Heinz Narjes: 'It was not until 1980 that the Community was able to take a strategic view of science and technology. It was then that that the Commission first stated its belief that it was not possible to devise a new model for society, to secure Europe's political and economic autonomy, or to guarantee commercial competitiveness, without a complete mastery of the most sophisticated technologies' (1988, p. 396). Narjes further argued that the Community had a responsibility to 'strengthen the scientific and technological basis of European industry', in addition to actively encouraging industry to become more responsive to the global competitive environment.

Thus, it is clear that at the most senior levels of Commission industrial policy-making during the 1980s, an active interventionist view was taken towards the European high tech industry's competitive enhancement. Evidence of this active interventionism can be found in a series of case studies which have been undertaken in the sphere of EU high-tech policies. So, for example, Sandholtz (1992b) has argued that with regard to the information technology project, ESPRIT, the Commission 'seized the initiative' and exercised policy leadership (p. 272). An integrationist agenda which sought to develop European collaborative R&D initiatives for high technology activities was advanced through the creation of an advocacy coalition (see below) based on a Commission–business partnership. The usefulness of the coalition from the Commission's viewpoint was that large firms exerted influence over their respective national governments and persuaded them to support the Commission's efforts. 'The Commission first mobilised a transnational coalition in the telematics industry; then, with support from those influential firms, it won support for the programs [ESPRIT and RACE] from the national governments' (Sandholtz, 1992b, p. 9).

European industrial policy from the early 1980s in the field of information technology thus reveals a highly activist

Commission, working to ensure that domestic bargains are shaped by prior supranational bargains, and that supranational bargains form the bases for supranational policies. The evidence does not support the view put forward by those who subscribe to a broadly intergovernmental view of the integration process that international organisations such as the Commission are marginal to analyses of international cooperation.

THE COMMISSION AGENDA FOR INTEGRATION: INDUSTRIAL POLICY IN THE 1990s

A significant development in the process of European industrial integration was the issuing in 1990 of a Commission communication to the Council which sought to clearly define and establish an EC industrial policy. The communication, which was adopted by the Council, was entitled *Industrial Policy in an Open and Competitive Environment*. It served, in effect, to establish a *de jure* industrial policy, albeit one of a somewhat general and ambiguous nature. Great stress was put on the concept of 'competitiveness' and on the notion that the attainment of competitiveness is primarily the responsibility of enterprises. However, it was also emphasised that there was a role for governmental actors, which should take the form of them being active 'partners' rather than silent spectators.

The European Council accepted the approach of the communication and in so doing paved the way for industrial policy to be given treaty status via the TEU as Article 130 (EC). The EC was thus, for the first time, given an explicit legal mandate in industrial policy.[8] This manadate was generic in nature, designed to include all areas of industrial activity. In reality, sectoral emphases still existed and has continued to exist. Commission attention has remained focused on sectors which are considered to be crucial to European competitiveness and industrial integration.

Commission-led coalitions for competitiveness

To say that the ultimate onus for competitiveness is on firms themselves, is to state the obvious. To say that this responsibility should be extensively supported by the public sector has major public policy implications. The Commission acknowledges that firms compete for world market share but it argues that they cannot do so alone. Thus, a middle-way is advocated, between governmental directed firm strategy and free market competition. The Commission has pursued this 'middle-way' through the creation of an advocacy coalition, having a Commission–(large) firm partnership as its nucleus. Sabatier (1993) argues that an 'advocacy coalition' comprises

> ... people from various governmental and private organisations who share a set of normative and causal beliefs and who often act in concert. At any particular point in time, each coalition adopts a strategy envisaging one or more institutional innovation that members feel will further policy objectives. (p. 18)

The 'shared normative beliefs' generally consist of policy goals. The advocacy coalition's intention is to manipulate legislation, public expenditure, personnel concentration and so forth, so as to attain mutual policy objectives over a period of time (Sabatier and Jenkins-Smith, 1993a, p. 5). This strategy encapsulates the purposeful opportunism of the Commission in the realm of industrial policy, and its integration by stealth approach which is implicit in a strategy of 'institutional manipulation over time'. In addition, Sabatier's advocacy coalition framework may be interpreted as being in part a function of external (global) competitive pressures instigating policy change. This would concur with our argument that globalisation precipitated a new policy fashion (transnational collaboration) in Western Europe. The advocacy coalition created for industrial policy hinged upon the Commission–big business relationship, but also included some like-minded national governments, the European Parliament, and smaller private interest groupings. Ross (1993 and 1995) lends support to the thesis that EC industrial policy has been shaped by an advocacy coalition which has at its core a Commission-large firm partnership. This applies in particular to EC collaborative R&D policies. Ross differs slightly from our analysis, however, in that he identifies big business rather than the Commission as the policy entrepreneur. He observes that EC policies for electronics have emerged during the 1990s as a result of large European electronics firms exerting pressure on the Commission to assist them. These industrial leaders played the political card, intimating that the Community's *raison d'être* would be questioned amongst the European business community if the Commission did not attempt to assist industry in times of stiff international competition (Ross, 1993, pp. 20–43). In these circumstances, not only did the Commission fear losing the confidence of European business (and thus losing power *vis-à-vis* national governments) but, as several observers have argued,[9] it also saw European industry – especially high technology sectors – as potential allies in the struggle to achieve a federal Europe. The increased role of Community institutions in policy for high technology industries thus had political undertones. The Commission saw European high technology companies – particularly in the information technology sector – as potential allies in the advancement of an 'ever closer union'.

As outlined in various Community industrial policy documents,[10] in Delors' Copenhagen European Council speech of 1993, and in statements by numerous senior level Commission officials,[11] the information technology sector in general, and the electronics industry in particular, have been seen as a 'priority' industry for EC industrial policy. The high proportion of R&D funding channelled to electronics under the Framework Programmes illustrates the industry's position as the vanguard of the Commission's post-SEA drive towards industrial integration. More especially, as an integral part of the move to deepen industrial integration, the policy for the electronics industry is seen as strengthening European economic and political integration.

As part of its industrial policy, the Commission believes that both it and large European firms benefit from working closely together. More particularly from its viewpoint, Commission efforts to enhance the global competitiveness of firms is accompanied by a closer relationship between Brussels and corporate Europe, and this gives greater political authority to the Commission vis-à-vis national governments. In this context, the Commission has for some time pursued a policy designed to convert Europe's largely sheltered, national high-tech companies into competitive multinationals, with a Europe-wide marketing base. This policy

> . . . would not only give them the size to stand up to the likes of IBM and Hitachi, but also the resources to turn an increased R&D effort into new, competitive products. One way to achieve this was to bring European companies together in research. Joint research would lead to joint ventures. A lot of small, national champions would become a few big, European ones, whose interests would lie with the Community, not with separate states. Once again, research was given a political role, this time through high-tech rather than nuclear power. (McKenzie, 1992, p. 7)

In reviewing this powerplay over the last decade it would seem that the Commission strategy has been successful. Large firms have indeed come to play a very significant role in the process of European integration. In the information technology policy sphere in particular, the Commission has had considerable success in creating a common area of action, and this has helped to solidify Europe's industrial integration. Moreover, information technology policy appears to have translated into greater political unity, as is evident in the secondary role of national governments in creating and controlling EC policy for key electronics industries. Mazey and Richardson argue that the movement from national policies to European-level initiatives for sectors of the economy as diverse as textiles and stock exchanges signifies political integration at work (1993, p. 251). Their conclusions concur with our findings for electronics.

INTRA-COMMISSION RIVALRIES IN THE CREATION OF EC INDUSTRIAL POLICY

The Commission's agenda for industrial policy integration is influenced as much by internal bargaining between Directorate-Generals (DGs) and between DGs and Commissioners *cabinets,* as it is by external pressures and negotiations. Ideological cleavages exist as much within the Commission as they do within the Council of Ministers. Thus, policy and industrial integration is in part an outcome of intra-Commission rivalries, and bargaining between

bureaucrats and Commissioners of different ideological per-
suasions (and, sometimes, different national loyalties).

Within the Commission, the industrial policy bargaining
process involves the *cabinets* of several Commissioners, including the Commission President, as well as a range of
different DGs. The DGs involved invariably include DGXIII
(Telecommunications, Information Market and Exploitation
of Research), DGIII (Industry), DGXII (Science, Research
and Development), DGIV (Competition) and, to a slightly
lesser extent, DGI (External Relations).[12] A number of other
DGs, such as DGXI (Environment) and DGXXIII (Enterprise Policy), may also enter the bargaining process at different
times (Lawton, 1995).

Contrary to popular belief, the Commission is not a monolithic entity. As a multinational institution, it endeavours to
contain several divergent political and economic cultures.
The most prominent and vigorous intra-Commission schism
in respect of industrial policy is the divide between the more
open market and liberal trade cultures of officials and Commissioners from the Union's northern members, and the
more protectionist, *colbertist,* cultures of officials and Commissioners from France and the Union's southern countries.
Tensions arise not only in the Council of Ministers but also
in the Commission between those who favour a 'minimalist'
approach – seeing competition policy as the main tenet of
industrial policy – and those who prefer a 'maximalist' approach – advocating an active, interventionist industrial policy
regime (Sharp, 1991, p. 177). A constant struggle exists
between individual Commissioners and DGs to determine
policies for so-called 'core' technology industries such as
electronics.[13]

DGIV is the most liberal DG. It has consistently been the
strongest opponent of interventionist policies for the European electronics sector and it has resisted the very notion
of 'strategic industries' as outlined in various Commission
documents of the 1980s and early 1990s. DGXIII, by contrast,
has been the most interventionist DG, the most consistent
supporter of strategic targeting, and the most collusive with
big business. During the early to mid 1980s, its *dirigiste* approach dominated key aspects of EC industrial policy, particularly collaborative R&D programmes. Its central role has,

however, subsequently been reduced, as the structure of Frameworks III and IV (with, for example, their increased emphasis on the role of small and medium-sized enterprises) has resulted in power shifting to less interventionist DGs.

Intra-Commission ideological divisions of the kind just noted were starkly illustrated in a 1991 Commission report on the information technology industry (Commission, 1991b) and in the reactions to the report. Drawn up by DGXIII, the report was highly interventionist in tone, which resulted in it being strongly criticised, both publicly and privately, by more liberal DGs such as DGIII and DGIV.[14] The report was subsequently revised and given a more liberal tone.

The reactions to the 1991 report were a foretaste of things to come. The 1990s have witnessed a strengthening of Commission liberals and attempts to develop a more market-friendly, 'competitive promoter', form of EC industrial policy. Although this transformation is not yet complete, a progressively more liberal direction has been pursued by the Commission with regard to industrial policy.

IMPLEMENTING THE AGENDA

It should be emphasised that the Commission's industrial policy agenda for integration extends right through the policy chain. This chapter has focused on the 'up-stream' parts of this chain, in particular agenda-setting. However, the Commission's 'purposeful opportunism' extends all the way downstream, to the policy implementation stage. As Mendrinou argues, the Commission's powers in the area of monitoring Member State legislative non-compliance are crucial for any analysis of the role of the Commission in European integration (1996, p. 1). Monitoring is a crucial process in EU policy and politics, taking place in the sensitive area of relations between Member States and European institutions and constituting a significant chapter in the Commission's developing role in integration (Mendrinou, 1996, p. 2).

In the industrial policy sphere, the Commission is highly active at the implementation stage of policy. In, for example, policing the use and abuse of trade instruments, the operation of collaborative R&D initiatives, and the overall competitive environment of the EU, the Commission's policy monitoring and (discretionary) enforcement mandates are important parts of its agenda for integration. Thus, although we have not dealt directly here with the implementation stage of EC industrial policy, it must be emphasised that the Commission's agenda for integration encompasses not only the formulation but also the application of industrial policy.

CONCLUSIONS

From the late 1970s, the Commission began to broaden its competence in industrial affairs. From its traditional industrial policy domains of coal, steel, and nuclear energy, it sought a competency in newer industries which were of core economic value to Community Member States. It thus focused its efforts on those groups of industries comprising the information technology sector. The Commission, assisted by a group of large firms, successfully wrested considerable policy power from national governments through developing a type of knowledge-oriented industrial policy known as innovation policy, and concentrating this policy on information technology industries such as electronics. As Cram (1994) attests, many national governments were not willing participants in this transfer of authority to Brussels, so to try and side-step the opposition the Commission pursued its integrationist agenda more by stealth than by candour.

Thus, EC industrial policy for the electronics industry evolved as part of the Community's efforts to create a common area of action for industrial affairs. This is evident from the 1979 Davignon 'round table' meetings with electronics leaders, through the creation of the EC-directed Framework and ESPRIT R&D programmes, and EC involvement in Eureka. The process culminated in the 1990 communication on industrial policy to the Council and later industrial policy documents wherein electronics were explicitly targeted for 'special treatment'.

The focus on electronics has been part of a broader Commission strategy which has seen European industry – especially large firms within critical, enabling industries –

as potential allies in the struggle to achieve a federal Europe. As McKenzie has noted, a lot of small, national champions would become a few, big European ones, whose interests would lie with the Community, not with separate states (1992, p. 7).

Such an approach signifies a complete reversal of earlier EC attitudes towards large corporations. As Green has argued, during the first twenty years of the EC's existence firms were kept largely outside of policy decisions (1993, p. 3). This was partly due to the antipathy of the EC's Founding Fathers towards big business: Jean Monnet, for example, viewed business as 'too nationalistic to support a European project' (ibid., p. 3). It was partly due also to the associated fact that business saw more benefit through their national political patrons than through the Community.

The post-1970s entrepreneurial Commission strategy has been based in large part on a belief that European industrial interests can be integrated through, in the first instance at least, co-ordinating policy for a few large firms within key technology industries. These sectoral common areas of interest will in turn 'spill over' to other industries. Neofunctionalist theory states that the next logical step will be a consolidation of wider economic integration, which will subsequently enhance political union. Therefore, the Commission's creation of an advocacy coalition, resting upon a policy partnership with large, critical technology firms, will serve to foster European industrial integration and, at the same time, gradually undermine the position of the nation state as a policy actor. Our arguments support this neofunctionalist interpretation of Commission strategy from the Davignon–industry meetings onwards, and particularly during the lifetime of the Delors-led Commissions. Moreover, the evidence indicates that the Santer Commission is continuing with this integrationist strategy.

Notes

1. The author wishes to thank Jeremy Richardson for his helpful comments on a previous draft of this chapter. The chapter derives from a research project financed through an EU Human Capital Mobility

Fellowship based in the Department of Government at the University of Essex.

2. Under the terms of the Treaty on European Union, legal competence for industrial policy rests with the European Community and not with the European Union. Thus, we refer to 'EC' rather than 'EU' in this chapter.

3. Title XIII, Article 130 of the Treaty on European Union contains the first Treaty provisions for what can loosely be called EC industrial policy. Although there is no specific reference to a 'policy', areas are identified within which the Community may act to improve industrial competitiveness.

4. Sabatier's (1993) concept of an 'advocacy coalition' will be discussed briefly further on.

5. For a detailed discussion of 'new institutionalist' theory, as applied to the EC, see Bulmer (1994a).

6. The corporate members of Davignon's round table were ICL, GEC, Plessey, AEG, Nixdorf, Siemens, Thomson, Bull, CGE, Olivetti, STET, and Philips.

7. The European Research Coordination Agency (EUREKA) was launched by seventeen European countries and the European Commission in 1985, in an effort to improve the global competitiveness of Europe's industries and economies through collaborative high technology R&D.

8. Work such as Ross (1993, 1995), Green Cowles (1995), and Lawton (1995) discusses how the Commission White Paper on industrial policy and the subsequent EC mandate for industrial policy, evolved largely from the efforts of a coalition of public-private interests, of which the Commission and big business formed the nucleus.

9. Most notably, the United States Office of Technology Assessment in their 1991 report on competitiveness, and Forum Europe in a 1992 document released by them.

10. These include the definitive industrial policy documents, *Industrial Policy in an Open and Competitive Environment* (1990), and *An Industrial Competitiveness Policy for the European Union* (1994); plus the Commission's (1992) *Research After Maastricht* report.

11. Some of these statements were made in private, in interviews conducted by this author with European Commission officials; others were made in public, for instance in a speech given by former Commission Vice President Pandolfi at the 'Horizons of Research' conference, 1992, Brussels.

12. Directorate General I is included here due to its competency for trade tools such as anti-dumping.

13. The vigorous intra-Commission rivalry in creating policy for information technology industries was brought to the author's attention in interviews conducted with several senior Commission officials, Brussels, 1994.

14. These ideological divisions in the Commission were emphasised to the author in meetings with Commission officials, Brussels, 1992 and 1994.

8 Safeguarding the Economic Constitution: The Commission and Competition Policy
Lee McGowan

INTRODUCTION

As academic interest in the development of the European Union has expanded, so attention has converged increasingly on specific policy sectors. An extensive literature now covers practically all areas of EU activity from agriculture to trans European networks and from foreign and security policy to social policy. Rather curiously, competition policy has been largely ignored by political scientists, though a substantial body of literature exists from legal and economics perspectives. This oddity can perhaps be explained by a reluctance to engage in an area heavily dominated by the intricacies of European law, but its omission overlooks the resonance of a highly significant policy area. There are two particular aspects of its significance.

First, competition policy represents one of the pillars on which the EU has been constructed. Logic necessitated a competition policy; after all, there was little to be gained from the removal of tariff barriers and quotas if having promoted the free operation of economic forces through the free movement of capital, goods, people and services, private companies were free to engage in collusive and other anti-competitive activities. A state of constant competition between firms was deemed to be fundamental to the success of the common market, on the grounds that it would help to generate a dynamism which would secure innovation, technological advance, and lower prices for the consumer. European competition policy gives priority to these goals, and beyond these goals is a crucial plank in the general process of European integration. It is neither fanciful nor unrealistic to argue that the competition rules have formed the economic constitution of the EU.

Second, competition policy embodies the first truly supranational policy of the EU, as power is vested almost exclusively in the hands of the Commission. The Commission operates as an autonomous agency that is largely free from interference by the Member States. The extent of its power is remarkable and in many ways unique. As the Commission's authority has grown, it has exerted an ever-increasing impact not only upon the activities of businesses, but also upon governments through its power to control state aids and nationally owned or sanctioned monopolies. The Commission's power has been demonstrated repeatedly, as it has taken action against industries engaged in collusive and predatory activity, and against Member State governments providing financial aids and security to public companies.

Unbeknown to many analysts and largely unrecognised for several decades by the Member State governments, competition policy is actually bringing 'federal' implications for the future administrative and governmental structure of Europe (Gerber, 1994). In operation, the EU regime incarnates the world's leading antitrust enforcement agency and, as such, it may serve as the ideal prototype for a larger international accord as pressure mounts for the establishment of some form of global competition rules. This chapter examines the EU's competition policy from the viewpoint of the role and function of the Commission. Particular attention is paid to the key position of the Directorate General for Competition (DGIV).

POLICY EVOLUTION

A desire to escape the damaging autarky and detrimental protectionist measures that had typified inter-war trade provided the basis for the fabric and foundations of EU competition policy. These were laid in the 1950s and the early 1960s: firstly, within Articles 65 and 66 of the 1951 European Coal and Steel Community (ECSC) Treaty, and secondly, and more significantly, within Articles 85 to 94 of the 1957 European Economic Community (EEC) Treaty. Essentially, intra-Community trade, backed by a vigorous competition policy, was expected to succour European prosperity and aid growth. Accordingly, Article 3(g) (EEC) sought the institution of a system ensuring that competition in the common market was not distorted. This aim constituted nothing less than a radical and complete break from the situation in all European states prior to 1945.

Yet, although the EEC Treaty clearly identified policy objectives, it failed to designate the means to secure these objectives. The onus was placed on the Council to provide a framework to such delicate questions as: which body would decide upon the application of the law?, what form would the administration assume?, how would the competition body acquire its information?, how it would enforce the principles of competition?, and would the sanctions be retrospective or merely prospective?

After four years of fervent deliberations on an administrative system, the legal competence of DGIV was established by the Council in 1962 through Regulation 17. This has served ever since as DGIV's 'procedural bible'. It accredited DGIV the crucial role of principal policy-maker and equipped it with the exclusive power to investigate, codify, exempt and fine, while simultaneously marginalising the role of the national competition authorities. Regulation 17 thus laid the foundations for a truly autonomous federal agency.

With hindsight, the Council in 1962 failed to recognise the overall significance of competition policy, but this was scarcely surprising given that only West Germany possessed such domestic legislation. This lack of recognition resulted in DGIV being accorded far more powers than it would be today were the Regulation being debated *ab initio* (Goyder, 1993). The lack of recognition also meant that DGIV's potential potency was not initially recognised – by either the outside world or by itself.

The Commission's handling of competition policy may be divided into two distinct periods, with the first extending from the creation of the EEC until the publication of the Cockfield White Paper on the internal market in 1985, and the second dating from 1985 onwards.

Laying the foundations of policy: 1958–85

In this first phase, activity was essentially low key and was focused on two specific areas:

i) *Cartels.* Article 85 (EEC) formed the backbone of anti-trust legislation. It prohibited and declared void all agreements between firms and concerted practices (such as price fixing and market sharing) which had the objective of preventing, restricting or distorting trade within the EEC and which affected trade between the Member States. Such arrangements were relentlessly pursued by DGIV from the outset, as evident in its 1969 *Aniline Dye* case.[1] Under certain conditions, however, the Commission was permitted to grant exemptions if the agreements were deemed to improve production and the distribution of goods or to contribute to technical and economic progress.

ii) *Monopolies and Dominance.* Whereas Article 85 was geared to agreements between undertakings, Article 86 was designed to counter the abusive behaviour of individual companies which held a dominant position in the market. The Article stated that 'any abuse by one or more undertakings of a dominant position within the common market or in a substantial part of it shall be prohibited as incompatible ... in so far as it may affect trade between Member States'. Such abusive activities were defined as consisting of imposing unfair purchase or selling prices, limiting production, restricting technical developments to the prejudice of consumers, applying dissimilar conditions to equivalent transactions with other trading partners, and making the conclusion of contracts subject to supplementary obligations which have no relevance to the original contract. However, in practice, the difficulties of providing an authoritative definition of what constituted a dominant position meant DGIV concentrated its efforts on restrictive practices. DGIV only began to make use of Article 86 in the early 1970s, but even then the number of cases examined were relatively few in comparison to its activities under Article 85.

DGIV's impact during this first phase was limited. In hindsight, it took another twenty five years after the passing of Regulation 17 before, in the late 1980s, it was really able to exert its supremacy, transform itself into one of the Commission's leading DGs, and earn its reputation as the world's most influential competition authority.

The transformation of DGIV: 1985 to the present

The time lag between actual inception and actual capability should not have been unanticipated, for all institutions take time to develop, attain confidence, and acquire legitimacy. DGIV was no exception. Five factors combine to explain the sudden metamorphosis in the 1980s from a small and sleepy backwater of Community administration into a formidable machine of economic integration.

i) *Economic.* By the start of the 1980s the spirit of neo-liberalism was sweeping across the Atlantic. Deregulation, privatisation and liberalisation suddenly became a new orthodoxy to restore European competitiveness and to replace the moribund *ancien regime* of industrial planning. The Single European Market (SEM) programme epitomised the efforts to invigorate European industry. Competition policy, although not explicitly mentioned in the Cockfield White Paper, naturally proved to be a corollary of the programme and the potential gains of competition were identified in the 1988 Cecchini Report (Cecchini *et al.*, 1988). In short, companies were forced to restructure, merge or withdraw from the market. In this environment, EU competition policy emerged as a central policy to keep the level playing field open, and the position of DGIV was thereby considerably enhanced.

ii) *Legal.* All too often the discussion of the EU in non-legal circles tends to dismiss the 1960s and 1970s as a period of stagnation and sclerosis. This is misleading, not least as regards the field of competition policy, in which, during this period, the European Court of Justice (ECJ) was highly active. It produced some of its most famous rulings as in *Aniline Dyes, Quinine, Continental Can, Consten-Gründig* and *Hoffmann La-Roche*. (On these cases see, for example, Whish,

1993; Korah, 1994.) The accretion of jurisprudence is of fundamental significance for, as competition law has expanded, so a powerful legal momentum has accumulated. The power of precedent and the rulings on competition have directly impacted on DGIV. Two rulings in the early 1990s are indicative of the authority of the European courts for DGIV's activities: in the 1991 *Italian Flat Glass* case, the Court of First Instance (CFI) castigated DGIV for 'doctoring' the evidence; and in the 1992 *PVC* case, the CFI overturned a series of DGIV decisions because of flaws in the Commission's own procedures during the investigations. Both rulings emphasised the judicial commitment to proper supervision.[2]

iii) *Generational.* Backed by legal precedent and an advantageous economic philosophy, DGIV became engendered with greater self-assuredness both to define and apply the competition rules. As Michelle Cini shows in Chapter 4, by the end of the 1980s a zealous dynamism had infected DGIV officials in their implementation of competition policy (on the culture of DGIV, see also Wilks, 1992a). The optimistic and confident mood of staff was noticeably different from the low staff morale of the early 1970s (Graupner, 1973).

iv) *The Competition Commissioner.* The personality and leadership qualities of Commissioners have often proven instrumental in the development of particular DGs. This certainly applies to competition policy, which was fortunate to be headed by a series of highly capable and adept individuals from the 1980s onwards. DGIV's changing fortunes were initially signalled by the arrival of Dutchman Frans Andriessen (1981–5), who was particularly intent on targeting state aids, but it was his successors, Peter Sutherland (1985–9) and Leon Brittan (1989–93), both staunch free marketeers, who really transformed DGIV. Both men seized the initiative presented by the favourable climate of the 1980s and the unique opportunity presented by the single market to advance the spirit of competition and to place DGIV squarely at the heart of EU activities.

They were both determined to tackle state aids (which amounted to a huge 3 per cent of EU GDP in the mid-1980s), to uncover and penalise restrictive practices, and to argue the case for EU competency over mergers and acqui-sitions. Indeed, it was Sutherland who seized Article 90 from the dusty DGIV shelves and sought to implement it to break public monopolies and to push the case for greater liberalisation, particularly in the airline and telecommunication fields. These priorities were reproduced in the appointment of the ultra-liberal Leon Brittan, who quickly emerged as one of the few intellectual heavyweights in the Commission and became a worthy opponent of Jacques Delors' attraction for *colbertism*.

v) *Merger Control*. The arrival of EU merger control, under Regulation 4064/89 in December 1989 (and effective from September 1990), modernised the armoury of DGIV almost at a stroke and greatly enhanced its position and authority. The Council had resisted granting the Commission power over mergers for 17 years, but finally acceded. It did so partly due to demands from industry for a one stop shop for merger control at the EU level, partly to provide greater clarity and certainty in this area, and partly to improve the Commission's attempts to tackle mergers under Articles 85 and 86. How-ever, the sensitivity of the issue was confirmed by the Member States' decision to provide for Commission competency to deal with a merger, but only if a concentration exceeded high thresholds of ECU 5 billion for aggregate worldwide turnover and ECU 250 million for aggregate EU turnover.

The period after 1985 thus witnessed the rapid rise of DGIV, intensified the salience of competition policy, and heralded a much more proactive approach to all restraints on trade. The eminence of competition policy has persisted under DGIV's current Commissioner, Karel van Miert. For van Miert, however, it is imperative that competition policy should be designed to serve the EU's citizens as consumers, employ-ers, employees and shareholders. He has adopted a much more pragmatic line to competition policy than his more dogmatic predecessors, by placing greater emphasis on con-sultation and consensus and by arguing that competition policy 'cannot be understood or applied without reference to the legal, economic, political and social context'.[3]

In the 1990s, progress has been particularly apparent in the following areas:

i) *Cartels.* DGIV's rejuvenated efforts to unearth and penalise cartels has led to the imposition of ever-higher fines for breaches of Article 85. The highest fine to date, 248 million Ecu, was levied on a group of 33 cement producers in December 1994.

ii) *Mergers.* The Merger Regulation created a Merger Task Force (MTF) within DGIV to process and investigate all notified cases. The nature of the Regulation has been well documented and the MTF has been praised for its efficiency, speed, and its handling of the cases by the business community, and on the whole has been judged as an administrative success (Bulmer, 1994h; Davies and Lavoie, 1993).

iii) *State Aids.* Although enshrined as an objective under Articles 92 to 94 of the EEC Treaty, this area was essentially neglected until the mid-1980s. It has since evolved into an urgent priority which is reflected in a shift of emphasis away from DGIV's habitual concerns with private behaviour towards the problem of government interference with the competitive process. This has been mirrored in its approach to the public utilities.

iv) *Nationalised Industries and Public Utilities.* Historically the large monopoly utility industries (energy, transport, telecommunications, water) were excluded from the scope of EU competition policy, but in recent years the Commission has eagerly pursued a policy, under Article 90, to de-monopolise these industries and thus to open up these markets to the force of competition. Its record in this area among Member States has been mixed, with advances having been most pronounced in the telecommunications and air transport sectors.

DIRECTORATE GENERAL IV

If the EEC Treaty was imbued with the philosophy of free competitive markets, then this philosophy found its natural home within DGIV. Although the Commissioner sets policy priorities, the overall responsibility for the administration

Figure 8.1   The Organisational Structure of DGIV

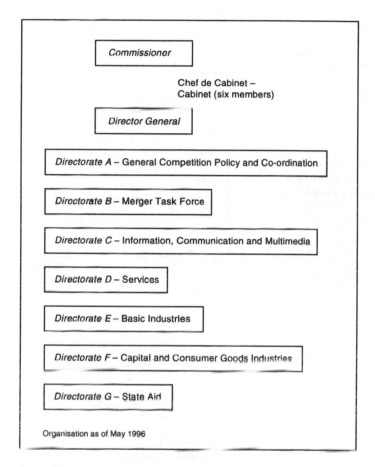

Commissioner

Chef de Cabinet –
Cabinet (six members)

Director General

Directorate A – General Competition Policy and Co-ordination

Directorate B – Merger Task Force

Directorate C – Information, Communication and Multimedia

Directorate D – Services

Directorate E – Basic Industries

Directorate F – Capital and Consumer Goods Industries

Directorate G – State Aid

Organisation as of May 1996

and functioning of DGIV rests with the Director General. The three Directors Generals of DGIV to date (Caspari, Ehlermann and Schaub) have all been German, a fact which reveals the interest taken by Bonn in competition policy matters. DGIV, which is basically structured along the lines of the German Federal Cartel Office, comprises seven directorates, as outlined in Figure 8.1. It has a total of just over 400 staff, of whom 51 per cent are 'A' grade officials (including some 25 national experts on secondment in Brussels). Of the available manpower, 44 per cent are allocated

Figure 8.2   The Decision-Making Process with Regard to Articles
85 and 86

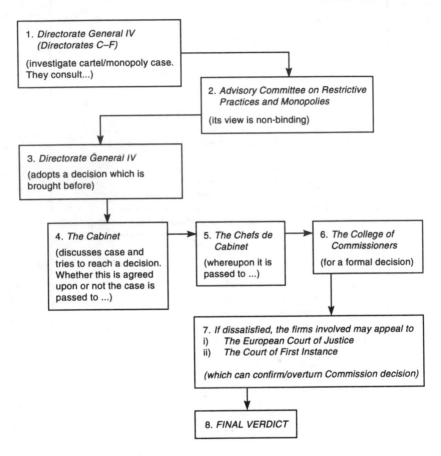

to work under Articles 85 and 86, 12 per cent to the Merger
Regulation, 3 per cent to work under Article 90, 21 per
cent to state aids, 9 per cent to international regulations,
and the final 11 per cent are clerical officers (Commission,
1994a, p. 111).

A closer breakdown of these bare statistics proves illumi-
nating and provides greater insight into the changing culture and norms within the DGIV. With regard to educational
background, the composition of the DG reflects the continental European preference for administrative specialists.

Economists and lawyers are dominant, with the lawyers comfortably outnumbering the economists by a ratio of 7:1. Parity only prevails within Directorates A and B (General Competition Policy Coordination and the Merger Task Force). This imbalance causes friction and is, in general, resented by DGIV economists who are prone to maintain that economic evaluations do not always receive the consideration they warrant and are often subordinated to legal considerations and practicalities.

THE FORMAL POLITICS OF THE DECISION-MAKING PROCESS

Different procedural actors and mechanisms within the Commission are responsible for different aspects of competition policy. Essentially, policy processes vary depending upon whether the Commission, and more especially DGIV, is dealing with cartels and abusive monopolies or with mergers. (For a full account of variations, see Cini and McGowan, forthcoming.)

As regards Articles 85 and 86, DGIV's caseload originates from three sources: complaints from third parties; DGIV's own *ex officio* investigations; and notifications. Of these three, notifications have been most important with regard to Article 85, while complaints have played a much greater role with regard to Article 86. The investigative and decision-making processes for both are lengthy and it takes, on average, two to three years before decisions are reached. As time has progressed, a backlog of cases has accumulated, thus delaying DGIV's initiation of proceedings. By the end of 1994, 1058 cases awaited attention and, according to Ehlermann (1994a), this backlog was unlikely to fall much in the foreseeable future.

The delay in processing cases has proved frustrating to the business community which demands speedy responses to take account of rapidly changing market circumstances. To overcome this dissatisfaction, the 1989 Merger Regulation established a distinct organisation within DGIV, the Merger Task Force, which was given exclusive responsibility to handle mergers, and to ensure efficiency the Regulation provided for the inclusion of a strict timetable. The procedure,

Figure 8.3   Procedure in Merger Control (as established under
Council Regulation (EEC) NO. 4064/89)

Phase 1: Initial examination.

This lasts for four weeks and results in a decision under Article 6:

Three possibilities:

  6a: the concentration is not within the scope of the regulation
  6b: the concentration does not raise any serious doubts: approval
  6c: the concentration raises serious doubts: investigate further

6c opens the way for Phase 2: Initiation of proceedings.

This involves a second and more detailed investigation which includes a statement of
objections, third party hearings and oral hearings. At this stage the Advisory Committee
on Concentrations (as set up under Regulation 4064/89) is asked for its opinion. This
second phase endures for four months before the outcome is known.

Article 8 provides for three possible outcomes:

  i)   The merger is deemed compatible with EEC law: approval
  ii) It is declared incompatible with EEC law: prohibition
  iii) It is compatible in view of commitments: approval by imposing conditions
       or obligations.

If a merger is prevented from its realisation under Article 8, the firms involved are entitled
to lodge an appeal to the European Court of Justice.

Source: Commission of the European Communities, *Community Competition Policy in 1993*, Luxembourg, 1994.

which is set out in Figure 8.3, involves a two-phase investigation and provides for a decision within five months.

In all types of competition work undertaken by DGIV,
individual cases are assigned to a *rapporteur* (of a particular
directorate) who has an extensive knowledge of the particular
market and the leading players within it. In practice it is
often the *rapporteur* who provides the decision-making
momentum and dynamics. He/she conducts an analysis (both
economic and legal) of the case, and then prepares a draft
decision which is referred to at least five other officials in
DGIV, the Commissioner's *cabinet,* and the Commission's Legal
Service. They debate the case and make known their opinions
to the *rapporteur,* who then produces a final recommendation

which is passed, via the Commissioner's *cabinet*, to the weekly meeting of the Commissioners' *cabinets*.

In competition policy, the importance of the Commissioner's *cabinet* is crucial to decision-making, with every *cabinet* having a competition policy specialist who has amongst his/her main duties keeping a close eye on, and if necessary protecting, the national interests of the Commissioner's home country. These competition policy specialists normally meet twice a week, in what are known as special chefs meetings. Recommendations from the special chefs are referred to the weekly meetings of the *chefs de cabinets*. If agreement is reached between the *chefs de cabinets*, the College of Commissioners almost invariably accept their recommendations.

Cabinets, and especially the *chefs*, must bear in mind not only the national implications of competition decisions, but also the portfolio implications. Given the portfolios of Commissioners, a conflict of interests can and does often ensue at College level, for competition policy is not generally perceived by the other Commissioners as having its own *raison d'être*. Consequently, DGIV's ambitions to promote competition through market integration is subject to repeated demands to link competition policy decision-making to the overall framework of EU economic policy. It is not altogether surprising that, in the final analysis, outcomes can be determined by other Commissioners intent on defending their own specific realms of interest, which can jeopardise the principles and priorities of DGIV. These principles and priorities can also be jeopardised by the 'turf protecting' tendency of DGs and the manner in which some are run almost as autonomous baronies. DGIV and its Commissioner clash most frequently with DGXI (Environment), DGXIII (Telecommunications), DGVII (Transport), DGXVII (Energy), but most notably DGIII (Industry) which has long sought to shelter European industrial 'champions' from the full rigours of competition. In his account of 'life inside' the Delors Commission, Ross (1994) has depicted a somewhat startling picture of the battles that raged between the *cabinets* and the DGs over competition policy, and especially over merger control (pp. 130–5).

Critics of the EU regime argue that the decision-making process is heavily politicised, as competition policy priorities can be torpedoed by industrial, regional and employment considerations. This is seen to be particularly acute with regard to merger control, and was most notoriously apparent in *Aerospatiale/De Havilland*. In this instance, the perennial split between DGIII and DGIV emerged. The latter deemed the proposed merger to be anti-competitive, while DGIII, backed by the French and Italian governments, sought its approval for employment reasons. A tremendous struggle ensued between the two camps as they sought to win supporters within the Commission. Although victory was narrowly conferred in the College upon the Competition Commissioner/ DGIV camp, by nine votes to eight, this was hardly deemed a success for competition reasoning. The conclusion seemed apparent: competition criteria were vulnerable. Vigorous leadership by the Commissioner and the services of DGIV officials was essential, but the overall key to progress was coalition building within the Commission.

If *Aérospatiale/De Havilland* is an example of DGIV and its Commissioner 'winning' a dispute over conflicting priorities, the 1994 renewal (with only minor changes) of the block exemption granted to the European car industry in 1985 is an example of a 'defeat'. The renewal was staunchly opposed by DGIV on the grounds that it ran contrary to consumer interests and all arguments of economic efficiency. DGIV officials were swift to rebuke their peers for mere politicking and argued that the decision was a shortsighted effort to protect Europe's largest manufacturing sector. The renewal was seen from DGIV as casting doubt on the sincerity of the Commission's commitment to free competition in the car industry and diminished its authority to enforce single market rules on recalcitrant Member States.

From an institutional and policy-making perspective, the degree of independence possessed by DGIV is striking. Its position is unique, for in stark contrast to all other policy areas it is not obliged, when taking most decisions, to seek approval from the Council of Ministers – though, of course, the Council is responsible for the overall framing and shaping of competition law. Nor does the Commission have to earnestly concern itself with the views of the European Parliament (EP) though this relationship is, it should be said, undergoing continual change as the EP accrues increased powers – as is reflected in the increasingly prominent role of the competition policy *rapporteur* from the EP's Committee for Economic, Monetary and Industrial Affairs.[4] When DGIV is investigating competition cases, the only bodies that it is obliged to consult for their opinion prior to any Commission decision are the Advisory Committee on Restrictive Practices and Monopolies (set up under Regulation 17) and the more recent Advisory Committee on Mergers. In practice, their opinions are not binding on the Commission and fall far short of the initial French intentions to equip the committees with the power of veto over DGIV decisions.

In practice, only the EU Courts, with their powers to interpret EU law, represent formidable checks on DGIV's powers and position.

THE INFORMAL POLITICS WITHIN THE DECISION-MAKING PROCESS

Beyond the formal framework of decision-making, DGIV encourages and seeks information from those groups which are directly effected by the implementation of competition policy. Two non-core actors predominate: business and associated interest associations, and national competition authorities.

Since the mid-1980s there has been a belated realisation of the European dimension among the *business community*. This is reflected in the ever-growing presence of business representatives based in Brussels and the development of links between these representatives and the Commission. The degree of informal politicking required to have an input into policy formulation is immense and is impossible to gauge accurately. In competition issues, DGIV is the natural focal point of business activity given its huge amount of discretion over competition cases. In considering cases, it not only decides which criteria to take into account, but it alone determines whether or not to prosecute in the first place. Accordingly, it can be depicted from outside 'as a force either for justice or injustice' (Middlemas, 1995, p. 507).

Close dialogue with DGIV enables the business community to keep abreast of present and future Commission priorities. More importantly, such exchanges provide companies with the opportunity to test DGIV reactions to certain agreements and thus identify the potential sticking points to formal approval. The proposals can be amended accordingly. It is crucial to recognise the importance of this relationship, for mere statistics can prove misleading. For example, in merger control, of the 400 notifications made to the MTF by the end of 1995, only four – namely *Aérospatiale/De Havilland* in 1991, *MSG Media Services* in 1994, and *Holland Media Groep* and *NSD* in 1995 – were prohibited. Initially this is gloomy reading and raises questions about the Commission's record, but many thorny issues were eradicated after informal meetings between DGIV officials and company lawyers before companies tendered any formal notification of their merger plans.

It is still premature to talk of the existence of a distinct competition policy network, as the coalition of interests varies from industrial sector to industrial sector and according to whether the competition issues in question relate to cartels or monopolies, state aids or mergers. Nevertheless, it is clear that there are many business firms and groupings which have a strong interest in policy outcomes and future developments and which aspire to be actively involved with Commission procedures.

It is the relationship, however, with the *national authorities* that has often been the most sensitive for DGIV. As the Commission's potency has expanded, so have Member States developed a marked interest in its application of policy. Most of the friction between the Commission and Member States originates from different cultural norms, conflicting policy priorities, and varying approaches to European integration. In terms of disaffection, a north/south divide can be identified. The northern states, and most notably Germany, have been constantly critical of the Commission's failure: firstly, to take a tougher stance on state subsidies to the Mediterranean states; secondly, to adopt a tougher stance towards mergers; and thirdly, to prevent political considerations from influencing competition policy decisions. In contrast, the Mediterranean states, and most notably France, have been brisk to castigate the Commission for its interference in their national economies. It is hardly surprising, therefore, that certain Member States are resistant to granting further powers to Brussels and were instrumental, for example, in preventing the reduction of the merger thresholds in 1993.[5]

PROBLEMS AND REMEDIES

It is not necessary to delve far into the vast literature on competition policy (or more accurately competition law and competition theory) to encounter hostility and criticisms of Commission procedures and activities. DGIV has been charged with an assortment of crimes: of being too bureaucratic, too inefficient, too politicised, too meddlesome, and even too cavalier in its approach (see, for example, House of Lords, 1993a). Although most criticisms can be classified as being relatively minor issues of particular interest to the legal practitioner, such as the issue of comfort letters[6] and the concept of access to file, which are being remedied without too much difficulty, some are inevitably more weighty (Ehlermann, 1995a). Five core issues can be identified:

i) *Inefficiency.* In administrative terms DGIV is charged with being too slow in dealing with cases. This is a fair criticism in respect of its handling of cartel and monopoly cases and stands in marked contrast to the MTF's speed in dealing with mergers.

ii) *The need for a separation of powers.* This arises from DGIV's combined role as policeman, judge, jury and executioner. As things currently operate, the *rapporteur* is absolutely central to the entire investigative process. Many observers regard this as a decidedly unhealthy state of affairs and seek greater openness and objectivity in the Commission's handling of policy and administration.

iii) *A greater demand for decentralised control.* The Commission has been pushing for the national courts to apply EU law ever since the *BRT/SABEM* case of 1973. The fruitlessness of its efforts culminated in 1993 in its *Notice on Decentralisa-*

tion to promote greater national authority involvement. From the Commission's perspective, greater Member State involvement in competition policy enforcement would enable it to concentrate on the most pressing cases and free resources to tackle the backlog. How effective any decentralisation of policy would be remains doubtful, however, so long as the Commission remains the sole body entitled to exempt agreements from the rules and so long as doubts persist as to the approach of certain Member States to the objectives of competition policy.

iv) *Politicisation.* The existing decision-making process has encountered criticism, particularly from the German authorities, on the grounds that it has proven prone to politicisation. Indeed, under existing procedures there can never be any guarantee that competition criteria will vanquish other considerations. On the contrary, as was noted above, other Commissioners are free to introduce industrial, political and social issues into competition deliberations. This reality led Wolfgang Kartte, a former president of the German Federal Cartel Office to condemn the Merger Regulation in the following terms:

'A congenital defect of this new Regulation lies in the fact that in critical cases, . . . the decision is not reached by DGIV, but by all . . . Commissioners' (Kartte, 1990).

v) *Transparency.* A criticism that is directly related to the variety of roles played by DGIV centres on the opaqueness of case investigations and the decision-making process. As things currently operate, informal bargaining prior to the Commission taking any formal action usually resolves potential difficulties for the parties concerned, even though this arguably works to the detriment of rival competitors. Recent annual competition reports indicate the necessity of greater openness, but ultimately how far it can be attained is limited due to the need to preserve business confidentiality.

These criticisms have multiplied the resonance of calls for the reform of existing structures and procedures. Unless problems and weaknesses are rectified they could ultimately undermine what is amongst the most integrationist of all

EU policies. Reform is thus squarely on the agenda for the late 1990s.

Discussions on the reform of EU competition policy need to reflect and appreciate the broader origins of competition policy in Europe. As essentially a post-1945 phenomenon in Western Europe, competition policy has evolved in a sporadic fashion and has been subject to divergent cultural, historical, and socio-economic considerations. From the outset, different national conceptions of competition policy were apparent in relation to the key questions: Should there be a judicial or a political approach? Should competition be subservient or superior to industrial policy and non-competition policy criteria? Could competition policy and market forces alone deliver dynamic economic benefits and would the social costs incurred in the process be too great? These sorts of questions were answered in different ways in Western European states, and to some extent still are so in the context of the EU. This has made attempts at brokering policy deals very difficult.

The most radical option on the reform agenda is a proposal to take the enforcement of law on Articles 85 and 86 and mergers out of DGIV's hands and entrust it to a new independent competition agency, a European Cartel Office (ECO). This option is backed strongly by the German Government, which envisages a body that mirrors the design and function of the German Federal Cartel Office. The proponents of this course of action argue that an independent body would solve some of the current difficulties with the implementation of competition policy (Wilks and McGowan, 1995) The idea certainly raises a number of very interesting, though controversial, issues. Would an ECO be responsible for all aspects of competition policy, or selected aspects of it such as merger control?; how would an ECO operate?; to whom would it be responsible?; would it rely on strict competition policy criteria as the German authorities insist?; and where would it be located? (On some of these issues, see Ehlermann, 1995b).

The continuing debate on an ECO throws into relief the whole issue of the current EU competition regime, by raising questions about existing procedures, the Commission's administrative resources and arrangements, and the logic

Table 8.1   The Plausibility of a European Cartel Office

Possible Advantages	Disadvantages/Problems
i) would strengthen the principle of competition in the EU	i) can politics be excluded from economics?
ii) political influence would be minimalised	ii) what are economic criteria?
iii) general interests of the consumer would be better represented	iii) it needs a treaty amendment
iv) freeing of much needed resources	iv) undermines the national authorities
v) greater transparency	

of establishing organisationally independent agencies on the American or UK models. At its heart, lies the question of how best to reform the EU regime. Any moves towards an ECO would necessitate a revision of the Union Treaties, which would undoubtedly engender substantial controversy. Significantly, however, as Figure 8.4 shows, there is no guarantee that an ECO would deliver the results which its advocates anticipate.

CONCLUSIONS

There are, as has been shown, many problems associated with the EU's competition policy and the Commission's management of it. Nevertheless, judged positively, competition policy has attained a considerable degree of maturity. DGIV has emerged as a potent force and an autonomous institution since the mid-1980s and arguably has become the most effective of the Commission's administrative units. It not only makes policy, but also enforces it. Accordingly, it has exerted an ever greater impact on the activities of businesses operating in Europe and on government state aid programmes. Beyond the specifics of competition policy, it must not be forgotten that the primary goal of EU competition policy has been market integration and in this context DGIV has determined many of the most important rules and conditions under which the European economy has integrated.

DGIV is facing a period of transition. A reappraisal of competition policy is high on the EU agenda. The pressure for a reappraisal stems from competitiveness and policy linkage issues. The successful implementation of a vigorous competition policy is one means to secure and promote European competitiveness. However, in current Commission considerations competitiveness policy is a portmanteau term which incorporates industrial policy. DGIV remains fearful of any emergence of interventionist economic policies and views with considerable wariness attempts at policy linkage in case the principles of competition policy are diluted to serve the interests of other EU priorities, notably regional, social, and environmental policies. Consequently, many advocates of competition policy (and many within DGIV) strongly favour the creation of a truly independent European competition agency. Such an agency, supposedly free from political interference, would be able to pursue its primary objectives of protecting and promoting competition. It is difficult at this point in time to predict the outcome, but it seems increasingly likely that such an agency will materialise in the medium-term. Its realisation would involve the 'hiving off' of much of DGIV's current responsibilities and staff, but it would complete the process of creating a legally independent agency which would symbolise the world's first supranational competition authority.

Notes

1. In this 1969 case, six EC firms, three Swiss firms and one British firm, all suppliers of industrial dyes, were charged with price fixing. All introduced similar price rises within a few days of each other on three separate occasions. This 'parallelism of pricing' is not sufficient in itself to determine anti-competitive activity, and naturally the firms denied that this was taking place, but DGIV was convinced that this was a prime example of concerted action and consequently fined all participants accordingly. The ECJ backed the Commission's findings.
2. The *PVC* judgement introduced a number of innovations, both procedural and substantive, that will have considerable impact on EU law and DGIV's investigations. These included the CFI's insistence that a thorough economic analysis must be carried out under Article 85.
   In the *Italian Flat Glass* case, three Italian glass producers lodged an appeal against a Commission ruling. (Incidentally this is another

industry that has become a focal point for Commission investigations following susceptibility for cartel formation.) Interest focused on the Commission's reliance on a theory of collective dominance, which although previously used by the Commission had not been approved by the Court. The CFI did not accept the concept of collective dominance under Article 86 but, more significantly, it also uncovered the Commission's 'doctoring' of evidence. See Pope (1993).

3. On a personal level, van Miert has been extremely fortunate. Due to external circumstances his position in the Commission, let alone as Competition Commissioner, was in severe jeopardy during 1994. Had the UK Government not vetoed the nomination of Jean-Luc Dehaene for Commission President, van Miert would have automatically lost his position, because Belgium is only entitled to have one Commissioner.

4. The annual Commission report on competition policy is placed before the EP's Committee on Economic, Monetary and Industrial Affairs (usually no later than 30 April). This committee appoints a *rapporteur* (a one-year appointment) to examine the Commission's report in detail, before it is discussed at the committee stage. During the deliberations and discussions, both the Competition Commissioner and the Director General of DGIV become directly involved in the process and appear before the committee's representatives to defend DGIV's actions and explain their priorities.

5. The 1989 Merger Regulation provided for a review of the thresholds before the end of 1993. The Commission and large sections of industry favoured a reduction, especially of the upper worldwide turnover threshold from Ecu 5 billion to Ecu 2 billion. However, the enduring economic recession and the continuing problems associated with the Maastricht ratification process led the Commission to readily accept a postponement of any decision on the thresholds until 1996 at the earliest.

6. The Commission has always taken considerable time to grant a formal clearance or exemption under Article 85. Since this is unacceptable to business and since the Commission only makes a small number of former exemptions each year, it prefers to send to the parties an informal letter known as a comfort letter. From the Commission's perspective a comfort letter means that there is no reason for it to intervene. In short, a comfort letter provides a firm with continued protection from fines.

9 The Commission Made Me Do It: The European Commission as a Strategic Asset in Domestic Politics
Mitchell P. Smith

A new language of semi-detachment is being created.
The world outside Britain is being recast in the hope
of making political life at home easier to manage.
Geoffrey Howe, *Financial Times*, 30 January 1995.

INTRODUCTION

With this comment, former British Foreign Secretary Geoffrey
Howe recognised a critical point: the myth of a grasping,
bureaucratic, centralising, unaccountable 'Europe' embodied in the European Commission can be extremely useful
in domestic politics. This chapter explores this 'leveraging'
role of the Commission in the critical policy area of Member State aids to industry. There are three principal reasons why this portion of competition policy creates an ideal
environment for political actors to gain leverage by invoking actions of the Commission. First, state aids are by nature transfers of government funds to public or private entities
with narrow but deeply committed constituencies. Even where
governments wish to curtail such transfers,[1] the political price
for deciding against powerful domestic constituencies may
be quite high, or the strength of the political opposition or
internal party rivals may in effect block such policies. Second, the Commission's demands may be credibly invoked
because the Commission has the legal authority to enforce

decisions on state aids. And thirdly, the review of state aids is a negotiated process that takes place privately between Commissioners and political executives of Member State governments. National parliaments and publics, as well as government ministers in policy areas outside the realm under consideration, lack information about the bargaining positions of their government ministers. Interacting with the Commission strengthens particular actors in Member State governments where costs of decision-making are high, the Commission has legal authority to decide, and decisions are privately negotiated.

For national actors, invoking the Commission becomes part of a bargain through which they increase their control over the political agenda. This may include narrowing the range of policy options or altering the cost of a particular option relative to others. Where 'Euroscepticism' features prominently, as in Britain, blaming 'Europe' helps politicians produce evidence supporting their world view of a grasping, bureaucratic Commission that encroaches on Member State sovereignty. What does the Commission extract from this bargain? While the European Community (EC) Treaty gives the Commission competence to regulate Member State aids, this legal competence does not translate directly into policy influence because of the impact of politics. The Commission cannot simply impose its will and antagonise Member States who could 'punish' the Commission in other areas of the integration project. The Commission must bargain and be willing partly to accommodate Member State interests. For the Commission, therefore, such bargains sometimes are necessary to move the integration process forward.

After describing more fully the conditions underlying these bargains, this chapter reviews two instances in which domestic political actors invoked the Commission in order to help secure desired outcomes or to lower the costs of achieving those outcomes. In the first case, Britain's Department of Trade and Industry (DTI) announced in July 1989 that the Sunderland yards of North East Shipbuilders, the last holding of state-owned British Shipbuilders, would be irrevocably closed because of a ruling by the Commission prohibiting the return of shipbuilding to these sites. Opponents of the move – including local Members of Parliament (MPs), a small number of Conservative MPs who were determined that the Government should participate in building competitive advantage for British industry, and the Labour Party leadership – attacked the Government on two grounds: incompetence and weakness. These critics alleged that the Government had failed to fully understand the terms of the aid approval from the outset, and had not lobbied with sufficient intensity in Brussels for the interests of British industry.

The argument presented here suggests an alternative explanation for this 'defeat' of British interests at the hands of the European Commission. The Government wished to diversify industry in Sunderland, and being 'forced' to do so by the Commission became a convenient means of minimising the political costs of adopting this policy. Indeed, constructing policy along these lines neatly fitted with the Thatcher Government's portrayal of a centralised, bureaucratic, unaccountable Commission aggressively intruding upon British sovereignty. Although unpopular, the policy preferences of the Conservative Government converged with those of a Commission intent on reducing shipbuilding capacity in the EC, and the British Government took advantage of the opportunity to shift the costs of unpopular policy to the Commission.

The second case involves the transfer, beginning in 1996, of substantial state resources to the Spanish air carrier Iberia for the second time in less than four years. In this instance, the airline's need for additional capital was caught between the views of contending factions within the governing Spanish Socialist Party (PSOE), one of which was determined to sustain the tradition of generous public investment, the other of which was committed to shrinking the state sector. In this instance modernisers in the PSOE found an ally in Transport Commissioner Neil Kinnock, who was determined to tighten implementation of state aids rules in the aviation sector but was unwilling and politically unable to force a national carrier into financial disaster.

Neither case is extraordinary. Political executives often are interested in acquiring additional leverage for austerity regimes, particularly in an era of fiscal austerity – which is partly a result of the Maastricht convergence process. 'Bargains' with the Commission can produce a range of austerity

170   *Mitchell P. Smith*

outcomes that the recipient of the aid and other constituents may be reluctant to accept, such as outright rejection
of a subsidy, a reduction in the amount of a state aid, or
the imposition of conditions on the granting of aid in the
form, for example, of market liberalisation or privatisation.[2]
Policy-making authority ceded to the Commission in the
treaties may thus sometimes restrict the autonomy of Member States, but it can also enhance the capabilities of Member State executives to achieve desired objectives in the
national political arena. The Commission participates in such
bargains with the aim of increasing its own capacities to
move forward the integration process.

STRENGTHENING DOMESTIC POLITICAL ACTORS:
THE COMMISSION MADE ME DO IT

European integration often is depicted as a special case of
a global integration process that constrains the autonomy
of domestic policy-makers. The agenda-setting role of the
European Commission, the Council of Ministers' weighted
majority system of decision-making, and the processes of
completing the Single European Market (SEM) and moving toward Economic and Monetary Union (EMU), typically
lead to the conclusion that European integration means a
substantial loss of policy autonomy for Member States.

This emphasis on constraints on domestic policy effectiveness and latitude yields considerable insight into the implications of integration processes. However, it provides us with
an incomplete story at best. First, even where strategically
positioned political actors can implement their preferred
policies, they may attempt to attribute political outcomes
unpopular with domestic groups to transnational or
supranational constraints. This may be an effective way of
reducing the political costs of securing a desired outcome.
And secondly, recent analyses suggest that the constraints
on autonomy implied by global economic integration are
circumscribed in important ways. This is equally true for
the European integration process.

The strategic interaction between the Commission and
national political actors is a specific case of the general in-

terpenetration of European Union (EU) and national politics. Historical experience provides numerous examples of this interaction. According to Milward (1992), the very founding of the European Coal and Steel Community (ECSC) represented an effort to 'rescue' the nation-state from the failings of the interwar years and the Second World War. Rather than relinquishing sovereignty to a supranational authority, European statesmen hoped to use European institutions to augment the capacities of their states and to enhance their abilities to win the allegiance and support of their citizens. More specifically, the Belgian Government used the desirability of integrating Germany into European structures to win support for the ECSC, which in turn altered the subsidy regime for Belgium's highly inefficient coal industry. Faced with a low productivity coal industry and an entrenched regime of heavy subsidisation, the Government wished to secure rationalisation of the industry, but simply could not countenance the political costs involved. The ECSC offered a way out of this quandary. As Milward argues, given substantial domestic opposition, 'The government might be able to use the new supranational authority to enforce a restructuring policy on the industry and do so in the name of Europe' (1992, p. 72).

The issue of European Community membership was transformed into a domestic political weapon in the partisan struggle over the supercession of the military dictatorship in Greece in 1972–3 (Verney and Tsakaloyannis, 1986). In particular, the reformist centre–right deployed the benefits of EC membership and the EC's declaration that only democratic states could accede to the Community as an inducement for a transition to a western-oriented, capitalist, democratic Greece. The centre and right seized upon EC membership as a unifying issue that could consolidate their position against the left in domestic politics (ibid, p. 191).

Sandholtz (1993b) argues that the decision by European governments to pursue monetary union was in part a strategic approach to securing the credibility of the commitment to low inflation made in the 1980s. As he argues, 'European governments favoured EMU because it would provide the highest possible level of credibility: monetary union would once and for all "tie their hands"' (p. 35). Speaking of the desire of Britain's Chancellor of the Exchequer to make such a commitment, Keohane (1991) writes that 'restrictions on operational sovereignty may benefit one not merely because of increased control over others, but because of restraints on oneself . . .' (p. 24).

Member State officials negotiating state aids cases with the European Commission are especially well-positioned to import the Commission into domestic political contests as a strategic asset. Invoking a Commission rule can be an effective strategic manoeuvre because it quickly alters the terms of political debate. If an actor can credibly establish that Commission decisions or regulations preclude particular domestic political outcomes, the policy preferences of actors favouring those outcomes will necessarily shift. Moreover, invoking the Commission is forceful because it appears objective. The irony is that strategic national actors may play a critical role in forging the very rules that constrain them, or may even cooperate with Commission officials to impose rules that alter the environment in which other domestic political actors form their preferences. Indeed, acting in the name of the Commission is not an uncommon means for strategically-positioned actors in Member States to generate political leverage to attain desired objectives or to diminish the risks of achievable but politically costly policies.

The Commission: bargaining for integration in small steps

One effect of completion of the internal market has been to amplify distortions implied by government intervention. With the removal of other barriers to competition, regulation of state aids therefore has assumed a greater significance for the European Commission. Reining in state aids is vital both for the functioning of the market and for sustaining cohesion across Member States with different capacities to aid their industrial enterprises.

The EC Treaty gives the Commission legal competence to regulate aids paid by Member States, but the Commission cannot exercise this authority simply by confronting Member States. Article 92 of the Treaty states that aid which distorts competition is incompatible with the internal market. Article 93(3) of the Treaty requires Member States to inform the Commission of plans to grant aid and stipulates that proposed aid measures may not be put into effect until the Commission has made a decision concerning the compatibility of the aid with the internal market. Article 93(2) gives the Commission authority to require that states 'abolish or alter' aid that it deems incompatible with the internal market. The procedure embodied in Article 93(2) allows the Commission to impose conditions on approved aid, including 'restrictions on the type, amounts, intensities, beneficiaries, purposes and duration of aid' (Commission, 1994a).

The fact that the Treaty allows broad discretion in regulating state aid is both a strength and a complication for the Commission. As Claus-Dieter Ehlermann (1994b, p. 412) has noted, the rules governing state aid in the EC Treaty depart fundamentally from those in the ECSC Treaty, which banned state aids in steel and coal under the assumption that ECSC aid would replace national assistance to these industries. In addition to permitting the Commission to make exemptions for aid to low income areas, to promote projects 'of common European interest,' or to 'remedy a serious disturbance in the economy of a Member State,' Article 92(3)(c) allows the Commission to authorise subsidies 'where aid does not adversely affect trading conditions to an extent contrary to the common interest.' Citing these exceptions, critics have argued that they 'open great gashes through which governments can – if the Commission approves – drive a coach and horses' (*Independent on Sunday*, 7 August 1994). Discretion invites politicisation.

The politics of state aid are explosive because in most cases jobs are at stake. In an economic environment characterised by persistently high unemployment, there is a general unwillingness to 'give in' to the Commission.[3] It is not uncommon for senior civil servants or government ministers to lobby key members of a Commissioner's *cabinet*, top officials in the administrative services, or Commissioners to make their case for the importance of a particular aid. The Commission must balance these political pressures against its concern that state aids can undermine the objective of social and economic cohesion given variations in the resources of Member States and its overarching commitment to developing the single market and improving the competitiveness of European industry.

Therefore, when ministers seek the active involvement of the Commission in reducing public sector spending or liberalising markets, the Commission must exploit such opportunities. Alliances of this type can advantage the Commission in pursuit of greater industrial competitiveness in Europe by fostering the use of the minimal amount of state funds required to achieve the maximum level of industrial restructuring. This type of cooperation is useful for the Commission because its legal authority to monitor and regulate state aids does not translate directly into an ability to influence the aid policies of Member States.[4] The Commission must build this capacity through judicious use of its legal powers and by seeking the political means to effectively apply its policies.[5]

Britain: North East Shipbuilders and industrial diversification

Given their large majority in Parliament throughout the 1980s, the Conservative Governments of Margaret Thatcher did not rely on the EC to help enact their policy of piecemeal privatisation of British Shipbuilders. However, by the late 1980s, recession, high interest rates and unemployment made it important for the Government to minimise the costs of implementing controversial policies. Moreover, while privatisation generally had its institutional and partisan opponents, closing down an industrial site and selling it for alternative development, which eventually took place in the case of shipbuilding, represented an especially controversial form of privatisation because of the dislocation caused to the particular industry and locale. With the prospect of such dislocation, the Government deployed the Commission as a constraint on domestic political choice, facilitating completion of the final and most contested phase of the shipbuilding selloff and undergirding the Government's plans for an enterprise zone to help diversify British industry, attract foreign direct investment, and enhance Britain's international industrial competitiveness. By invoking a Commission ruling, the Conservative Government secured its most favoured political result and eliminated the prospect of achieving only a 'second best' outcome.

The shipbuilding industry was nationalised only in 1977 in response to a crisis of British shipbuilding associated with the rapid transfer of British technology abroad, particularly to South Korea (*The Independent*, 4 September 1994). The newly-elected Conservative Government began to rationalise the state's holdings in the early 1980s, starting with ship repair and general engineering sites and moving on to privatisation of warship building in 1985–6. Consolidation and selloff of merchant ship building followed. By 1988, the 27 companies and 87 300 employees vested in British Shipbuilders in 1977 were reduced to just four companies and three subsidiaries with total employment of 6300 (HC 517i: 1). Global overcapacity in shipbuilding convinced the Government to bring an end to state-subsidised shipbuilding in Britain. In April 1988, the DTI announced plans to sell the remaining holdings of British Shipbuilding to the private sector. Buyers were found for all of these companies (or their assets), with the exception of North East Shipbuilders Limited (NESL), a company located in Sunderland employing 2800 workers and equipped to build large merchant ships. With no orders on its books after a contract for 24 Danish ferries collapsed in mid-1988, it remained the only British Shipbuilders subsidiary for which no private offer had been made (*Financial Times*, 16 June 1988, p. 6). Hoping to complete the privatisation of British Shipbuilding by the end of 1988, the Government closed NESL in December, gaining approval for £45 million in redundancy aid from the European Commission.

By mid-1989, lobbying by local political interests and the labour movement for a reopening of NESL's two yards intensified as global demand for merchant shipbuilding increased.[6] The DTI pledged to keep the yards' equipment in place through June 1989 to allow time for any buyers to emerge in response to changed market conditions. Although the Government conducted preliminary negotiations with at least two interested potential buyers, the yards were pronounced unequivocally closed in July 1989 following a Commission clarification that aid approved in December 1988 was conditional on the permanent termination of shipbuilding at the two NESL sites.[7] Any attempt by the British Government to negotiate a return to shipbuilding, even by a private buyer, would result in the Commission's reappraisal of aid approved in late 1988 (Hansard 156, p. 1145;).

The Commission's ruling appears to have been a constraint on the Conservative Government's policy-making autonomy. However, this perspective incorrectly assumes a tension between British Government and Commission objectives. Consonant with its larger privatisation programme, the Conservative Government was committed to ending subsidisation of British shipbuilding. In May 1988, the Minister of Trade and Industry, Kenneth Clarke, argued before Parliament that the Government had spent £250 million on Intervention Fund support to subsidise shipbuilding orders and an additional £1.4 billion to subsidise losses and costs of maintaining excess capacity (Hansard 133, p. 1123). In testimony before the House of Commons Trade and Industry Committee in June 1989, the (new) Minister of Trade and Industry, Tony Newton, spoke of the 'aim of the British government, in common with the European Community collectively, to move away from subsidised shipbuilding' (HC 517(i), p. 17). When Prime Minister Thatcher appointed Leon Brittan as the senior UK European Commissioner in late 1988, it was on the understanding that he would vigorously pursue steep reductions in state aid to industry throughout the Community. Brittan, along with the British Government, viewed state subsidies as a distortion of competition that would undermine the benefits of the single market.[8] A general cutback of subsidies across the Community would benefit British industry on balance, given its below-average subsidisation level.[9]

Robert Atkinson, Chairman of British Shipbuilders in the early years of the Conservative Government, reports being told by a senior civil servant that Margaret Thatcher 'wants rid of shipbuilding' (*The Independent*, 4 September 1994). Government policy favoured the creation of economic dynamism, jobs and industrial diversification through investment incentives such as those embodied in enterprise zones. Thus the preferences of the British Government were consistent with the pronouncement of the Commission on the termination of shipbuilding at Sunderland and with the

Commission's broader aim of reducing shipbuilding capacity and improving overall industrial competitiveness. Moreover, the Government did not contest the Commission's decision. Indeed, investigations by the Commission of state aids in accordance with Article 93 were common where subsidies were *not* coupled with plans for capacity reduction and restructuring. Yet in the British case aid unquestionably had been tied to privatisation and restructuring. Additionally, while the Commission certainly had the power to reconsider its approval of aid to Sunderland workers, were the shipyard to continue operating in private hands the Commission would not likely have imposed unilaterally a ruling to which the British Government vehemently objected. The Commission's approach to state aid, especially in steeply declining sectors, had been cautious and pragmatic rather than unyielding (Scott, 1992, p. 74).

Defending the Government's policy in Parliament, successive Ministers of Industry argued that continuation of shipbuilding at Sunderland would jeopardise aid already approved and disbursed as well as alternative development plans for the area. In July 1989, Tony Newton asserted that 'it has been made clear' by the Commission 'that the Sunderland enterprise zone . . . could be called into question' (Hansard 156, p. 1145). Asked if the Commission had warned that it would kill the enterprise zone if the DTI pursued private shipbuilding bids for the Sunderland yards, Newton replied only that Commissioner Brittan had 'made clear that the Commission could not rule out reopening the question of the enterprise zone' in such a case (Hansard 156, p. 1153).

Members of the Trade and Industry Committee suggested that there was an understanding between the DTI and the Commission about a reduction in British shipbuilding capacity (HC 517(i)). Labour MP Bob Clay, of the Sunderland North constituency, maintained that the Sunderland site was a 'sacrificial lamb' for assistance to other shipbuilding locations (*The Guardian*, 13 April 1990). Bill Scott, Director of NESL at the time of the closings, has since suggested the Government sacrificed the Sunderland site in exchange for gaining EC approval to privatise remaining holdings, and that this deal was fixed in early 1988 (*The Independent*, 4 September 1994). Whatever the precise explanation, bargaining took place between the Commission and DTI without the participation of representatives of British Shipbuilders, who may have preferred privatisation of shipbuilding with subsidies to sweeten a private sale (HC 517(i), p. 14). Ultimately this helped make it possible for the British Government to strategically invoke the Commission's ruling to defuse opposition to its plans for an enterprise zone and industrial diversification in Sunderland.

In Parliament, the DTI came under attack for failing to contest the Commission's position. Bryan Gould, Labour spokesman for industry, challenged Tony Newton to 'tell the Commission that he and his Government are not prepared to sit back and allow Britain ... to be reduced to a situation where it no longer has any major merchant shipbuilding capacity...' (Hansard 156, p. 1146). Another MP asserted that the Minister 'should have made a strong case out to the Commission' and been prepared 'to fight ... to keep the yards open' (Hansard 156, p. 1151).

Parliamentary debate about the NESL shipyards illustrates both the Government's invocation of the Commission as a constraint on the outcome and the suspicion of opponents of the yard closure that the Government ministers or senior civil servants conspired with the Competition Commissioner, Leon Brittan, to secure the constraint. Opening the Commons debate about the European Commission's decision that the yard not reopen, Industry Minister Douglas Hogg[10] asserted that in a discussion prior to the Commission's official letter on the decision, 'Sir Leon Brittan made it plain that he would not accept any proposal predicated upon a return to shipbuilding ...' (Hansard 167, p. 779). One Labour MP questioned the logic by which a government committed to privatisation wished to prevent the private takeover of the Sunderland yard. In reply, Hogg reiterated that 'in so far as the proposals are predicated on a return to shipbuilding, the Commissioner has made it wholly plain to me that such a proposal would not be acceptable to the Commission' (Hansard 167, p. 782). In essence, whatever the preferences of the Government, the option of reopening the yards for shipbuilding under private ownership was simply out of the Government's hands.

Pressing the Minister on the issue, another opponent of

the yard closure hinted at the possibility of Government complicity in the Commission's ruling:

> The Minister has sought to blame Leon Brittan for the decision, but has also sought to argue in the House that it was the right decision. Will he clarify whether, in talking to Leon Brittan, he urged the case for the consortium to be allowed to go ahead on behalf of local jobs or simply accepted Leon Brittan's decision – or even welcomed it? (Hansard 167, p. 785)

Citing the widespread support for the private takeover of the yard from British Shipbuilders, the local government council, local MPs, and the North East region's Members of the European Parliament (MEPs), a Labour MP referred to the 'hidden agenda that leads the British Government, in the most subservient way, to give in to every arbitrary and legally dubious whim on which Sir Leon Brittan decides' (Hansard 167, p. 781).

By invoking the European Commission's position, the DTI altered the environment in which actors outside the Government formulated their policy preferences. Prior to the import of this constraint on domestic policy alternatives, opponents of the Government's programme of industrial diversification, defeated in their efforts to sustain Government subsidisation of British shipbuilding, could still pressure the DTI to keep the Sunderland yards intact in the hope of finalising terms with a private buyer. By bringing in the European Commission, the Government ruled this out. Now opponents of the termination of shipbuilding, largely local MPs, could do no more than attack the Government and the Commission rhetorically, and stand aside to avoid blame in the event that the DTI's planned enterprise zone for Sunderland failed. The cause to save shipbuilding in Sunderland was already lost when a parliamentary delegation travelled to Strasbourg in July 1989 to ask MEPs to help change the Commission's ruling. Moreover, for Britain's Conservative Government, invoking the Commission as a 'constraint' brought the added benefit of reinforcing the Government's depiction of a federalising 'Brussels' representing a pervasive threat to parliamentary sovereignty epitomised by Margaret Thatcher's 1988 Bruges speech to the College of Europe.

Spain: Iberia and state shrinkage

In January 1995, the Spanish Government officially informed
the European Commission that it planned to invest 130 billion pesetas of capital in its state airline, Iberia, as part of
the terms of a restructuring plan designed to restore the viability of the carrier. Iberia had accumulated losses of approxi-
mately Pt200bn, or about £1bn, between 1990 and 1994.

Iberia's new Chairman, Javier Salas, who was, behind Industry Minister Juan Manuel Eguiagaray, EU Transport Commissioner Neil Kinnock's secondary interlocutor on the Iberia
case, announced that it would be difficult for Iberia to convince the Commission of the viability of its restructuring
plan and so obtain the Commission's approval of the aid
(Reuters News Service, Western Europe, 10 January 1995).
It appears that Salas was placed at the head of Iberia to
fundamentally alter the way that Iberia conducted business,
shifting from a short-term, politically-driven management by
ex-ministers or executives of other public sector enterprises
to a professional, market-disciplined management by private
sector executives (*Business Spain*, November 1994). Iberia's
problematic investment in Aerolineas Argentinas, part of a
payment of Argentine debts to the Spanish Government,
was symptomatic of this politically-driven management.

Late in 1994, Iberia's new Chief Executive, Juan Saez, and
Salas stepped up cost-cutting efforts, informing employees
that average wage cuts of 15 per cent and substantial re-
dundancies would be required to keep the company viable.
They warned that the European Commission would not
approve a desperately-needed capital infusion from Teneo,
the state holding company, without agreement on such a
wage package (Reuters News Service, Western Europe, 24
October 1994). When employees failed to agree in initial
bargaining rounds and staged a one-day strike, Salas warned
that the alternative to the pay accord was to sell off substantial parts of the company. Coinciding with Salas' warning, Competition Commissioner Karel Van Miert publicly
rejected the Spanish Government's claim that Iberia's need
was legitimate due to special circumstances, principally a
sharp devaluation of the peseta and huge losses on the
company's Latin American assets. Salas, in turn, warned that

without the pay agreement demanded by the Commission, Iberia would be bankrupt by March 1995 (*Flight International*, 23 November 1994).

In November 1994 the Commission opened a breach in its previous formulation of a 'one-time, last-time' policy for capital transfers to troubled public airlines, announcing that aids could be approved in exceptional circumstances. While the Transport Minister, Jose Borrell, argued publicly that Iberia had a legitimate case for receiving assistance due to the special circumstance of the peseta's sharp devaluation and the unexpected length of Spain's recession, Industry Minister Eguiagaray repeatedly warned that the Commission would not approve the capital infusion unless the cost cuts pushed by Salas and Saez were achieved and Iberia's board of directors was reorganised. In mid-March 1995, the Spanish press and Eguiagaray reported that the Commission would not authorise aid to Iberia unless political appointees on Iberia's board were replaced with business professionals from the private sector. Replacement of directors would institutionalise a more market-oriented approach to the management of Iberia (*Gaceta de los Negocios*, 17 March 1995). This step to alter Iberia's corporate culture reflected an emerging tension within the Government over macroeconomic policy between those favouring state shrinkage and those more deeply committed to public investment and ownership. Economy Minister Pedro Solbes appears to have been the primary proponent of state shrinkage, with Eguiagaray a critical ally and Transport Minister Borrell opposed.

Acceleration of the drive to cut Spain's budget deficit came in part from the EU itself, following a July 1994 meeting of Finance Ministers. In accordance with the terms of the Maastricht Treaty, the Ministers recommended a set of macroeconomic policy guidelines for 1995 calling for the reduction of public sector deficits. The recommendations cited Spain's need to take action in response to a deteriorating budget picture. Solbes sought to put Spain on the path to a reduction in the public sector deficit to 3 per cent by 1997, partly through large-scale privatisations in the telecommunications, oil and banking sectors, and partly through cuts in public investments. Solbes emphasised the critical importance for Spain to move in its 1996 budget toward the convergence criteria for the third phase of EMU, and underscored that the required reductions in Government spending would come through cuts in Government transfers to public and private enterprises rather than reductions in social spending (*La Vanguardia*, 10 September 1995, pp. 62–3).[11]

Keeping a close watch on the Iberia case, Industry Minister Eguiagaray was one of Solbes' allies in this endeavour to shrink the public sector (*El Pais*, 28 April 1995, p. 57). Once the Commission, in March 1995, opened its investigatory procedure into the intended payment to Iberia in accordance with Article 93 of the EC Treaty, Eguiagary intensified pressures to change the composition of Iberia's board as a step toward withdrawing the Government from management of public enterprises.

After nine months of deliberations, the Commission, in January 1996, approved a transfer of 87 billion pesetas rather than the 130 billion originally requested. The Commission ruled that with Iberia divested of its holding in Aerolineas Argentinas, the principal condition of the approval, the transfer would resemble an investment consistent with the behaviour of a private investor rather than a state aid (*Financial Times*, 20 December 1995, p. 3). Eguiagaray pronounced that he was 'reasonably satisfied' with the decision, while Economy Minister Solbes commented that the amount 'is a figure with which we can live and with which we can resume the modernisation and adaptation programme as planned' (*Aviation Europe*, 21 December 1995, p. 1).

CONCLUDING IMPLICATIONS

It is clear that the actions of the Commission have important implications for the *policies* of Member States. This chapter has suggested that the Commission also matters in the *politics* of Member States.

The Commission is a significant presence in the industrial policies of Member States, not least because of its activist role in the state aids policy area which is central to the fulfilment of the SEM. Yet due to the political weight of Member State governments, the Commission needs allies in the Member States to advance its agenda, especially when dealing with aids to the public sector, typically involving large numbers of jobs and strong political support. In the two cases examined here, actors operating from a strategic position in Member State governments benefited by invoking the Commission. The UK Government could deploy the Commission's decision on the Sunderland shipyards to its advantage because it already had used its political resources to narrow the range of possible outcomes to include just two alternatives, enterprise zone development and privatisation – its first and second preferences. Bringing in the Commission ruled out the UK Government's second-ranked preference and enabled it to secure its preferred outcome at a reduced political cost. Similarly, Spain's modernisers negotiated with the Commission to advance their broader economic objective of slimming the public sector while averting financial disaster for a huge public sector employer. Members of the Government favouring a continuation of traditional subsidisation policies were weakened by the Commission's effort to apply a market investor principle to capital transfers to public enterprises and by the demands of the EMU convergence process.

While the Commission was a strategic asset to particular political actors in Member States in the cases discussed in this chapter, it, too, achieved critical objectives through its cooperation with government ministers. In the case of NESL, the Commission achieved the permanent reduction of excess capacity in shipbuilding, and also contributed to the credibility of its effort to tighten state aids policy in the runup to the single market. In the case of Iberia, the Commission sought to sustain the credibility of its commitment to combat state aids by approving a limited capital infusion that 'pared Iberia to the bone' (*Financial Times*, 20 December 1995, p. 3). Indeed, the Commission emphasised that the Iberia case represented the first time it had demanded divestment 'of major direct investments in civil aviation' of an EU airline (*Aviation Europe*, 21 December 1995, p. 1). The Commission thereby lent support to modernisers seeking to reduce the burden of Iberia on the Spanish state, facilitating Spain's economic convergence with the EU's stronger economies. In addition, in the process of negotiating Iberia's restructuring plan, the Commission advanced its objective of liberalising ground handling services (aircraft, passenger, cargo and mail handling) at Spain's airports, part of the Commission's larger objective of fulfilling the single market by opening up the public procurement process. In 1995 and 1996, AENA, Spain's airport authority, moved to end Iberia's monopoly and overcharging on ground handling at Spain's airports (*Aviation Europe*, 14 March 1996, p. 5).

On a broader front, Transport Commissioner Kinnock ultimately hoped to use the Iberian case to gain, through liberalisation of the European aviation market, a more central role for the EU as a negotiator for aviation agreements with third parties. This is a direct response to the lessons of the 'open skies' agreements negotiated between individual EU states and the US, which Kinnock believes will intensify competition between EU Member States for access to the American market (*The Economist*, 18 March 1995, p. 55). The Transport Commissioner aims to create a single aviation market, in which EU Member States could do better negotiating as a unit.

Though it may reap benefits, it should, however, also be noted that the costs may be high for the Commission when political actors invoke its requirements as a strategic asset. The case of NESL had a negative impact on the Commission's image in Britain. When one of Britain's Industry Ministers explained before the House of Commons in July 1989 that the Commission would not permit the revival of shipbuilding at the Sunderland shipyards, a prominent response was an attack on the EC for its encroachment on British sovereignty. One Conservative representative of shipbuilding interests asked if it would 'not be infinitely better for a Conservative Government in a free-market economy to leave such a decision to the market and not to non-elected bureaucrats in Brussels?' (Hansard 156, p. 1152). In a subsequent debate, the same MP requested that the Minister for Industry 'consider that there is a serious democratic problem when a non-elected civil servant in Brussels can instruct the British Government and Parliament, irrespective of their wishes, that shipbuilding without special aids cannot continue in a part of this country' (Hansard 167, p. 780). Another MP spoke of a 'surrender to Brussels' (Hansard 156, p. 1147).

Bryan Gould, Shadow Industry Minister, labeled the Commission's decision 'an intolerable interference by Brussels,' ironically endorsing the image of a meddling European bureaucracy nurtured by Conservative critics of the integration process (*Lloyds List*, 20 July 1989).

However, where a Commission decision endorses more disciplined management of a public sector enterprise, the Commission is likely to gain supporters as well as detractors in the relevant Member State. In the Spanish case, the costs to the Commission were not as high because the Commission ultimately acknowledged the legitimacy of Iberia's claim and did not completely reject the planned capital injection. The approved infusion of capital allowed the company to continue to operate by making some difficult decisions designed to ensure its viability. Nonetheless, in this instance the Commission incurred other costs, coming under sharp attack from Member State governments, private air carriers, and economic liberals in the European Parliament.[12]

As for other policy areas, building an effective state aids policy requires not the confrontational 'get tough' approach advanced by many neo-liberal critics of the Commission, but cooperation with Member States to steer a middle course between economic objectives and political realities. Therefore, as the Santer Commission seeks to do 'not more, but better', it must increasingly rely on strategic relationships with well-placed politicians and officials in Member States to realise its objectives.

Notes

1. Aid may come in the form of government grants; interest subsidies; research and development assistance; tax credits, exemptions, or deferments; reductions in social insurance contributions; state equity participation; and loan guarantees. See Commission, (1995d), pp. 51–2.
2. While the Commission cannot impose privatisation as a condition of approving aid for restructuring, privatisation can be a central factor in a Commission evaluation of the viability of a restructuring programme.
3. Personal interview with Commission official, July 1995.
4. For another example of this principle, see Walter Hallstein, *Europe*

in the Making, p. 113. Hallstein points out that while Article 57 of the EC Treaty codified mutual recognition of diplomas and professional degrees in the Community, the existence of craft guilds and professional bodies created barriers to such recognition in practice.

5. For details on how the Commission has done this with good success, see Smith (1996).
6. *Lloyd's Register* reported in June 1989 that world shipbuilding orders had reached their highest level in four years (*The Times*, 7 June 1989, p. 26). Hearings of the Commons Select Committee on Trade and Industry took place on the day following release of the report, and committee members criticised the Government for so thoroughly reducing capacity that British Shipbuilders was left unable to take advantage of the market upturn, especially strong in merchant shipbuilding, the forte of NESL (HC 517(i), pp. 7–9).
7. See the *Financial Times*, 11 July 1989, p. 10; 14 July 1989, pp. 10 and 20; and *The Times*, 14 July 1989, p. 13.
8. For a discussion of Brittan's war on subsidisation, see the *Financial Times*, 10 March 1989, p. 18; 1 August 1990, p. 18; 12 October 1990, p. 22; 19 November 1990, p. 6; and *The Economist*, 9 June 1990, p. 13. In July 1989, the Commission's annual report on competition policy announced a review of existing state aid. See the *Financial Times*, 27 July 1989, p. 24.
9. British manufacturing received average subsidies of ECU 757 per worker as compared with an EC average of ECU 1774, swollen by Italy's average subsidies of ECU 5951 per worker.
10. In July 1989 Tony Newton left his post as Minister of Trade and Industry when he was appointed Secretary of State for Social Security.
11. Foreign Broadcast Information Service translation.
12. British Prime Minister John Major was one of the most vocal public critics of the Commission's Iberia decision. A Danish Liberal member of the European Parliament sought a motion condemning the Commission's state aids policy. See *Aviation Europe*, 15 February 1996; 22 February 1996; and 7 March 1996.

10 The Commission and Implementation in the European Union: Is There an Implementation Deficit and Why?

B. Guy Peters

INTRODUCTION

The frequently identified tension in the study of the European Union (EU) between international relations approaches and comparative politics approaches persists. Both approaches are absorbed with the great questions of sovereignty and the future shape of the political system in Europe. We more mundane scholars, however, can identify a political system already in place, already churning out a large number of laws and regulations which are implemented through somewhat cumbersome mechanisms. Attention to the great issues, important as they are, may deflect attention from the workings of the system that already exists and especially from 'boring' administrative questions such as policy implementation.

All political systems are complex, but the EU has evolved into a particularly complicated system. The structure of decision-making in the system is complex enough, given the increasingly intricate interactions among institutions formally required to make decisions (Kassim, 1994; Tsebelis, 1994). However, the implementation process for the decisions produced by the EU is, if anything, even more complex and demanding. For almost all of its policies, the EU depends upon the governments of the Member States for implementation, having only limited capacity to enforce Union policy

directly itself. The national governments, in their turn, often rely upon subnational or third-sector organisations (Hood
and Schuppert, 1988) for implementation of both their own
policies and also European policies. Indeed, the increasing
decentralisation of national administrative systems into 'agencies' and the like tends to diminish hierarchical control even
within government. This multi-tiered and loosely coupled
system is hardly an enviable implementation structure for
government attempting to impose its policies and its will
over a territory.

This chapter will examine certain key aspects of the implementation of EU policies, with particular reference to the
role of the Commission and whether there can be said to
be an implementation deficit. (For a thorough description
of the nature of EU policy implementation, see Siedentopf
and Ziller, 1988). The first question is whether there is indeed an implementation deficit that some analysts of the
European system claim exists. We will point out that the
perfect implementation process implicit in the 'deficit' argument rarely exists, even within individual nation-states,
so that perhaps any deficit that exists is not peculiar to the
EU. This argument does not mean, however, that implementation problems are unimportant and that citizens and governments should accept implementation failures. We will examine
the existing barriers to effective implementation of EU policies, using the several varieties of theory that exist in implementation theory. The chapter will conclude by speculating
on the further development of implementation within the
EU, and the impact of implementation questions on the
general development of the system of governing.

IS THERE AN IMPLEMENTATION DEFICIT IN THE
EUROPEAN UNION?

It has become almost axiomatic that the European Union
has an implementation or management 'deficit' (Metcalfe,
1992). The Sutherland Report, published in 1992, placed
the management issue squarely on the EU agenda and it
has not gone away (Sutherland, 1993). The apparently monu-
mental difficulties that any policy would face being trans-

lated from just a stated policy to operational policy within the EU are taken to mean, prima facie, that policies will not be implemented. This deficit argument appears to be based implicitly on an idealised picture of what implementation should be. More precisely, the argument appears to reflect a model of 'perfect administration' (Hood, 1976) in which decisions taken by legislatures or political executives are translated almost effortlessly into action. In reality (as Hood demonstrated clearly) implementation almost everywhere encounters formidable barriers and involves bargaining, negotiation, and the use of a variety of other political devices before anything actually happens. Therefore, despite the pessimism of some commentators, implementation difficulties in the EU may be more normal than exceptional.

A particular problem for the EU is that it has no single pattern of policy implementation (Héritier, 1996). It has become engaged with an increasing range of policies and each policy raises its own implementation questions. Most policies must be implemented through the Member States, but a small number of policies (competition, fisheries) are implemented at least in part by the EU itself via the Commission. Therefore, a study of implementation requires some attention to the relevant differences between policies which are largely implemented through agencies in the Member States. Further, some policies may have only a single implementing agency, or at least only a few agencies, in some member countries, while other policies may involve a large and disparate number of organisations (Lavoux, 1986, p. 101). These differences mean that to understand implementation in the EU requires some differential understanding of different ways of putting policies into effect. There is an increasing number of sectoral studies of implementation in the EU, (see, for example, Sbragia, 1996; Zimmerman, 1995) but care must be taken not to generalise from any of these.

Evidence/arguments for the deficit

The most fundamental argument for the presence of an implementation deficit is that the EU depends heavily upon its Member States for implementation. There are two aspects to implementation: incorporation and application.

Regarding incorporation, when the EU adopts new, non administrative, legislation, its Member States are required to incorporate the legislation into national law (Nugent, 1991, pp. 87–93). This results in EU law being accorded similar status to independent acts of national parliaments (primary legislation) or national administrations (secondary legislation). (The status of EU and national laws is not identical since the principle of primacy applies to EU law in the event of there being a conflict between the two.) The problem with the requirement of legal incorporation is that not all countries are as responsive as they might be to the necessity of making the incorporations. Since the incorporation process generally must be performed through national parliaments there is no guarantee that the issues will not become entangled in national politics, if only as a means to embarrass the government of the day. Even if political embarrassment is not a motive, national governments may have genuine concerns about EU policies, or may interpret the meaning of a policy differently from the Commission's and Council's original intentions.

Regarding application, legal incorporation does not guarantee that there will actually be effective translation of EU laws and policies into action. National bureaucracies must still act and must actively pursue the implementation of laws and policies before they can become operative. In respect of national policies, bureaucracies have some capacity to sabotage a policy by inaction or by excessive attention to procedural detail, and that action may be more common for policies that are initiated elsewhere. Even the exercise of normal administrative discretion may undermine the intentions of the framers.

The limited resources of the Commission bureaucracy makes it difficult for it to monitor the incorporation, and more especially the application, behaviour of the Member States as closely as is ideally desirable. The critics of the EU, inside and outside the governments of the Member States, are very keen to talk about the expansionist and unreasonable bureaucracy encountered in the EU, but the Commission is actually a very small organisation (see Chapter 1). Certainly an organisation that wishes to implement, or monitor the implementation of, diverse policies over such a huge territory and population, should be larger than a few thousand employees, no matter how skilled they may be. Further, although the Commission administrators are skilled, their skills appear to be more in the area of policy formulation than implementation (Ludlow, 1991, p. 107). Thus, just on the basis of Commission personnel alone, we might expect the EU to have a severe implementation deficit.

Further, the EU is moving from its original competencies into a wider array of issues. Some of these issues have emerged through the Maastricht Treaty and others have emerged through interpretations of the meaning of the Treaty of Rome and of the Single Europe Act. So, just as the interstate commerce clause of the United States Constitution has provided the foundation of a wide range of federal government powers, the mandate to eliminate barriers to competition provides a rather wide grant of power for EU activity. As the range of EU activities increase so too do the Commission's implementation difficulties. These difficulties arise in part through the relative inexperience of Commission officials in these policy areas, and also because some policy areas – such as environmental policy and social policy – are less tractable than the original areas of EC activity.

The final reason to be concerned about the real or perceived implementation deficit is that the EU is not a 'normal' political system. It is still in the process of state-building and therefore its capacity to enforce its policies throughout its territory is of particular significance. If, as Scharpf (1994) and others have argued, the policy-making capacity of the EU has not yet made up for the loss of capacity of individual Member States, then implementation becomes even more crucial for state-building. A failure to enforce laws effectively is no real threat to the continued sovereignty of, say, the United States or France, but it may be to a new political system – whether that system is the EU or a newly democratic government in central Europe. However, the Commission, when undertaking its implementation responsibilities on behalf of the EU, faces the challenge of balancing the need for uniformity and legality with the need to utilise some 'rule of reason' to prevent offending the less committed Europeans – whether governments or private citizens.

Evidence/arguments against the deficit

The reliance of the EU on its Member States for implementation makes implementation more difficult than in more linear administrative systems. In many national political systems (especially, but not exclusively, federal systems), this same problem often arises when central government must rely on the constituent components of the country for implementation. There are any number of cases in which federal proposals in the United States have been modified, or in effect defeated, by the states during the process of implementation. The legalistic administrative culture of Germany makes this type of nullification through implementation less likely, but even there implementation problems (of both national and EU policy) do exist (Philip, 1988, p. 116).

We could argue that this pattern of opposition to policies, or at least non-compliance, might be less likely in the EU than in many nation states. For many policies the EU cannot have acted without the agreement of all the member countries. Even for the policies that can be adopted by qualified majority voting (qmv), the coalition required appears sufficiently large, and bargaining principles sufficiently well-established, that few countries would be in the position of implementing a policy with which they disagreed fundamentally (Hosli, 1996). There are certainly such cases, seeming to appear most frequently in the United Kingdom, but they should be less frequent than in the average nation-state, especially the average unitary nation-state.

In undertaking its implementation responsibilities the Commission has the advantage of being concerned largely with regulatory policies (Majone, 1994a, 1995). Most heavily budgetary-dependent policies – such as education, health, and social services – are delivered to citizens by national and subnational administrative levels. Moreover, the Commission's implementation duties mainly involve monitoring the actions of others rather than delivering a service directly itself. These two factors – the regulatory and monitoring nature of policy responsibilities – mean that the Commission is relieved of many 'conventional' administrative duties and in many policy areas does not have to concern itself unduly with complex and detailed questions of service quality.

The Commission has allies in the implementation process. Its primary ally is the European Court of Justice. If a Member State chooses not to incorporate EU law policy into national law, or decides to incorporate it in a manner that is deemed to be inappropriate, then the Commission can appeal to the Court. Further, the various treaties and acts serving as the working constitution of the EU give citizens the right to appeal directly to the Court concerning inadequate national implementation of EU regulations. This provision gives the Commission an additional 'fire alarm' (McCubbins and Schwartz, 1984) for monitoring implementation in each country. That does not mean that implementation will be swift and untroubled, especially since the sanctions imposed by the Court tend to be more informational than directly punitive (Pollack, 1996). It does mean, however, that the implementation process can be monitored with less direct public cost than might be true in many other political systems that lack this popular device.

UNDERSTANDING IMPLEMENTATION DIFFICULTIES

A well-developed body of theoretical literature on implementation now exists as a means for understanding the process. These existing theories are generally characterised as having either a 'top-down' or a 'bottom-up' perspective (Sabatier, 1986; Linder and Peters, 1989) depending upon the perceived locus of the impetus for the pressure for putting laws into effect. The top-down perspective assumes that law should drive policy and that the most appropriate guide for implementation is the formal statement of what the 'formators' wanted (Lane, 1983). The bottom-up view, on the other hand, assumes that implementation is best understood as a process of bargaining and negotiation, with the needs of the lower echelons of organisations at least as important as the formal desires of the centre of government. In many ways, the EU corresponds to the bottom-up view, given the number of relatively autonomous implementors. Despite that, we will argue that the most analytic leverage can be gained from taking the top-down perspective and thinking about the problems of control and accountability within the system.

The bottom-up perspective

Proponents of the bottom-up perspective argue that implementation inevitably involves decisions by 'street-level' officials (Lipsky, 1980), so it is therefore crucial to understand the behaviour of those officials. Whereas the top-down approach to implementation tends to focus on a 'single lonely organisation' charged with implementing a policy, the bottom-up approach points to the interorganisational networks and 'implementation structures' actually responsible for most implementation (Hjern and Porter, 1980; Hanf and Toonen, 1985). More normatively, proponents of the bottom-up perspective (such as Elmore, 1982) argue that policies *should* be designed from the bottom-up, with implementation and the policy preferences of the implementors clearly in mind from the outset. Designing programmes from the bottom-up will minimise the probability of programmes encountering the administrative failures that fuel the source of many top-down arguments for greater hierarchical control.

It is easy to contest some of the normative premises of the 'bottom-up approach' to implementation. Designing policy in accordance with taking into account all the wishes of prospective clients appears to argue for policy as the lowest common denominator that would be acceptable to every possible client and implementing group. Government may get into the business of doing what is easy to do, rather than perhaps what it should do or would like to do. Further, while serving the client is certainly a part of the logic of the New Public Management (Pollitt, 1993; Hood *et al.*, 1996), and more basically a component of democracy, following legal mandates is also a crucial component of governing and should not be ignored.

The EU appears to be particularly suited for the bottom-up approach to implementation. In the first place the variety of national policy styles (Richardson, 1982) and the variety of national administrative styles appear to make developing workable policies from the top down difficult. These long-standing differences will be hard to overcome unless the EU is willing to invest heavily in implementation, and is willing to take a great deal of political heat as a result of policy choices (Page and Wouters, 1995). Whereas we have argued elsewhere (Peters, 1994b), that the multiplicity of ideas and functioning policies within the EU makes agenda-setting easier than in most national policy systems, this diversity appears to make implementation more difficult.

Also, the general European style of implementation has been described in a number of places (Vogel, 1986; Lundquist, 1980; Majone, 1989) as being based more on bargaining than upon the strict imposition of legal mandates as is more characteristic of regulation in the United States (Bardach and Kagan, 1982). Thus, any attempt to impose a top-down approach for implementation (especially of regulatory policy) is not likely to be as effective as it might in other settings.[1] The negotiated, bottom-up character of policy-making within the EU is enhanced by emerging arguments that uniformity, or harmonisation, ultimately may be counter-productive for the Union. The emerging regime is manifested by an emphasis on 'mutual recognition' as opposed to the previous concern with 'harmonization' of policies. There is also now advocacy of 'regulatory competition', in which the Member States would not implement policies uniformly but rather ' . . . market forces would respond to differences in national regulations' (Sun and Pelkmans, 1995, p. 70). In other words, national differences in regulation and implementation might become a virtue rather than a vice as a means of enhancing the overall efficiency of the European market.

The bargainable nature of policy in Europe may be enhanced by the continuing absence of effective coordination in the centre of the Brussels machine. Most studies point to the decentralisation of power to the Directorate Generals within the Commission bureaucracy, and their links with their functional counterparts in other countries (Peters, 1992; Mazey and Richardson, 1994). This decentralisation at the policy formulation stage in turn implies that the subsequent supervision of implementation will inevitably also be decentralised. Thus, although there may be an aspiration for uniformity and coordination, there inevitably will be some slippage.[2]

Finally, the subsidiarity principle also appears to make the EU more amenable than most political systems to arguments favouring bottom-up policy implementation. If policy is to be made at the lowest possible unit within the EU, the possibility that policy may be interpreted differently in different settings appears to be an acceptable proposition. If policy is defined, as it often is in the literature, through implementation, as an evolutionary process (Majone and Wildavsky, 1978), then understanding implementation from the bottom-up is crucial for understanding the way in which policy is actually made. In summary, the bottom-up version of implementation does not conform to the idea of perfect administration usually taken as the standard for good implementation. Implementing 'from the bottom-up' implies a great deal more diversity in implementation and in the interpretation of policy than is sometimes thought appropriate. If intellectual (and legal) resistance to that diversity and substantial local influence can be overcome, then this may be the most appropriate manner in which to conceptualise implementation in the EU, and with it the implementation role of the Commission.

The top-down perspective

When Pressman and Wildavsky (1974) brought the concept of implementation to the attention of political scientists the perspective they used was, in essence, what has come to be labelled the 'top-down' perspective. They were concerned with the failure of an economic development programme adopted in Washington to go into effect in Oakland, California as was planned. The failure of government programmes to function as planned was hardly a new phenomenon, but now there was a label to attach to that failure, and a better means of understanding the consequences of many of the problems normally encountered in administrative life. The Pressman–Wildavsky book and the subsequent literature may place too much of the blame for failure at the doorstep of implementation, as opposed to the initial policy formulation, but it did provide a way to comprehend failures.

The model of implementation developed by Pressman and Wildavsky was based on 'clearance points', or the number of separate decisions required before a policy decision made in a national capital could actually be put into effect somewhere in that country. In the case of the Oakland Bay project, there were some 70 independent clearance points that had to be negotiated before the policy could be implemented successfully. Even with hard work by the advocates of the programme and good will on the part of other participants in the process, this number of necessary decisions made successful implementation extremely unlikely.[3] Implementation of EU legislation appears to involve the Commission relying on an inordinately large number of clearance points, given particularly the key position of Member States in respect of most implementation.

If the number of clearance points were not a sufficient problem for the Commission, the existence of a variety of administrative and legal traditions makes the problem even more difficult. Programmes that might be put into effect easily in the legalistic culture of Germany or Austria can encounter real difficulties in the common-law cultures of Britain or Ireland, or in the Napoleonic systems of France and Spain. Programmes and policies must be converted to operational elements in order to be implemented and that conversion is more difficult when there is such a variety of formats that must be matched before they become operational. There are also different levels of effective national strength within the implementation process, so that a decision by Germany to go slow on implementing a major economic programme is perhaps more important than a similar decision taken by Portugal or Finland (Wilks and McGowan, 1995).

The top-down perspective thus provides a number of insights which can be used to explore EU implementation, and more especially Commission control of that implementation.

THE PRINCIPAL–AGENT MODEL OF IMPLEMENTATION AND THE EUROPEAN UNION

The top-down perspective on implementation in the EU demonstrates many of the features of the principal–agent problem common in rational choice analyses of public administration (Horn, 1995; Calvert, 1995). In this perspective, the Commission ordinarily would be conceptualised as the principal, with its basic problem being to control defection on the part of the agents – the national governments and their bureaucracies. This problem is not confined to the

EU but is a common problem in all bureaucratic systems. Bureaucracies, and in this case national governments, have the tendency to pursue their own interests and to serve their clients to the possible rejection of the mandates imposed upon them by their principals.

The case of the EU is complicated by the fact that national governments are not only agents of the Commission but are also, by virtue of their membership of the European Council and the Council of Ministers, simultaneously its principals. Decisions about the policies for which the Commission has implementing responsibilities must be approved by the national governments, operating either on a unanimous or a qmv basis. Moreover, the national governments have established a variety of mechanisms, such as the 'comitology' procedure, to help bind the Commission's actions to their wishes (Docksey and Williams, 1994). The Commission is, therefore, subject to extensive direction and restraints regarding its implementation duties. However, it is by no means completely locked in, and in important respects national administrations can certainly be thought of as being its agents.

The tendency of these agents towards defection – in the sense of seeking to pursue their own agendas rather than the agenda required by the Commission – may be increased by managerial changes occurring in most national bureaucracies. The current style of reform in administrative systems is to delegate increasing amounts of authority to the lower echelons of organisations and to diminish the degree of hierarchical control exercised by central agencies and political officials (Aucoin, 1995). Further, another part of the 'New Public Management' is the redefinition by agents of principals as 'political masters' to principals as 'clients' or 'customers'. These changes make *ex ante* control over national bureaucracies exercised by the Commission much more difficult to make truly effective.

Implementation within the principal–agent model would not be such a problem if monitoring and control of agents were costless activities, but they are not. Therefore, the EU, and more especially the Commission, must determine how much to invest in control of its agents. In other words, how much defection is the Commission willing to permit, given the inherent difficulties in detecting deviations and then forcing the Member States to comply? Given the limited staff resources of the Commission, awkward decisions must be made about whether it is worthwhile to invest those resources in attempting to ensure implementation within the member countries and, if so, what level of monitoring it should generate in that effort.

An additional consideration is that the costs which the Commission must bear in performing its implementation tasks are more than just economic costs of time and administrative salaries: important political costs are involved as well. We noted above that the EU is still in the process of state-building and that it must create legitimacy for its actions. There are threats to legitimacy whichever way the Commission decides to play the implementation 'game'.[4] If it is excessively draconian, the Commission encounters the risk of offending the less committed Member States – notably, the United Kingdom. On the other hand, if it is too lenient it runs the risk of offending the more legalistic members, as well as indicating to many citizens within the Member States that it is not an effective political system.

It must also be remembered that the Member States and their bureaucracies can claim somewhat more legitimacy as independent actors than the principal-agent concept of implementation might accord most agents. It is not unknown for national leaders to argue that national governments have substantially greater political legitimacy than the Commission, and therefore to suggest that they may be justified in considering carefully the regulations coming to them from the EU. Within the language of this paradigm, national governments may believe that they must play the role of the agents of their citizens, at least as much as the agents of the Commission, and that as such they have an obligation to protect the interests of those citizens even if they conflict with Commission views and/or instructions.

The claims of national governments to have as much or more legitimacy as the Commission is strengthened by the feeling that the Eurocrats sometimes violate their own obligations not to act as the agents of national governments (Nugent, 1994, p. 91) – the 'commitment problem' in principal–agent theory. Thus, from time to time Member States may feel that they have to counteract the 'biased' behaviour of the Commission. Spence (1994, pp. 79–80), for example, points to examples of apparently country-biased allocation of industrial contracts. In short, national bureaucracies may feel justified in adopting their own course of action in implementation when they believe that their nation is possibly being treated unfairly.

CONCLUSION: QUESTIONS ABOUT THE FUTURE OF IMPLEMENTATION

As the EU moves forward in coping with the requirements of the Maastricht agreements, and the potential for further integration, a number of questions about the future of implementation arise. These questions to a great extent address the various perceptions of the future of the Union and its several possible configurations. The capacity to implement policy is one central defining feature of any political system, and if in the future the EU is to be a functioning government then implementation becomes a crucial question. Implementation is often forgotten as political systems and their policies are designed, but this is a crucial activity for any government, and often defines what policies actually mean (Peters, 1994b).

One of the questions arising in implementation will be the degree of policy uniformity expected and required. A top-down perspective would mandate very stringent requirements for similarity across the Member States, with Greece and Sweden presumably doing almost exactly the same things as they implement EU law. A less stringent, bottom-up answer to the uniformity question might permit Member States much greater latitude to define their own patterns of adherence to the spirit, if not the letter, of EU regulations. Most federal governments permit substantial variation among their constituent units in the manner in which policies are implemented locally, and there may little reason to expect the EU to be substantially different. What may be different are the strict formal requirements contained in the implementation process of the Union (Mény, 1993, pp. 28–35), and hence an even stronger appearance of failure if full uniformity is not achieved. Clearly, this question of uniformity of implementation has considerable implications for the role of the Commission.

Another question is whether the need to perform similar tasks in a similar manner will produce greater homogenisation of the implementing structures of European governments, especially their public bureaucracies. There is some evidence that the countries with perhaps the least similar administrative systems – such as Greece, Portugal and Spain – are converging toward some common European model (Spanou, 1996; Alvarez, 1996). A great deal of variation remains in national administrative systems, but there are continuing pressures toward greater similarity if not absolute uniformity. This convergence almost certainly will not guarantee perfect implementation of EU policy but it may make designing policy for implementation, and subsequent monitoring of implementation by the Commission, somewhat easier.

As well as possibly being smoothed by structural convergence, implementation may ultimately be facilitated most by individual convergence. That is, as individual civil servants have increasing amounts of contact with EU legislation and the Commission, and as in the course of their ordinary working lives they increasingly function as the agents of Brussels (Cassese and Cananea, 1990), they may come to perceive the difference between national implementation and EU implementation as minimal or non-existent. Further, Commission officials may produce an EU bureaucracy that helps make EU policies that are more compatible with national patterns (Christoph, 1993). Such changes would not guarantee perfect administration, but they may eliminate, or at least lower, any artificial barriers to the administration of EU policies and laws.

This chapter has sought to demonstrate that implementation is not simply a boring, mechanical administrative activity. Rather, implementation processes can illuminate a great deal about the nature of the political system that is performing the implementing. They can also say a good deal about the nature of the policies that are being implemented. In the case of the EU as an emerging political system, implementation is an increasingly important element and the role of the Commission in that element is crucial.

Institutional developments over the past decade have helped address at least a part of the democratic deficit in the EU system. The complementary implementation deficit is perhaps overstated, being based upon an implicit model of perfect administration, but it is, and will remain, a real challenge for the Union and, more particularly, for the Commission.

Notes

1. Most of the studies of regulation argue that the negotiated style is, on average, more effective than the more draconian style.
2. Cassese (1987a) argues, however, that this fragmentation in the systems allows greater interpenetration and somewhat greater possibilities for convergence.
3. Pressman and Wildavsky worked out the probabilities. If each clearance point had a 99 per cent probability of being passed, the likelihood of all 70 being passed successfully still was only 0.489. At 95 per cent, the probability dropped to a minuscule 0.00395. A mere fourteen clearance points reduces the *a priori* probability of implementation to less than 50 per cent at 95 per cent.
4. For a conceptualization in these terms, see Bardach (1977).

11 Managing the Managers: The Commission's Role in the Implementation of Spending Programmes
Roger Levy

INTRODUCTION

No matter how good a policy may be, it cannot succeed unless somebody implements it, and whoever implements has a key influence over what and how much is delivered, and to whom. It is thus surprising that the Commission's role as an implementer, as opposed to a maker, of policy has generally been neglected as a field of study. While this role does not lend itself to easy generalisation, in most areas of policy the Commission implements at arm's length via the Member State governments and their agencies, only implementing directly in a few areas, such as competition law (Shaw, 1993; Nugent, 1994). In Nugent's phrase, it is primarily a 'supervisor and overseer' of frontline implementation (Nugent, 1994, p. 107).

In the implementation of European Union (EU) programmes, the much discussed principle of subsidiarity generally prevails, whereby Member State bodies act as agents for the Commission. In practice, relationships are intricate, fractured and diverse in the extreme, as might be expected in a system of multi-level governance. In managing a vast and varied army of managers to a greater or lesser degree, the Commission performs a wide range of implementation functions, both simple and mechanical, and complex and judgemental in character. In the context of the oft-noted slender manpower resources of the Commission, it is hardly surprising that the practice of implementation often leaves much to be desired.

Yet in describing the Commission as the 'motor of European unification', the President of the Commission, Jacques Santer, identified implementation as one of the Commission's three principal roles, and also referred to the 'profound reform of financial management practices' taking place under the direction of the Commissioner for Budgets, Erkki Liikanen (Santer, 1995). Indeed, one of the few areas of Commission implementation subject to really extensive external and academic scrutiny has been budgetary management and control. A combination of political interest in the European Parliament (EP) and among Eurosceptical politicians in the Member States, media interest in good copy, institutional function (of the European Court of Auditors (ECA) and the Parliament's Budgetary Control Committee), and academic analysis have conspired to highlight the problems of EU financial management, particularly fraud and irregularity.

While it would be unfair to heap sole blame on the Commission for poor implementation of the budget, weaknesses and shortcomings have been exposed over the years. Work by Norton (1986), Tiedemann (1988), Mennens (1986), the House of Lords (1989, 1992, 1994), Tutt (1989), Levy (1990, 1991), Passas and Nelken (1991), Sherlock and Harding (1991), Vervaele (1992), Mendrinou (1992), Huybrechts *et al.*, (1994) and Ruimschotel (1994) among others, has variously investigated the type, level, causes and possible solutions to budgetary irregularity and fraud. However, the most consistent observer and sternest critic of the Commission in this regard has been the ECA, whose annual and special reports since 1978 have provided the most detailed external insights into financial management by the Commission.

Given the predominance of agricultural price support spending within the budget and its legendary opportunities (real or imagined) for fraud, such a focus was inevitable. More recently, interest in the Commission's broader managerial capabilities has been growing both among external commentators (see Metcalfe, 1992, 1994), and from inside the EU institutions themselves. For example, the 1990 Financial Regulation and the 1992 Treaty on European Union (TEU) allocated new managerial responsibilities to the Commission, the European Parliament called for a report on evaluation and monitoring in the Commission in 1994, and the Commission itself has established units, working groups, initiatives and studies to look into and improve its own managerial processes.

This chapter will focus on the implementation of spending programmes, and is divided into four sections. The first will differentiate between different types of implementation, will outline the legal basis, and will consider the impact of the subsidiarity principle. The second will locate the Commission within the overall system of EU policy implementation. The third section will review the practice of implementation in different spheres and analyse the major common problems facing the Commission. The final section will discuss recent changes and alternative pathways for the future.

LEGAL BASIS, IMPLEMENTATION TYPE, AND SUBSIDIARITY

The key treaty provisions defining the Commission's general role in implementation are Articles 5, 155, and 169–171 of the Treaty Establishing the European Community. They make it clear that the Commission essentially implements via the Member States. So, Article 5 states that 'Member States shall take all appropriate measures . . . to ensure fulfilment of the obligations arising out of this Treaty or resulting from actions taken by institutions of the Community'. The Commission's implementation duties and powers as specified in Article 155 include ensuring that 'the provisions of this Treaty and the measures taken by the institutions pursuant thereto are applied', and exercising 'the powers conferred upon it by the Council for the implementation of the rules laid down by the latter'. Articles 169 to 171 confer enforcement powers on the Commission enabling it to refer Member States to the European Court of Justice (ECJ) for failing to implement their obligations.

In specific reference to the Commission's budgetary powers, Article 205 places an obligation on the Commission to 'implement the budget . . . on its own responsibility and within the limits of the appropriations having regard to the principles of sound financial management'. At a more detailed

level, the Commission's role is defined by the regulations
affecting particular programme areas and by the Financial
Regulation (as revised in 1990) applicable to the general
budget of the European Communities. The latter requires
the Commission to analyse the financial management of the
previous year's spending (Article 3), and places a general
obligation on the Commission to ensure that there is 'sound
financial management' of Community finances and to set
and monitor objectives (Article 2). This has been taken to
mean the achievement of value-for-money (VFM) in programme delivery, and has greatly increased Commission
activism in the field of implementation, as we shall see in
specific cases later.

The distinction between 'direct' and 'indirect' implementation used by Shaw is useful in alerting us to the fact that
the Commission implements at second hand in most policy
areas. She notes that most instances of direct implementation concern 'activities of the Commission aimed at protecting the legal fabric of the Community' (Shaw, 1993, p. 58).
So, for example, in the case of competition law, the Commission uses both its own powers and its powers of referral
to the ECJ to enforce the rules. Indirect implementation
mainly concerns spending programmes such as agriculture
and regional policy, but also includes purely supervisory
regimes such as external trade and customs policy, and social security arrangements for migrant workers. In all such
cases, it is the Commission's job to ensure that Member
States implement EU policies.

However, it can be argued that the process of implementation is fundamentally different where the Commission is
providing direct financial support for a policy. While not in
contradiction with the basic distinction used by Shaw, Strasser's
model of Commission financial management distinguishes
between direct, decentralised and shared programme management (Strasser, 1992). The vast majority of expenditure
falls into the categories of decentralised or shared
management.

i) Direct management refers to all parts of the budget managed solely by the Commission: primarily its own administrative expenditure and those limited areas of operational

management, such as the Joint Research Centre at Ispra, which are directly under Commission control. General Research and Development (R&D) expenditure financed by Directorate-General DGXII (Science, Research and Development) is more difficult to classify. On the one hand, DGXII seeks to implement an overall programme via a series of projects, so there is a direct relationship between the beneficiary agency (usually a university or research institute) and the Commission without the interposition of a Member State government agency. On the other hand, it is the beneficiaries which actually implement the research projects and manage the funds operationally rather than the Commission itself. Moreover, DGXII draws on panels of external experts to evaluate which projects should be approved in the first place. Excluding the considerable number of jointly funded projects which would come under the shared management category, R&D expenditure is thus a hybrid of direct and decentralised management.

ii) In *decentralised management*, the Commission delegates frontline implementation to national and local agencies, supervising them in turn through regulations and directives specific to those programme areas and functions. Thus, the implementing agencies have more or less discretion over how to achieve the specified objectives. Commission implementation functions, therefore, tend to be concentrated at the macro and evaluative levels, but there is a range of variation, with regulations being more prescriptive than directives and regulations themselves varying from the very detailed to the quite general. The collection of EU revenues is an example of an implementation area that is mostly governed by directives, whilst the Common Agricultural Policy (CAP – by far the biggest item in the spending budget) is an example of an area that is governed by heavily prescriptive regulation. Thus, the Commission is involved in far more implementation functions in the administration of the CAP than in the collection of revenue sources such as Value Added Taxes (VAT).

A good example of decentralised management is foreign aid programmes and projects. In those countries in receipt of aid through the Lomé Convention (the legal instrument which sets a multi-annual trade and aid framework), implementation is effected through local programme management teams approved by Commission delegations in those countries. Overall supervision remains the responsibility of DGVIII (Development) in Brussels. There are similar arrangements in the case of aid to Central and Eastern European countries and the Commonwealth of Independent States (CIS) through programmes like PHARE and TACIS, although local management is more devolved and the supervising agent in the Commission is DGIA (External Political Relations). As the focus is on the achievement of programme objectives rather than the process per se, the management of these funds is fundamentally different from decentralised management in agriculture where there is little local discretion.

A different sort of decentralised management is seen in the dozen or so new agencies established by the EU in late 1993 – including the European Trademark Office, the European Environment Agency, and the European Patent Office. Funding for these agencies comes from the Commission, but is managed by the agencies locally.

iii) Shared management covers programmes jointly funded by the EU and other partners – usually the Member States, but other partners include universities, research institutes, and third countries in the Lomé regime where projects are joint funded. This type of arrangement includes many of the characteristics of decentralised management insofar as frontline implementation and the determination of local projects making up the programme are basically left to the partner bodies.

The major area of shared management is the structural funds. Subsequent to the revisions of the funds in 1988 and 1993, Commission financial support ranges from 25 per cent to 75 per cent of programme costs. The regulatory framework is less detailed and prescriptive than the regulations governing the CAP, with an emphasis on delegation to the Member State agencies and on regular monitoring, review and evaluation by both the Commission and the partner agencies. The Commission establishes the overall implementation framework consistent with the policy goals of the regulation, and approves particular Community Support Frameworks

(CSFs) in consultation with the beneficiary Member States. Partial exceptions to this model include Commission-sponsored initiative programmes within the structural funds such as RECHAR, RENAVAL and RESIDER, over which the Commission has far more detailed control. In general, programme and project management on the ground is handled by locally based Programme Management Committees which contain a nominated Commission official to link local implementation with Brussels.

The principle of subsidiarity as reaffirmed in the Common Provisions and Article 3b of the TEU is supposed to help clarify the allocation of managerial (and indeed policy-making) responsibilities between the Member States and the Commission (Duff, 1993, Scott *et al.*, 1994). However, the concept is vague and ambiguous, and leaves everything to a case by case judgement of whether EU or Member State action is the most effective in any particular circumstances. As the onus is now on the Commission to prove that every proposal meets the test of subsidiarity as an efficiency criteria for implementation, it could be used as 'an instrument of member states to protect national interests' (van Kersbergen and Verbeek, 1994, p. 277).

On the other hand, subsidiarity is a 'two edged sword' (Duff, 1994, p. 29) which can also be used by sub-national authorities as a weapon against centralisation by national authorities. If this is coupled to the conception of subsidiarity which was achieved by Jacques Delors – that Commission action is often preferable for efficiency reasons – then national authorities are in potential danger of being by-passed in the management process. In his evidence to the House of Lords European Communities Select Committee in 1991, the then UK Secretary of State for Trade and Industry, Peter Lilley, stated that it was 'one of the ambitions of the Community to involve (local authorities) more extensively and national governments less extensively' in the policy and management of the structural funds (House of Lords, 1991, p. 155), so establishing a direct partnership between local and Commission managers.

The subsidiarity debate has thus done little to clarify implementation responsibilities regarding EU programmes.

There is still much disputed territory between the Commission and the Member States. The only iron rule is that when policy implementation fails, Member States and the Commission generally blame each other.

THE STRUCTURE AND ORGANISATION OF IMPLEMENTATION

EU policy implementation, like EU policy-making, is part of a multi-level system of governance. In simple terms, there are three levels of management – supranational (the Commission as a whole and the individual DGs); national (ministry or other agency); and local (field agency, local authority, programme managers and project managers).

The management framework for the Commission on a year to year basis is set by the multi-annual financial framework for EU spending programmes (last agreed at the Edinburgh summit of 1992), the annual budget document (over 1900 pages long for the financial year of 1995), and the regulations governing particular programme areas. Within this framework, spending programmes are subject to the implementation cycle that is set out in Figure 11.1 (see also Levy, 1990, 1994). The stages in the cycle, after the overall budgetary allocations, are as follows:

The *authorisation phase* involves the processing of requests for funds and the approval of particular programmes or projects. This phase is executed at three levels, two of which are located within the Commission. The levels are: the Member State agencies dealing with the overall programme area, the relevant spending DG in the Commission (e.g. DGVI for agriculture, DGXVI for regional development), and DGXX (Financial Control). The spending DGs essentially examine and approve plans and/or requests from the Member States for funds, while DGXX examines the requests coming down from the spending DGs (visa préalable) and is the ultimate source of financial authorisation in the Commission. According to the Acting Director General of DGXX, some 150 officials were responsible for authorising 360 000 requests for spending in 1995, in addition to other tasks (for example,

Figure 11.1   Implementation cycle of EU funded programmes

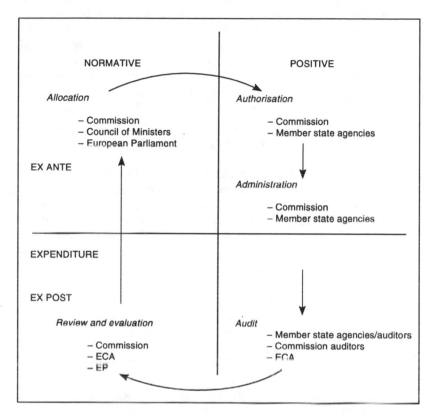

on the spot controls), so the level of scrutiny is not always optimal (Pratley, 1995). Nevertheless, DGXX has resisted all attempts to transfer this function to authorising officers in the spending DGs.

An important aspect of the authorisation stage is virement. The Commission does have some discretion to transfer funds from one heading to another, but the highly prescriptive nature of the budget document means that DGs (principally those dealing with the CAP and the structural funds) frequently have to seek authorisation from the EP for virement from one budget line to another during the course of the year. Thus, it is common to find Commission officials at meetings of the EP's Budgetary Control Committee for this purpose.

The *allocation and administration stage* refers to the operational management, including financial management, of programmes. As outlined earlier, there are a variety of models of Commission involvement here. In the rare instances of direct management, the Commission performs routine operational tasks and directs payment to final beneficiaries. Normally, however, the spending DGs are not directly involved in routine administration as this is left to national and local agencies in the Member States. The main role of the Commission is to ensure that funds are transferred to managing agencies in the Member States after approval by DGXX.

At *the audit stage*, the Commission has a far more substantial range of functions, although this too is shared with the Member States and the ECA. Audit is both an internal process within the Commission and Member State agencies, and an external process visited on local, national and Commission managers by national and Community auditors at a later date. It usually occurs after spending has taken place, but the visa préalable system amounts to an ex ante audit of claims before funds have been transferred. As DGXX is also involved in ex post facto audit, it has been argued by the ECA that the Financial Controller should be relieved of this responsibility so as to avoid a conflict of interest (Court of Auditors, 1989). However, this move has been successfully resisted by DGXX, which has also been developing its capacity for effectiveness audit through the establishment of a Cost Benefit and Cost Effectiveness Studies Unit – which perhaps duplicates some of the work of the ECA itself. This growth of audit capacity in DGXX is symptomatic of developments within the Commission as a whole. Indeed, DGXX shares its responsibility for effectiveness audit with DGXIX (Budgets) through the advance financial statements which line managers in the spending DGs have to submit to DGs XIX and XX. These include a statement of objectives, cost effectiveness and evaluation arrangements of the project concerned, and they are later (in theory) checked against final account statements. However, the two biggest budget items – CAP guarantee and structural funds expenditure – are as yet excluded from this system.

As in the case of the ECA, Commission VFM audit is really

an audit of the VFM arrangements put in place by spending DGs (and ultimately by programme managers in the Member States). It is not a methodology as such, but rather a series of questions to managers. Insofar as this system puts the onus on line managers to ensure that VFM is achieved, it could be a catalyst for a radical change in culture. On the other hand, the submission of financial statements in the required format can become a mere exercise in bureaucratic processing without any real substance if there is no effective follow-up later. This system is still in its early stages of development in the Commission.

Specialist auditors from DG XX also participate in audit visits with host DGs (for example, DGs V and XVI in the case of the structural funds, DGVI in the case of agriculture), and some of these visits involve auditing VFM arrangements. Practices vary considerably according both to programme area (and hence from DG to DG) and Member State. It is self-evident that the audit of a complex series of entitlement programmes based on daily market management (the CAP guarantee) is a very different proposition to the audit of carefully-framed multiannual programmes (such as the structural funds, R&D, or the European Development Fund (EDF)). Different legislative requirements, Commission–beneficiary relationships and organisational cultures further complicate the picture. For example, DGVIII (responsible for the EDF) has developed a system of programme evaluation (the project cycle management model), including VFM audit, which is not used much elsewhere in the Commission. Another contrast is between, on the one hand, the DGs responsible for the structural funds – notably DGV (Employment, Industrial Relations and Social Affairs) and DGXVI (Regional Policies) – which have to manage VFM arrangements at a distance, via regulations which place obligations on the implementing agencies in the Member States, and, on the other hand, DGXII (Science, Research and Development), which audits beneficiaries directly, having developed its own form of ex-ante financial monitoring well in advance of the system now deployed by DGXX.

Review and evaluation is a natural progression from VFM auditing. While each DG tends to regard its own system as superior, external bodies are not so partisan. The ECA's criticisms of development aid management made in its 1991 annual report, for example, were sharp and were reiterated in a House of Lords report (House of Lords, 1993b). In addition to the often sloppy formulation and execution of projects and project evaluations identified by the Court, the report noted that only 12 permanent staff in the Commission were employed on evaluation work in this sector (the number has subsequently been raised to 15 with the occasional use of external evaluators).

There are now stronger pressures from within the Commission itself to improve audit and evaluation. These emanate both from DGXIX and DGXX, and from internal control and evaluation units within other DGs. In the case of DGVI for example, the internal control unit spends much of its time on control visits in the Member States auditing the operation of CAP regulations, reporting back to the Director General, and making proposals for improved control features. It also transmits these observations to the evaluation unit in DGVI which is charged with the review and evaluation of the different sectors of the CAP. Studies carried out there feed directly into the policy-making process, although their impact is variable. As is the case with all other DGs, there are horizontal linkages between the control unit in DG VI and the officials who are responsible for CAP matters in DGs XIX and XX.

Evidence collected by the Commission on its own evaluation capabilities suggests a fragmented picture in which horizontal and vertical coordination is weak in many cases. Thus, while the largest spending DGs have evaluation units, there is little sharing of learning or methodologies between them. Within DGs, evaluation functions tend to be isolated and misunderstood by those not directly involved. The overall budget for evaluation is low, and there is a focus on outputs rather than outcomes. As we observed in earlier work on budgetary control (Levy, 1990), the problem of measurement in evaluation is critically related to the absence of clear policy objectives. In common with systems elsewhere, the link between budgeting and evaluation is weak, and there is a problematic relationship between policy cycle decisions and evaluation findings and use. Thus, the considerable effort which does go into the evaluation of some programme areas not infrequently fails to produce any learning. One of the results of this is a proliferation of control and evaluation units within the Commission which get in the way of each other and inhibit the development of high level specialised technical skills where they are really needed.

In addition to localised units in the DGs, there are central control and evaluation bodies, most notably the anti-fraud unit (UCLAF), and the Inspectorate-General. Set up by the Commission in 1988 under pressure from the EP, the anti-fraud unit's role was initially low key, with coordination and public relations/information as its most important functions. At the insistence of the Parliament's Budgetary Control Committee, its numbers have been increased to over 70 so as to give it the potential to undertake effective implementation. However, its actual powers to implement or enforce are weak, since there is no independent legal base for the Commission to prosecute fraudsters in the Member States.

THE PRACTICE OF IMPLEMENTATION

As we have argued, Strasser's model provides a basis for classifying implementation mode. In terms of practice, the general pattern of implementation is one of complexity, competition, overlap, low trust, and variations in style, procedure, and standards. Two contrasting examples will be taken to illustrate some of these aspects of the practice of implementation

i) The structural funds. The management of the structural funds is based on an attenuated chain of command stretching from the Commission (where three DGs are involved), through to national and, in several cases regional, ministries and agencies, local programme management structures (the monitoring committees), and project managers at grassroots level.

Within the framework of the overall objectives and the financial and geographical package for structural funding which are set by the Council of Ministers, individual programmes have be agreed between the Commission and the Member State agencies. These take the form of Community Support Frameworks (CSFs) or, more commonly, Single Programming Documents (SPDs). Within these plans, individual projects are devised and managed locally. The Commission does have a direct link into local implementation through its nominated representative on the local monitoring committees, which are the Community's statutory instruments responsible for the implementation of each CSF. In addition, desk officers in DGXVI (which is 'the lead' managing DG) seek to maintain open and regular communication with local programme managers as an informal mechanism for ensuring the achievement of common purposes. More formally, the Commission conducts its own ex post evaluations (usually via external consultants) of programmes, and monitors *in situ* through audit visits by officials from DGs V, XVI, and XX.

Since 1990, the Commission has produced an annual report on the implementation of the funds which, for the most part, provides commentary on how the Member States have set about fulfilling the requirements for implementation and evaluation, the take up of funds, and the Commission's own actions. It is clear from the early reports that the Commission tried to ensure VFM evaluation by the Member States by building it in at the stage of formulation of the CSF. The Commission also sought to establish 'a generalised methodology of assessment', as no single pattern was emerging from the external consultants reports sponsored by the Commission or the Member States' initial CSF submissions (Commission, 1990b, p. 63). However, this objective was not achieved. The 1992 report observed that it had 'proved difficult to carry out . . . (and) consequently, the approach taken is based on what is eligible' (Commission, 1992b, p. 24). Undaunted by failure at the ex-ante stage, DG XVI then launched a series of mid-term evaluations covering all areas of the CSFs, while DGXX continued with its 'programme of on the spot checks centred on the systems of monitoring and financial inspection' (Commission, 1993b, p. 72).

This situation was less than satisfactory from a VFM point of view, and it is significant that the Commission tried to improve matters for the new round of structural fund programmes due to commence in 1993/4. Thus, it sponsored the MEANS pilot study in 1992 (still ongoing) 'in order to arrive at a better match between the methods used to evaluate structural policies' (ibid., p. 82), and the cost-benefit analysis unit of DG XVI introduced a pro-forma guidance note for Member States for the formulation of their CSFs to achieve a more consistent approach. With the Member States, it also sought to define 'financial, physical and economic impact indicators' (ibid., p. 92), and DGXX has conducted an audit of evaluation systems used by the Member States on structural fund programmes. However, in a debate in the EP held on 19 January 1996 on the 1993 report, the Commission was still being criticised for a lack of precision in measuring the effects of structural fund measures (Scotland Europa, 1996, p. 61).

The view taken by both the Commission and the ECA of the Member States' own efforts to secure VFM objectives has generally been negative, although less so in the case of the Commission as the monitoring committees responsible for managing the CSFs locally each have a Commission representative on them. The 1993 ECA annual report observed that there had been 'little evidence of real improvement in the financial management of the reformed structural funds' at the Member State level, citing weaknesses in 'planning, coordination, monitoring and evaluation' (Court of Auditors, 1993, pp. 6–7). It is clear that the extent of these weaknesses varies between Member States depending on the sophistication of local administrations.

The view from the Member States is rather different. They generally criticise the Commission rather than their own arrangements for VFM evaluation. As Bruce Millan, the former Commissioner for Regional Policy, observed in his evidence to the UK House of Lords Select Committee on the European Communities 'we are under a lot of pressure to set up a new evaluation mechanism . . . the member states do not appreciate (our involvement) very much. They would rather like to be left to get on with things under their own steam' (House of Lords, 1991, p. 96). Thus, it is not surprising that the UK Government, for example, has characterised the Commission's procedures as overly bureaucratic and interfering, and has accused the Commission of looking for excuses to increase its own control through bolstering its initiative programmes such as RECHAR (House of Lords, 1991, pp. 22–3; School for Advanced Urban Studies, 1992).

Given that structural fund subventions are based on co-financing arrangements (usually 50 per cent, but up to 75 per cent in the case of some spending), Member States naturally sometimes carry out their own evaluations on their own terms. There are three potential problems with this however: as already noted, some Member States do not have the capacity to keep good records let alone conduct effective evaluations; the additionality problem makes it difficult to assess the impact of Commission funding in states which are net contributors to the Union budget such as the UK, France and Germany; and national and EU audits may be geared towards different objectives and clients. This latter problem is by no means unusual, and reflects a tendency for each actor in the process to discount the efforts of others as of little value or relevance.

An example of local VFM monitoring is seen in one of the biggest CSFs in the EU, the Strathclyde European Partnership (SEP) in Scotland. Project managers must report on performance, outputs and impact in order to receive funding from the managing agent (Scottish Office Industry Department (SOID)), and have to send quarterly reports to SEP. For their part, SEP officials have a programme of on the spot visits to the 500–600 'live' projects so as to monitor the achievement of objectives and targets. These visits, along with the project managers' reports and specially commissioned interim and final evaluations of activities, provide much of the information used by SEP for an annual report it produces for the Commission (via SOID). An important feature of the SEP is that the VFM requirements of the Commission have been supplemented by the development of a local management culture in which VFM evaluation is routine.

ii) The CAP. As indicated earlier, Commission management of the CAP is far more detailed than is the case with the structural funds. This is inevitable given that the CAP is a mixture of a market management system and an entitlement programme where expenditure cannot be absolutely determined in advance. Although payment to direct beneficiaries and local enforcement of the regulations is the responsibility of agencies in the Member States (usually agriculture ministry paying agencies and customs/law enforcement agencies), DGVI can in theory exercise almost daily control of expenditure via adjustments to regulations governing intervention in particular markets. These adjustments are effected on advice coming from market management committees, from DGVI's own internal control unit, and, more broadly, from advisory committees of various kinds. Often adjustments stem from problems flagged up in the monthly 'early warning system' reports which DGVI compiles. However, there is an inevitable lag between the appearance of a problem, the analysis of it (whether it is a short run aberration or a long term difficulty), and when action is taken and takes effect.

While it is Commission officials who actually frame any changes to market management regimes, the key role and composition of the market management committees gives Member States and, less directly, farming interests, an input at this level of implementation. It is almost a reverse image of structural fund management, where the Commission has representatives in Member State field management structures, for in CAP management clients have representation in Commission structures in Brussels.

Overall budgetary management is executed via the multi-annual planning framework for agriculture spending, the annual budget plan which is based on the annual review of prices negotiated in the Council, and the 'early warning system'. The latter is something of a misnomer as it is comprised of actual expenditures which are three months old when notified to DGVI by the Member State paying agencies on a sector by sector basis – it is measured against averaged sector figures drawn from the previous three years. Should actual expenditures deviate from the averaged totals, the Commission may seek to adjust the particular sector regime in question if analysis indicates a long term problem. While this may be a useful monitoring tool for the Commission, it somewhat obviates the need for a detailed annual budget for agriculture spending; indeed, early warning system figures may contradict planning totals. It is an example of a management tool which has been developed as a response to political pressure rather than as a logical outcome of existing processes.

On the audit side, DGVI has a special unit dealing with the annual clearance of accounts process and the enforcement of control regulations by Member State agencies. The latter activity is at once operational and strategic, and is effected by a monthly cycle of on the spot control visits in the Member States and reporting back by DGVI officials. This leads in many cases to the reporting of infringements on the one hand, which can lead to penalties in monthly payments and in the annual clearance procedure, and proposals for regulation change on the other. The Commission does not have power to prosecute instances of fraud (that is the prerogative of Member State authorities), but only to see that Member States comply with specific control regulations. In this regard, Regulation 4045/89 (dealing with the scrutiny of commercial documents) is particularly important. Member States are obliged to submit an annual report on their implementation of the Regulation, thus enabling the Commission to assess its overall effectiveness and make ongoing monitoring visits. Council Regulation 386/90 and Commission Regulation 354/90 set down minimum standards for physical checks and export documentation, while Council Regulation 3508/92 provides for the establishment of an integrated administration and control system for the crop and livestock sectors at Member State level. In the latter case, there is provision for Commission funding to assist in the development of the system. The main regulations governing the agricultural reforms which were introduced in the early 1990s (the MacSharry reforms) all place responsibilities on Member States for routine monitoring and control.

The annual clearance procedure represents a peculiar kind of audit based on bilateral negotiation and compromise between Commission auditors from DGs VI and XX and the Member States, although the Commission can simply disallow, and can seek to claim back, expenditure. Subject to continual and serious delay because of Member State obduracy in reaching agreement over disputed payments, the clearance process used to be a source of frustration within the Commission and the object of perennial criticism by the ECA. However, since the Commission abandoned its former practice of paying in advance for Member States' estimated expenditure in favour of paying for expenditures actually made, the clearance process has become easier from the Commission's point of view, as payments can be withheld and rudimentary ex ante checks can be made by both DG VI and DG XX. Nevertheless, clearance represents a huge audit task as it covers expenditures totalling around 50 per cent of the EU budget.

The evaluation of the CAP is a complex multi-level process within the Commission, in which DG VI is the principal, but not the sole, actor. The process is difficult because of the rolling character of CAP spending and the lack of clear, quantifiable and time limited objectives in most of agricultural legislation. Evaluation priorities tend to be driven by sector size and immediate political imperatives. Measures of success or failure are rare unless reference is traced back to original treaty objectives (which are very general), or to expenditure guidelines placed on particular sectors. The MacSharry reforms mark something of a watershed, however, as they were accompanied by policy statements which set targets in the biggest sectors.

DGVI evaluation is characterised by the acceptance of market management norms, the use of in-house modelling techniques and databases, consultation with only a limited range of stakeholders, and restricted use of external consultants. It tends to steer clear of whole policy evaluation, adopting instead a sector by sector approach (with the partial exception of the study leading up to MacSharry). Given the limited resources available, this means that no single sector has yet been evaluated twice and the only recent whole policy evaluation of the CAP has been carried out by DG II (Commission Directorate General for Economic and Financial Affairs, 1994).

PROBLEMS AND SOLUTIONS

Writing in 1992, Metcalfe identified a mismatch between the Commission's management capacities and its increased responsibilities. He termed this mismatch the 'management deficit'. He focused particular attention on the Commission's need to establish performance indicators, better coordination, information systems and strategic management capabilities, and to create administrative networks in the Member States (Metcalfe, 1992, pp. 118–19). This lack of management capability has been regularly documented in the annual reports of the ECA, which have been highly critical of the Commission's own financial management and its seeming inability to eradicate poor management in the Member States.

Others have pointed to a loss of capability, directly attributable to the adverse impact of subsidiarity on the Commission's powers which has leached away at the direct implementation and control functions of the Commission in favour of the Member States (Kok, 1989, p. 347; Court of Auditors annual reports, 1987 and 1989) It is argued that direct beneficiaries have acquired responsibilities previously in the hands of the Commission for managing their own performance and checking whether they are spending EU receipts in accordance with the criteria laid down in the regulations.

An alternative interpretation to the 'golden age' theory is that the Commission has until very recently been dominated by a spending culture in which the influence of control and accountability imperatives has been relatively weak (House of Lords, 1994). Within such an environment, policy-making and programme spending are the main activities, and it is only later, when programmes start to produce outputs, that accountability and control issues assume greater significance. At this point, weaknesses become apparent and there is a gradual refocusing of organisational priorities.

All these views contain substantial elements of truth. The Commission has always suffered from a lack of enforcement powers in its stewardship of EU funds, relying on the Member States to detect and prosecute fraudsters and to manage programmes directly. It is certainly the case that while the Commission's responsibilities have grown almost geometrically, the resources available to manage them have not. Moreover, those resources which are available have not been used to best effect. The problem of implementing legislation which is vague and contradictory is longstanding, and the Commission has to rely on information from Member State agencies which varies greatly in quality and quantity, and on local management systems which are sometimes non-existent. An additional difficulty is that Member States jealously guard their autonomy in implementing EU programmes, and try to increase it where they can.

It is inconceivable, however, that the Commission will assume more direct control of its spending programmes in the foreseeable future, since that would imply a substantial increase in Commission staff and/or other resources. On the contrary, it is more likely that local control will increase. The question arises then of how to re-engineer Commission management for the next century. So far, the evidence suggests the Commission has embarked on a twin strategy of regulatory centralisation and system standardisation on the one hand, and the encouragement of partnership on the other.

i) Regulatory centralisation and system standardisation. Within the Commission, initiatives have been taken under Article 2 of the 1990 Financial Regulation which makes the achievement of economy and cost effectiveness goals a requirement. DGXX in particular has used this to advance centrally driven systems (Pratley, 1995, p. 253). For example, over the last few years, DGXX has introduced and spread a standardised *fiche financière* for spending proposals to most programmes. Since the installation of the new Commission at the start of 1995, a three-phase programme of action has been in place to consolidate *Bonne Gestion Financière* (BGF). The first phase involves the modification of internal rules, the rationalisation of internal procedures, and the raising of awareness among officials. Significantly, it is designed to strengthen the role of the financial controller, DGXX. In the second phase internal organisation of the Commission and the regulatory framework as a whole is to be reviewed. The final phase is intended to 'reinforce' partnership with the Member States (Commission, 1995b).

In parallel initiatives on programme evaluation, DGs XIX and XX have been collating and reviewing practices within the programme directorates with the intention of raising standards and standardising systems where possible. These same DGs have also been attempting to impose some kind of commonality of approach on other DGs in regard to how they manage Commission–Member State relations on implementation matters.

Another development has been the creation and strengthening of the centralised management agencies referred to earlier in this chapter, both within spending DGs and across the Commission as a whole via UCLAF and the Inspectorate General. Whilst units within the DGs tend to have specific and limited functions, the role of the Commission-wide units is as yet unclear but is developing beyond simple coordination and facilitation.

The final strand of the centralist approach has been the imposition of detailed audit and evaluation requirements on Member State agencies via regulation. At the most general level, Article 188c of the EC Treaty requires the sound financial management of all spending programmes by managing agents and a statement of assurance from the ECA as to the underlying legality and regularity of the accounts. Moving down to the programmatic level, the most recent regulations governing the structural funds (Council Regulations 2081/2/3/93) impose comprehensive ex-ante, ex-post and ongoing evaluation requirements and standardised formatting of proposals on potential beneficiaries. At the most detailed level, CAP regulations impose minimum standards on Member State agencies for such matters as physical spot checks (Council Regulation 386/90), export documentation (Commission Regulation 354/90), and an integrated administrative system for agricultural holdings, livestock, and aid applications (Council Regulation 3508/92 and Commission Regulation 3887/92).

ii) The encouragement of partnership. The EU's spending programmes require that the Commission works closely with the agencies in the Member States which are responsible for policy implementation. In recent years the Commission has done much to promote partnership between itself and these agencies, as is witnessed by legislation which provides for cooperation in respect of audit and evaluation. So, for example, under Regulation 3508/92, there is provision for part-funding of control systems at Member State level by the Commission. Less formally, the Commission encourages and facilitates cooperation between customs and other enforcement agencies involved in the audit process through meetings, circulars, seminars etc. Indeed, this was a role the anti-fraud unit was originally supposed to fulfil. However giving it, as some commentators on the EU advocate, 'hands on' powers may actually prove counter-productive from a partnership point of view.

The management of the structural funds has been one of the principal areas for the development of audit and evaluation partnerships. Given that joint EU–Member State funding is the norm in these programmes, what is surprising is not that this is starting to happen, but that it has taken so long to get underway. However, as we saw earlier in our review of the current arrangements, audit and evaluation partnerships in this policy area are still beset by enormous difficulties. There is an often adversarial relationship between the Commission and the Member States at the outset of the policy cycle (in the drawing up of CSFs for example), which may linger throughout the implementation phase. Any move by the Commission to establish closer liaison at the local or regional level once programmes are running is often viewed with great suspicion by national governments, where ministers and officials are concerned not to be by-passed. A competitive culture has thus not been conducive to developing mutual trust, recognition, and learning amongst audit and evaluation actors.

In very crude terms, the twin strategy of centralisation and standardisation on the one hand and partnership on the other, represents a carrot and stick approach which applies at all levels, but in widely varying degrees. Such is the uneven distribution of coercion and reward that a coordinated system based on partnership is unlikely to emerge of its own accord. As the strategy itself was never coordinated in the first place, that is hardly surprising. And, owing to the complexity of the politico-organisational environment, a rational order imposed from above is a chimera. It also assumes a competence on behalf of the Commission and many of the Member State agencies which is simply absent.

12 The European Commission and the Politics of Legitimacy in the European Union
Helen Drake

INTRODUCTION: LEGITIMACY AND AUTHORITY IN THE EUROPEAN UNION

In the would-be polity of the European Union (EU), legitimacy is experienced as a problematical political phenomenon. Accounts of legitimacy in the EU frequently treat 'legitimacy' as if it were synonymous with 'democracy', yet the EU was originally designed to give priority to efficiency rather than democracy; to bureaucracy rather than to politics; and to rationality rather than representativeness. This was a design reflecting how the founders of the European Communities prioritised the institutionalisation of authority and the administration of things over the organisation of democracy and the governance of people (Shackleton, 1994, p. 5; Rose, 1995, p. 67).

To define legitimacy more precisely as the acceptance, tolerance or 'rightness' of authority (Lodge, 1994, p. 365) is one step towards an empirical analysis of the politics of legitimacy as practised in the EU, which invites a focus on the Commission, and offers the prospect of comparative analysis. By examining more closely the bases and exercise of the Commission's authority, and considering how its authority is legitimated in theory and in practice, the aim of this chapter is to develop a conceptual perspective on the conundrum of legitimacy in the EU context. The chapter focuses on the decade from 1985 to 1995, when Jacques Delors was Commission President. This provides us with manifestations of the Commission's range of possible claims to authority, and the relevance of the Commission President to making such claims.

In formulating our approach, we use a terminology of authority derived from Max Weber's theory of modern politics (Beetham, 1974). Weber's conceptualisation of authority as a political resource intimately linked with societal development provides a perspective on the dynamic mix of the forms of authority underpinning democratic legitimacy: first, the rules and conventions structuring institutional authority ('rational-legal' authority); second, the dominant and time-honoured norms, values and traditions of society ('traditional' authority); and third, the authority of individuals legitimated on the grounds of personal, possibly exceptional, characteristics and claims ('charismatic' authority).

When we use the Weberian terms 'rational', 'legal', and 'bureaucracy' in relation to the Commission, we seek primarily to distinguish the Commission's authority as it is set down in the treaties ('legal') and in its internal working norms and practices ('rational'), from its ill-defined authority to act politically; and to differentiate its role in executing and implementing political decisions taken elsewhere (its 'bureaucratic' roles) from its more political duties of initiative and representation of the general interest of the EU. We also use the term 'rational' in a more general sense to describe the conforming to rules and procedures.

We interpret 'charismatic' leadership as the relationship that pertains between an individual leader and the rules and procedures of his/her leadership position; that is to say, as the ways in which the individual interprets his/her post on the basis of his/her unique set of leadership skills, and the claims s/he makes in interpreting the rules, in part through discourse. 'Traditional' authority we see as a potential resource of the charismatic leader. It describes a form of authority which, in its emphasis on the individual and his/her ability to articulate values and principles shared by given groups of followers, can be seen to operate in contemporary democratic society as a leadership resource. In the EU context, this seems to be the most problematic form of authority, since 'Europe' has yet to develop an undisputed sense of identity and belonging. Some authors have identified this problematic dimension of EU legitimacy as relating to myth, or 'social' legitimacy (Obradovic, 1996; Weiler, 1993); we consider this approach in our conclusions.

Despite its limitations and internal contradictions (Gaffney, 1989, pp. 18–21), Weber's classification of ideal-types of authority provides us with conceptual and terminological tools for developing our understanding of the more intangible aspects of politics such as authority and legitimacy. Viewing legitimacy as a dynamic combination of factors is particularly valuable in the case of the EU, where authority may be legitimate without being formally democratic, and where formally democratic procedures are not necessarily perceived as legitimate by all affected elites or publics.

THE EUROPEAN COMMISSION: BUREAUCRACY AND POLITICAL LEADER

Structurally and functionally the Commission is both a bureaucracy and a political leadership. This distinction and its tensions may be well-worn (see, for example, Coombes, 1970), but they are still relevant to discussions of the Commission's future. The reasons for the Commission's dual roles are to be found in the federalist-functionalist mode of politics launched by the founders of the European Communities.

The Communities' federalist potential was contained in Robert Schuman's declaration of 9 May 1950 calling for an unspecific 'federation of Europe' at an unspecified time in the future. This goal of federation was taken up implicitly in the subsequent treaties establishing, and then reforming, the Communities. Some of the institutional provisions of the Founding Treaties were, accordingly, drafted with this federal end-point in mind, most notably that for a directly-elected European Parliament (EP), by which one day a European electorate would elect representatives to a European legislature. The founders of the Communities, therefore, made provisions for democratic political representation at the European level. In this sense, the founders built the contours of a federal system of which the logic, although such may not have been the intention, was that the Commission might one day become the government of a federal Europe.

The Communities were also functionalist, since they were first and foremost economic communities designed to 'ensure the economic and social progress of their countries by common action to eliminate the barriers which divide Europe' (Preamble to the European Economic Community [EEC] Treaty). New institutions were devised to achieve such goals: the High Authority of the European Coal and Steel Community (ECSC), and later the Commission, were bodies of experts each sworn by oath to uphold their independence from national governmental instructions in their work. The national governments were not to interfere with the work of a 'supranational' body which, by virtue of its independence, would have in mind the European 'general interest',[1] not the clash of national interests, in the pursuit of limited economic goals. The members of the High Authority and the Commission were not supposed to be divorced from national interests, but to see these interests in the wider context of the general Community interest. The Commissioners derived their significance and authority from powers which were given to them in the treaties, so as to enable them to pursue this general Community interest, at the core of which was economic integration.

By emphasising the general interest of the Community, and by linking this interest to the independence of Commission members from their national governments, the Founding Treaties suggested a new framework for political representation. In respect of the Commission, five features of the framework were especially important. First, the implication was that there would emerge from the Communities an interest that would transcend and claim equality with existing national, partisan and sectoral interests. Second, the High Authority, and then the Commission, by means of their independence and expertise, would play a significant role in formulating, securing and promoting this interest. Third, there was a body of Europeans – the peoples of Europe – that would perceive, articulate and claim this interest. Fourth, the interest would be mediated coherently between national and European levels. Fifth, in the Commission President there was the potential for the individual, personalised articulation and representation of the general interest. The Community's federalist-functionalist method of politics, therefore, had created an institution with both bureaucratic capacity and political, representative, potential.

The Commission as a bureaucracy

In the Founding Treaties' provisions for functional integration, and in their creation of new institutions, most notably the Commission, there arose an example of the primacy of what Max Weber termed legal-rational authority, with an emphasis on the bureaucratic form of such rule. Much of the responsibility for the daily development of the new Communities was entrusted to experts acting in the general interest of the Communities; to bodies of officials charged with respecting and implementing the legal rules for integration contained in the Founding Treaty texts. The High Authority, and then the Commission, constituted the major bureaucratic source of such legal-rational authority.

Several studies of the Community and the Commission have emphasised the Commission's role as a bureaucracy, and have enquired whether it can be judged by the criteria of modern bureaucracies. Is it efficient, effective and well organised? Are its members suitably trained and recruited from the right pools? Are its internal rules and procedures such that it can function as a bureaucracy in the contemporary, civil service sense of the term? Can it fulfil the full range of its tasks under the terms of the Founding Treaties? The Commission's authority has, and can be, challenged on all of these bureaucratic grounds: for doing too much or too little, and inefficiently at that.

There is a further sense in which the Commission's bureaucratic tendencies point to a problem of authority in the Union, and that is in relation to popular perceptions and misperceptions of the Commission's activity and role. In popular terms, 'bureaucracy' has come to symbolise the perceived distance between citizens and decision-makers, and the inability of citizens democratically to affect the decision-making process – the unaccountability of the bureaucrat. In the specific context of the Commission, the 'Brussels bureaucracy' has often been portrayed as a particularly notable example of the loss of political control over bureaucratic machinery: 'Never without an image problem, the

Commission is widely viewed, in Sir Leon Brittan's words, as "a secretive, self-inflating bureaucracy bent on over-regulating the lives of [the EU's] citizens just to keep its staff in business"' (Dinan, 1995, p. 13). Perceptions of Commission excesses, however, relate equally to the Commission's political existence and capacity. From the perspective we have adopted here, this point is central to our understanding of the Commission's legitimacy, and that of its President, Jacques Delors, in the period 1985–95.

The Commission as political leader

A form of political control was established within the Commission itself alongside its bureaucratic incarnation, in the form of the College of Commissioners. The Commissioners, we have seen, are sworn to independence from the Member States. Nevertheless, they are appointed by the national governments, who can choose to renew their term of office, or not. The Commissioners are, therefore, appointed by democratically-elected national politicians, and in this way derive a form of delegated political authority (Page and Wouters, 1994, p. 450). This link between Commissioners and representative politics is further reinforced by two sets of treaty provisions. First, under the Founding Treaties, the College of Commissioners is answerable to the EP.[2] (In practice, the EP has never carried a motion of censure against the Commission, and even if it did there is nothing formally to prevent national ministers from reappointing the same College [Clergerie, 1995].) Second, under the Maastricht Treaty. (i) the Commission's term of office is closely aligned with that of the EP; (ii) the EP must be consulted about the person whom the national governments intend to nominate as incoming Commission President (it was obvious when this provision was first used in 1994 that the EP had, in practice, a veto over the appointee); and (iii) the incoming College is subject as a body to a vote of approval by the EP (on the first usage of this practice in 1995, the plenary vote was preceded by EP committees holding US-style 'hearings' with all Commissioners on an individual basis).

Despite, however, the growing potential political authority of the Commission, it is clear that in the EU system political authority has been and is fragmented and shared between the central institutions and the Member State governments (which act both within and outside these institutions). In this system, moreover, provisions for collective and collegial forms of political leadership outweigh those made for individual leadership. In these respects, the question of who or what would control the bureaucracy set up by the Founding Treaties was never really addressed in explicit terms, nor, more to the point, has it been resolved by experience. Because authority has been fragmented, it has proved difficult, in reality, for political leaders (whether in the Council of Ministers, the EP or national capitals) to exercise effective control over the Commission bureaucracy under the terms of the treaties. The Commission, in implementing the rules of the treaties, has increasingly come to be seen as at the hub of a new polity which has been described as a 'leaderless pluralism', to express the fact that '. . . authority is not the property of an individual, but is exercised either as delegated authority or as the result of an extended process of negotiation between a variety of institutions' (Page, 1992, p. 193).

The fact of having being established by written and binding texts, moreover, meant that the Communities tended towards becoming a polity in which authority was intended to be derived from rational-legal provisions, rather than from 'traditional' or 'charismatic' forms of legitimacy, since these latter forms would imply and require either that the Community was built on a shared set of traditions and sense of the 'eternal yesterday', or that the people of the Community would be able to agree that a particular 'charismatic' leader represented their best interests. Neither of these requirements was likely in a multi-national, multilingual community based on many different national (and infra/sub-national) traditions.

According to the Community design, the most logical place for 'European' political leadership to emerge was thus the Commission. It was invested with the authority to formulate and safeguard the 'general interest of the Communities', implying that it could see beyond, and reconcile, divisive national and partisan interests. It was given the bureaucratic authority to implement the general interest, and the authority associated with technocratic methods of politics, but it was also linked, indirectly, to the representation of 'Europeans' (through the EP and through the democratically elected national governments), and so enjoyed the sort of political authority which Weber deemed undesirable in a bureaucracy. On all of these grounds – its responsibility to act in the general European interest, its technocratic authority, and its indirect political and partisan links to a 'European' electorate – the Commission logically could be expected to provide a form of leadership in the sense of fulfilling the federalist hopes for a Community based on a sense of community and shared values and organised on majoritarian political beliefs that representative European leaders would subsequently be able to incarnate as the basis of claims to charismatic and traditional forms of authority.

The Commission as mixed-mode political actor

In Weberian terms, the Commission's nature as part-bureaucracy, part-political institution and leader, is problematical to the extent that, for Weber, state bureaucracies were ideally removed from all forms of political responsibility and should not be linked to representative politics. Weber's view was based on the belief that bureaucracies did not contain the right sort of individual to ensure the provision of politics as he defined it: politics had to be left to the professional politician driven by ambition, political beliefs and convictions. However, the Commission system does in fact allow to some extent for the separation of politics and bureaucracy, both in terms of control and in terms of the type of person recruited for each type of activity; the College of Commissioners (and in some respects their *cabinets* too) are appointed essentially on political grounds, whilst staff in the administrative services are recruited and trained in the manner of a bureaucratic civil service.

Within this 'mixed-mode' context, the position of the Commission Presidency is very interesting, for it can be interpreted as a potential source of the kind of charismatic leadership that Weber considered necessary for unifying and integrating societies: as a position from which the incumbent can claim authority on the grounds of both personal qualities, and the 'traditional' values and expectations that

follow from being a 'European leader'. The ways in which
Jacques Delors occupied the Presidency during his decade
in office are instructive in this regard. The following section provides illustrations of Delors' enactment of the Presidency, and emphasises two points in particular: first, a
powerful and authoritative President is implied in the logic
of the Community system; second, the President has been a
central figure in formulating and advancing Commission
claims to the legitimate exercise of authority.

1985–1995: THE PRESIDENCY OF JACQUES DELORS – EUROPEAN STATESMAN

Jacques Delors' Commission Presidency was political in two
important and related senses. First, over time he increasingly treated the EU as if it were a polity with its own unique
set of ethics, ideals, values, institutions, peoples, electorates
– and leader, a role which he increasingly saw as falling, by
default, to him. He himself behaved, as President of the
Commission, as if there were 'constituents' and 'constituencies' to which he could appeal, in the style of an elected
national leader. These included political representatives
(Members of the European Parliament) and their constituents (European citizens); national decision-makers (Heads
of State and Government); elements that he referred to
collectively as 'civil society' (organised interests such as workers
and employers); and third parties (most notably foreign
governments). He addressed these various constituencies via
different personalised discourses, and in this respect made
claims to legitimate authority mediated through discourse
and appeals, emerging gradually as the EU's foremost states-
man as a result.

The second sense in which Delors' leadership was political was that the grounds on which he appealed to 'his' constituencies were progressively 'European', or 'supranational',
based on interpretations of the general interest of the Communities. He presented himself as a figurehead for Europe,
with a blueprint for the future. The Founding Treaties, as
we saw above, had made such leadership logically possible,
if not inevitable, by linking, however tenuously, the Com-

mission Presidency to a European electorate and to Community-based criteria of responsibilities and achievements. The Treaties contained the space from which a leader such as Delors could emerge, enacting and voicing a transcendental European interest (transcendent of partisan and national divisions) as a leader who was representative, however indirectly, if not of a union of peoples, then certainly of pro-European elites and of a permissive consensus at the mass level.

Illustrations of these points can be drawn from an analysis which contrasts Delors' language and method of change at different points during the decade of his Presidency. Drawing on a larger study of two specific moments in Delors' Presidency – the production and promotion of the Commission's 1985 and 1993 White Papers on the internal market and on economic growth and employment, respectively, (Drake, 1996b) – and, for the purposes of exposition, with an emphasis on Delors' discourse, we can demonstrate the evolving nature of Delors' claims to authority over time, the significance of these claims to an understanding of his reputations, and their importance in conceptualising the politics of legitimacy in the EU.

1985: legitimising the task

In 1985, the Commission adopted the concept of the White Paper as the ideal format for a document intended to relaunch the integration process by means of a series of specific actions based on what we have called the Commission's rational-legal authority, programmed to occur within a specified time-frame and as part of an overall package of measures. The 1985 White Paper, entitled *Completing the Internal Market*, was primarily a list of measures to be accomplished within eight years – by '1992', the date that became the promotional symbol and real target of the single market programme. The measures contained in the Paper were derived from the provisions in the original EEC Treaty for completing an internal European market; indeed, the Paper was justified in terms of it providing for the implementation of the EEC Treaty's provisions for the free movement of goods, persons, services and capital. The Paper was presented to the Commission's several 'constituencies' (specifically, the EC Heads of State and Government, organised interests, and MEPs) for discussion, consultation and approval, and subsequently became the founding text for completing the single market.

In the production and promotion of the 1985 White Paper, Delors constructed a discourse of rationality, pragmatic solutions, daring, activism, and *volonté* on a European scale (Drake, 1995, 1996a; Ross, 1995, p. 31). This he used in his relations with national governments and leaders (his appointers); the EP (his keepers and minders); and European business (his supporters and promoters). This discourse portrayed a Commission President apparently acting within the bounds of the Commission's habitual practice of politics, that is to say based on national legitimacies and intergovernmental bargains. Delors seemed to be activating the Commission as a modern executive, leaving control in the hands of the national political masters. The single market initiative was not only tolerated but welcomed by these masters. This was a discourse, too, which consisted in creating, or at the least confirming, a space in which Delors and the Commission could act legitimately; the space consisting of the Commission's authority to enact the EEC Treaty.

In 1985 Delors had already started to style the role of Commission President by bringing his personal capacities – what we can term his leadership skills – to bear on it, and by getting the federalist-functionalist rules of integration to work without challenging national sovereignties. The national leaders subsequently renewed Delors as Commission President and the EP saluted him: European integration appeared to be back on course, offering a reassuring sense of purpose in its promise of fulfilling economic pragmatic needs. Delors, in 1985, had charismatically optimised the Commission's rational-legal authority and exploited the ripening intergovernmental consensus for more integration by presenting the single market, in the White Paper, as 'an ideologically neutral program around which the entire European polity could coalesce in order to achieve the goals of European integration. In this respect [the White Paper] was tapping into an interesting feature of the pre-1992 Community – the relative absence of ideological discourse and debate on the Left–Right spectrum' (Weiler, 1993, p. 33).

1985, moreover, represented a Delors on the offensive, defining the balance of political power between the Commission and the other EC institutions according to the founding constitutional texts of the EC, and acting as if he were the leader of these institutions, in the sense of providing the means to progress from good intentions to concrete and positive action. By recalling that the founding texts provided the Commission with circumscribed authority in low, functional politics, Delors contributed to the Commission's regaining its legitimacy in the Community system as an institution charged with the general interest on the basis of its rational-legal authority. It was not, at this stage, a discourse which drew on what we have previously defined as the traditional type authority logically available to a Commission President, and in this it differed considerably from the discourse of 1993, in which the theme of a critical choice to be made by the Member States, between Europe's 'survival' or 'decline', was to the fore.

1993: legitimising Europe

In contrast to 1985, the 1993 White Paper, entitled *Growth, competitiveness, employment. The challenges and ways forward into the 21st century*, was a White Paper in name only. Whereas the 1985 White Paper had recommended specific actions to be taken at the Community level, the 1993 White Paper was essentially a compilation of analyses of Europe's declining economic and competitive situation, and contained neither a firm timetable of the 1992 kind, nor detailed, specific recommendations for action. Moreover, whereas the 1985 White Paper had the direct effect of marshalling, enacting, and then expanding the Commission's rational-legal authority, the 1993 Paper explicitly revealed the limits to the Commission's own authority, and did not ask for additional competences. By the same token, the Paper signalled the limitations, for the Community, of these very limits. The Paper had the effect of highlighting the absence of an intergovernmental consensus on the scope and goals of integration, even economic integration, and of identifying the possible consequences of such a situation.

The very different content, intent and style of the 1993

White Paper can be explained with reference to the altered state of the integration process itself. By 1993, the intensely political nature of integration had revealed itself to political elites and peoples alike, with the effect of uncovering political union as a serious item on the European agenda. Member States reacted differently, but those applying the brakes to the integration process had in common a discourse of national sovereignty and how to keep it national; those urging further integration used a discourse of the sharing or pooling of national sovereignty, implying that national sovereignty did not have to be national after all.

The acceleration of integration, as promoted by Delors in the 1980s, seemed to bear out the intuition of the federalist-functionalist Founding Fathers, and the logic of their formula: that European functionalism could bring about European federalism; what Weiler has called the unitarian as opposed to communitarian ethos of integration (Weiler, 1993 p. 38). However, as Weiler also noted, 'the life of the Community (like some other things) is not logic, but experience' (p. 39), and the question of sovereignty and the legitimacy to act politically, filtered and amplified through twelve national prisms, suggested an EU of Member States in which certain elites (governing and in opposition) were perplexed and unprepared for the turn taken by the integration process. In this setting, President Delors had become emblematic of the new order.

The 1993 White Paper and its presentation by Delors illustrated the later stages of these developments, and of Delors' interpretation of them. First, Delors adopted a discourse of limited responsibility as a means of securing government approval for the Paper. This was a discourse in which he underlined the limitations of his and the Commission's authority in the Union of the 1990s, whose agenda was increasingly dominated by high politics. Second, Delors began to lay claim to traditional-type authority (the appeal to European values and principles; a discourse of atavistic appeals) as a valedictory warning message to Europeans of the dangers of halting integration. He presented the White Paper in terms of the choice between Europe's survival and its decline; of Europe's morality and civilisation; of the 'model' its economic and social structures represented. Delors' 1993 discourse in this respect can be seen as the script of the first European statesperson, pointing to the potential crisis for Europe if Europe's Member States failed to unite and establish European authority on the 'traditional' grounds of perceptions of collective memory, values and goals.

The 1993 White Paper is to be interpreted as an appeal to the Member States to recognise the consequences of EU inaction in low politics. The Paper did not itself request additional rational-legal authority for the Commission in the field of employment policy, but had the effect, and intentionally so, of demonstrating the consequences of the lack of such authority. The script written by Delors for the promotion of the Paper corresponded in tone: it reflected the mood of the 1990s by self-consciously depicting the Commission's limited responsibility and circumscribed authority in the politics of integration; it also responded to the state of integration and aimed to act upon it in its restatement of the Commission's duty to the general interest of the Communities. In 1993, through the voice of its President, the Commission was fulfilling its functions of *mémoire and provocateur* in respect of Europe's well-being to address the principal problem of the day – unemployment. It was seeking to cast the Union's most pressing economic problems into a new mould, and attempting to change minds on the causes and consequences of, and solutions to, unemployment.

In 1993, Delors' appeal to charismatic and traditional authority was greater than in 1985, yet at a time when the Commission was contested both as bureaucracy and as the conscience of Europe. The strength of his appeal aimed to compensate, as it were, for the weaknesses in the EU's provision for stable forms of authority in low and high politics. Delors himself explicitly said that the White Paper of 1993 had to be different from that of 1985, not because the Commission should not have authority in the areas it covered, but because its authority, including his own, was by then contested (Delors, 1995, p. 12). The case of the 1993 Paper in this respect demonstrates a tactical retreat by Delors, on behalf of the Commission, in order better to advance the Commission's strategy in the employment domain and, more generally, its vital role in articulating the European general interest.

Delors' language of leadership in 1993, rather like a medical

register of diagnosis, prognosis and prescription, emphasised
the spectre of decline if the patient – Europe – deterio-
rated, and sternly proposed treatments to prevent or arrest
the decline. In 1985 the note of diagnosis had been similarly strong, but the prescription less severe. Delors' language was a resource used charismatically throughout his
Presidency, and is to be seen here as part of a process of
discursively constructing a new EU order.

CONCLUSIONS: THE POLITICS OF LEGITIMACY IN THE EUROPEAN UNION

Legitimacy in contemporary democracy amounts to more
than the strict observance and daily enactment of democratic structure and process. Its multiple components have
been variously described as 'formal' v. 'social' legitimacy
(Weiler, 1993); reality v. 'myth' (Obravodic, 1996); and, using
the Weberian terminology that has been adopted in this
chapter, 'rational-legal' v. 'charismatically' or 'traditionally'-
legitimated authority. Identifying the constituent parts of
legitimacy in the EU is particularly problematic, and conceptually significant. This, essentially, is because 'the starting point for the exercise of political authority is the existence
of a state' (Rose, 1995, p. 68), and in the EU statehood has
always been, and remains, the object of controversy and doubt,
as has been the nature of the EU's demos, ethic and values
(Weiler, 1995). Although the EU has formal legitimacy in
the sense of its structures and processes being legal, being
established, and being repeatedly ratified and confirmed by
due democratic process, it lacks, or at least is deficient in,
so-called 'social' legitimacy or a constituent legitimising myth.
The reasons for this deficiency equate to the Union's lack
of 'traditional' type authority, taking traditional in the
Weberian sense to denote accepted and shared perceptions
of collective memory, values, ethics and goals.

Delors' political leadership – his statesmanship – consisted
in behaving as if grounds for traditional legitimation already
existed, or should and would do so. He consistently called
for Europe to sustain its unique model of development and
civilisation according to a visionary blueprint for the EU

order; and in the institutional conclusions he drew from such calls (for example, that Europe needed a European leader), he laid claim to leadership legitimacy based on the Founding Treaties. A key implication of the Treaties was seen as being that the Commission was to be indirectly representative of an anticipated European-wide and potentially trans-party consensus at popular and elite levels in favour of increasing integration and, ultimately, union.

Delors' Commission Presidency was instrumental in enacting the logic of the Community method by activating the Commission's potential to provide a non-partisan and European (or supranational) orientation of the integration process in the general interest of the Communities. Paradoxically, it was because Delors was the first Commission President to act charismatically in the broader sense of the Weberian term – that is to say, offering a form of personalised European leadership intended to transcend partisan and national differences and conflicts, and this on the basis of a set of personalised political convictions and leadership skills – that his Presidency highlighted the Community's problematic democratic credentials. Delors' leadership, while logical given the Community's design, represented (and was represented as) both an overestimation of the extent to which the peoples of Europe and their leaders felt inclined to enter into ever closer union (and so potentially to grant Delors legitimacy on traditional-type grounds), and an underestimation of the limitations of the legitimacy of functional representation. Delors, furthermore, in enacting the Community's arrangements and potential for new levels of popular political representation, challenged the dominant discourse of many Member States, in which political representation is a purely national matter.

Our analysis, including our focus on the discursive claims to legitimacy made by Delors, has offered a particular way of seeing the EU, and has suggested that Delors' leadership highlighted and exacerbated a situation in which disintegration is as much part of the Community logic as integration (Shaw, 1995). It is so in that the distribution of authority and power is fragmented and contested, and the values and ethic of integration do not constitute a common reservoir of memory or belonging. Delors liked to say that he was always 10 or 15 years ahead of his time. Insofar as his Presidency revealed and exacerbated the effects of a Europe not yet ready to legitimate European leadership on 'traditional' grounds – in the sense that it had not yet developed a sense of the eternal yesterday or tomorrow – Delors was certainly out of step with his times and with the state of the existing EU order.

The relationship between Delors' leadership and the state of integration, however, is not to be seen simply as a question of timing, but must also be seen in terms of the ambiguities and spaces in the structures of the EU put there by the EU's treaties. These allow for, and in certain circumstances encourage, leaders to make the type of claims to authority made by Delors. They explain the variety of reactions to such claims and they point to the ongoing need to challenge assumptions relating to the political and constitutional, if not philosophical, principles underlying the EU (Weiler, 1993, pp. 40–1).

A significant outcome of Delors' leadership, therefore, when seen from the conceptual perspective we have developed here, is to raise questions pertaining to what we could call the first principles of integration; namely, authority, power and legitimacy in the EU order. By focusing on the EU's ordering of forms of authority – theoretically, historically and in practice – we have been able to demonstrate that the Commission is as much part of the so-called 'democratic deficit' of the EU as, say, the EP, despite the Commission ostensibly not being a representative institution. We have shown that the Community and Union treaties provide for a matrix of co-existing forms of representation – functional, institutional, national, supranational – and so potentially for a hierarchy of legitimacies. The foregoing analysis suggests, moreover, that the rearrangement of legitimacies which the Community system created did not explicitly expect or anticipate that the role of the Commission would be in opposition to that of Member State governments or bureaucracies, but assumed that national governments would share authority with the new institutions, in the general interest, even to the extent of sharing the task of representative government (Shonfield, 1965; Lenaerts, 1991; Ludlow, 1991).

The intergovernmental consensus on which the Community was established suggested that Member States were in agreement on a system in which they would share authority with the new institutions, as if in a positive-sum game. This was the idealistic, quasi-utopian character of the Community-building exercise. The history of the Community's development, however, and specifically the evolution of the Commission's position, attests to the fact that the Community has often been seen by Member State governments as a zero-sum game, in which the Commission's authority challenges their own, and in response to which they devise methods of strengthening the 'intergovernmental' procedures for decision-making (Lindberg and Scheingold, 1970, p. 94). This is as true of the 1990s as of the earlier years of Community-building.

The politics of legitimacy in the EU thus represents the most intangible and immeasurable of the tides and cycles at work in contemporary politics: namely, the nature of individual authority and claims to charismatic authority; the nature of the combination of the forms of authority developed to organise and manage modern mass democracies; the extent to which the object of politics – society – is organised around a legitimising myth (or myths), or tradition, or culture; and the politics of meaning, such as the differing definitions and interpretations of terms such as 'bureaucracy' and 'legitimacy'.

In the case of the Commission, our focus upon these complexities of legitimacy has demonstrated that the authority of the Commission as an institution, and the authority also of its President, are derived from forty-year old expectations of a fundamental shift in the politics of legitimacy for a new European space and time. The 'failure' of the EU Member States – their governments, their populations, their political parties, and their medias – to fulfil these expectations is an empirical reality of European integration, with which any normative theory of legitimacy for the EU must necessarily begin. Furthermore, at a time when politics at national and EU levels is increasingly characterised by an emphasis on the immediate, the sound bite, the short-term, the personal, the individual, the said and the projected, the gaze upon the individual leader is inevitable. Such developments not only form the context of politics, but in turn act upon it and its rules, and thus become formative and not simply contextual factors. Modern politics in these crucial respects heightens expectations of the political individual's potential to lead and, as intangible and hard to measure as such phenomena might be, affects the political process with identifiable and consequential effects.

On these grounds, it seems appropriate that the analysis of politics in the EU contains a reappraisal of the components and ingredients of legitimacy, including a consideration of the degree to which legitimacy is portrayed and mediated through images recognised as quintessentially 'political', such as the protocol and trappings of political office increasingly conferred on Delors over time. In the specific case of the EU, faced increasingly with situations where what is required is both more democratic efficiency and more efficient democracy, such a focus seems indispensable. In the 1990s, as the EU undertakes the process of reviewing, if not rewriting, its existence as a political entity, the Commission's centrality to the Union's self-definition in political terms therefore becomes all the more apparent and problematic. Is it the quintessential provider of technocratic expertise, with a manager-President? Or is it the European government-in-waiting with, as President, a European statesperson?

Notes

1. The Paris and Rome Treaties both cite the 'general interest' of the Communities: ECSC Treaty Article 9; EEC Treaty Article 157. The wording of the article is virtually the same in both cases. ECSC Article 9: 'The members of the High Authority shall exercise their functions in complete independence, in the general interest of the Community'. EEC Article 157: 'The members of the Commission shall, in the general interest of the Communities, be completely independent in the performance of their duties'.
2. EC Article 144: 'If the motion of censure [on the activities of the Commission] is carried by a two-thirds majority of the votes cast, representing a majority of the members of the European Parliament, the members of the Commission shall resign as a body'.

13 The Commission and the Intergovernmental Conferences

Desmond Dinan

INTRODUCTION

Since the mid-1980s, the European Community/European Union (EC/EU) has been immersed in a seemingly continuous round of constitutional reform, centred on four separate but closely related Intergovernmental Conferences (IGCs). The first three of these IGCs transformed the European Community in the late 1980s and launched the European Union in the early 1990s. However, the IGCs that brought the EU into being also contributed directly to a crisis of European integration that overshadowed preparations and expectations for the fourth IGC, which began in 1996. Little wonder that, although virtually unknown during the Community's first thirty years, IGCs have become increasingly complex, controversial, and time-consuming.

The first IGC began after the European Council decided in June 1985 to revise the Founding Treaties in order to complete the internal market, deepen economic integration, and formalize foreign policy cooperation. Negotiations lasted from September to December 1985; Member State Foreign Ministers signed the resultant Single European Act (SEA) in February 1986; and, after a ratification delay caused by a constitutional impediment in Ireland, the SEA came into effect in July 1987. The entire process lasted a little over two years.

Less than two years later, at its June 1989 meeting, the European Council decided in principle to hold another IGC, this time to negotiate the treaty amendments necessary to achieve Economic and Monetary Union (EMU). By the time that the European Council decided, at its December 1989 meeting, to begin the IGC on EMU no later than the end of 1990, momentous events in Central and Eastern Europe had brought the Cold War to a sudden and unexpected end. The European Council responded in June 1990 with a decision to convene a separate IGC on European Political Union (EPU), focusing mostly on a putative Common Foreign and Security Policy (CFSP). Both conferences began in December 1990 and ended at the Maastricht Summit a year later; Member State Foreign Ministers signed the ensuing Treaty on European Union (TEU) in February 1992; and, after a bruising ratification crisis throughout the Community, the TEU came into effect in November 1993. The Community's second and third series of constitutional reform lasted more than three years.

The TEU specified that a follow-up review IGC would begin in 1996. As a prelude to the 1996 conference, the European Council instructed a group of Member State and EU institutional representatives – gathered in what was called the Reflection Group – to set the agenda and explore possible areas of agreement. The Reflection Group met from June to December 1995, and the IGC itself was opened in March 1996. Even before the negotiations formally began, the preparatory phase of this fourth IGC had thus lasted almost as many years.

Despite its name, an IGC is not exclusively inter-governmental. The EU's three supranational institutions are all involved to a certain extent. The Court of Justice and the European Parliament (EP) contribute to IGC agenda setting, whilst the EP participated in the pre-1996 Reflection Group, was given formal reports back from 1996 IGC meetings, and has an important voice in the ratification debate. The Commission, however, is the only supranational institution involved in the entire process, including the key negotiating stage. This is based on precedent rather than legal obligation. The treaty article covering treaty amendment – which prior to the TEU was Article 236 of the European Economic Community (EEC) Treaty and is now Article N of the TEU – stipulates only that the Commission may submit to the Council proposals for treaty amendment, and that, 'where appropriate', the Council will consult the Commission before deciding to call 'a conference of representa-

tives of the Governments of the Member States . . . (to determine) by common accord the amendments to be made
to this Treaty'. Despite this thin legal base, from the outset
the Commission became a player in the entire IGC process.

Few doubt the SEA's relevance for the EC's revival in the
late 1980s, or the Maastricht Treaty's impact on European
integration in the 1990s. Indeed, the EC/EU's vicissitudes
during the past decade have sparked a lively debate about
the extent to which either supranational institutionalism
(essentially neofunctionalism) or liberal intergovernmentalism
(large Member State politicking) account for the acceleration of European integration in the late 1980s.[1] Controversy
mainly surrounds the role of supranational actors (EC institutions and leaders, and transnational interest groups) in
the SEA's origin and negotiation, for a liberal intergovernmentalist interpretation of Treaty reform (including
the Conferences' causes, conduct, and consequences) would
seem more compatible with what is, after all, primarily an
intergovernmental affair. Accordingly, the extent and effectiveness of the supranational Commission's involvement in
the IGC process has important implications for the theoretical debate about contemporary European integration.

Inevitably, a Commission-centric assessment of the IGCs
is bound to emphasise and possibly exaggerate supranational
explanations for recent EC/EU developments. Nevertheless,
this chapter argues that, despite the constraints imposed by
a strongly intergovernmental Community system and an
avowedly intergovernmental reform process, the Commission
– more specifically, an elite group of Commission leaders
and officials – has played an important role in the IGCs. Its
influence was decisive in shaping and exploiting the SEA
and in launching the EMU IGC, and it was prominent in
the IGC negotiations which began in 1996. Only in the EPU
IGC was it somewhat on the margins (though this was not
for want of trying). Overall, the Commission has been more
effective in the economic oriented IGCs (the EMU IGC)
and economic aspects of IGCs (the policy aspects of the
SEA) than in the political-oriented IGCs and political aspects of IGCs. It has also been more effective at the beginning than at the end of the IGC process. The Commission's
ability to get the ball rolling and to set the terms of the

subsequent negotiations does not necessarily endorse supranational institutionalism, but it does point to a major weakness of liberal intergovernmentalism, which tends to dismiss
the contributions of non-state actors to treaty reform and
integration acceleration in the 'new' EC of the late 1980s,
and to the emergence and development of the EU in
the 1990s.

THE COMMISSION'S RECORD

As an instigator of (and lobby for) deeper integration, the
Commission has traditionally pursued two primary objectives:
to broaden the EC's competence and to replace unanimity
with qualified majority voting (qmv) in the Council of Ministers. These objectives (a means toward the ultimate end
of 'ever closer union') are clearly in the Commission's interest: the greater the EC's scope of action, the greater is
the Commission's involvement in public policy; and the
greater the Council's use of qmv, the greater is the Commission's influence, as a broker and coalition builder, in
the decision-making process.

In theory, IGCs present an ideal opportunity for a 'big
leap forward' in European integration. In practice, they involve
intensive bargaining between actors with varying degrees of
commitment to further integration, and inevitably favour
lowest-common-denominator compromises. Nevertheless, the
Commission's strategy in the first IGC was to press almost
indiscriminately for additional Community competences and
for an extension of qmv. Although it by no means got all
that it wanted in the 1985 IGC, the Commission was nonetheless satisfied with the SEA, both in terms of its actual
provisions and its potential for spillover of Community activity
into new areas.

Similarly, the Commission attempted during the seemingly
all-encompassing IGC on Political Union once again to introduce a number of new Community competences and to
broaden the scope of qmv. However, the most far-reaching
new competences under discussion in 1991 (foreign policy,
security, justice, and home affairs) proved too controversial
to be included in the Community's quasi-supranational

structure. Hence their inclusion instead in new intergovernmental 'pillars' as part of an overarching European Union.
At the same time, 'co-decision', a new legislative procedure
in the Community pillar, extended the EP's power but reduced the Commission's mediatory role *vis-à-vis* Parliament
and the Council during co-decision's final stage.

As a result of these developments, and of the public reaction in 1992 against the fledgling EU and against the Commission as its supposed architect, the Commission's previous
strategy of advocating more competences was neither practical nor politic in the run up to the 1996 IGC. Notwithstanding the EU's 'single institutional structure', the
Commission was marginalised in pillar II (Common Foreign
and Security Policy), and effectively excluded from pillar
III (cooperation in the fields of Justice and Home Affairs)
of the EU. Given that the acquisition of new or strengthened
Union competences might reinforce intergovernmentalism
rather than supranationalism, it was no longer in the Commission's interest to make such sweeping demands. In a climate of creeping Euroscepticism (throughout the Union,
not just in Britain), and because of its hypersensitivity to
the concept of subsidiarity, the Commission could not in
any case advocate a broad extension of EU authority. As for
decision-making, the EU's plethora of pillars and procedures
cast in doubt the Commission's ability automatically to increase its influence, and the EU's ability to grow 'ever closer',
simply through wider use of qmv.

Under the circumstances, it is hardly surprising that the
Commission was more circumspect and discriminating in its
approach to the 1996 IGC. Commission President Santer's
motto – 'Do less, do it better' – applied as much to the
Commission's involvement in the IGC as to the Commission's
other work. The surprising thing, therefore, is not that
the Commission was relatively unassertive in the prelude
to the IGC, but that its pre-IGC 'opinion' (position paper)
was in some respects categorical and emphatic.

The following sections examine in more detail the Commission's involvement in the pre-SEA, pre-Maastricht, and
post-Maastricht IGCs, focusing on the initiation, preparation,
negotiation, ratification, and implementation stages.

Initiation

The constitutional reforms of the mid-1980s and early 1990s would have been impossible without President Mitterrand's 1983 'conversion' to European integration, and the 1984 resolution of Britain's budgetary dispute. More specifically, the European Council's decision in June 1985 to hold an IGC stemmed from Member State determination to complete the internal market, frustration with their joint inability to enact legislation, and concern about the likely institutional strains of Spanish and Portuguese accession.[2] In late 1984 and early 1985 an ad-hoc Intergovernmental Committee on Institutional Affairs (the Dooge Committee) had explored ways to improve the Community's decision-making capacity (through qmv) and broaden the Community's scope of action (through completion of the internal market, greater economic integration, and tighter foreign policy coordination). The Dooge Committee recommended that a conference of Member State representatives negotiate treaty revisions along those lines. The surprise at the June 1985 Milan Summit was not that the Heads of State and Government endorsed the Dooge Committee report, but that the Italian presidency circumvented British, Danish, and Greek opposition to an IGC by calling for a majority vote on whether or not to hold one under Article 236 of the Rome Treaty. The issue was decided by a show of hands.[3]

The Milan Summit was Jacques Delors' first. Because he attended in his capacity as Commission President, and not as a Head of State or Government, he was unable to cast a vote. Delors' role in the intergovernmental European Council personified the Commission's role in the IGC process: present but not quite a full participant. Nevertheless, Delors' contribution to the IGC's initiation was characteristic of the Commission's contribution in the subsequent IGC itself: adventurous, assertive, and active behind the scenes. Delors had spent his first few months in office preparing the White Paper, a blueprint and timetable for completing the Single European Market (SEM). Without decision-making reform, Delors argued, the SEM would never be implemented. Accordingly, publication of the White Paper shortly before the Milan Summit fuelled a growing demand for qmv in the

Council. At the Summit itself, Delors pressed the President-in-office, Italian Prime Minister Bettino Craxi, to call for the fateful vote. Thus, in two important respects the Commission helped to initiate the Community's first round of constitutional reform.

EMU had always been a goal of European integration; its revival in the late 1980s was due largely to the effectiveness of the European Monetary System and the success of the SEM Programme. Delors was especially keen on EMU, both for economic reasons and as a means of federalising the EC. Indeed, linking the SEM Programme to EMU was a classic example of what George Ross has called Delors' 'Russian Doll' strategy: by successfully Communitising market liberalisation, Delors exposed another layer (macro-economic management and monetary policy) to Community action, thereby moving the EC closer to a federal core (Ross, 1995, p. 39).

The SEA IGC led directly to the EMU IGC, not only because completion of the SEM (including liberalisation of capital movements) was the most important rationalisation for EMU, but also because the SEA included a commitment to 'enhance the Community's monetary capacity with a view to economic and monetary union', by means of an IGC. Delors had pressed hard during the 1985 negotiations to include monetary policy provisions in the SEA. Andrew Moravcsik, the main proponent of liberal inter-governmentalism, cites the SEA's weak EMU declaration, and EMU's conditionality on a later IGC, as evidence of how national governments triumphed over the Commission in the SEA negotiations (Moravcsik, 1991, p. 66). If Moravcsik is right, then it was a pyrrhic victory for the anti-EMU Member States, for within twelve months of the SEA's implementation, the European Council not only agreed to hold an IGC on EMU, but also charged Delors with chairing a decisive preparatory committee.[4]

Delors deserves much of the credit for advocating monetary policy cooperation during the 1985 negotiations, and for advocating EMU so soon after the SEA's implementation. Of course, the post-SEA political environment favoured a move in that direction (Sandholtz, 1993b, pp. 95–128). France wanted EMU, and Chancellor Kohl's reluctance (because of the Bundesbank's opposition) could eventually be

overcome (because of his long-standing commitment to
deeper integration, reinforced in 1989 by events in Central
and Eastern Europe) (Baun, 1996, pp. 155–6). A booming
European economy increased EMU's appeal. In addition to
convincing the European Council to appoint him chairman
of the preparatory committee, Delors recommended that the
committee consist of central bank governors, thereby giving him a chance to co-opt a key EMU constituency. Delors
and a small team of Commission officials drafted the influential committee report, while Delors himself lobbied at the
Madrid and Strasbourg Summits for a decision on whether
and when to hold an IGC on EMU. It is unlikely that the
European Council would have agreed in 1989 to convene
the EMU IGC without Delors' dogged advocacy.

EMU raises weighty issues of political control, institutional
restructuring, and democratic accountability in the Community – issues which could have been addressed in the
EMU IGC itself had the EPU IGC not been called for unre-
lated reasons: the collapse of communism in Central and
Eastern Europe, the fall of the Berlin Wall, and imminent
German reunification. In a series of speeches in late 1989
and early 1990 Delors argued the case for deeper integration, encompassing also foreign and security policy, that would
bind a united Germany firmly into a federal Community.
But it was an ebullient Kohl and a fretful Mitterrand, not a
more circumspect Delors, who advocated an early IGC on
political union. The Commission was already over-extended
preparing for the EMU IGC and coping with a host of unexpected demands (mostly related to the Cold War's end)
on its time and slender resources. As part of his 'Russian
Doll' strategy, Delors certainly wanted an IGC on Political
Union, but later rather than sooner. Accordingly, Delors
supported, but did not initiate, the European Council's
decision in June 1990 to launch two IGCs at the Rome Summit
six months later.

In a departure from earlier IGCs, the European Council
did not take a formal decision to launch the 1996 IGC.
Instead, the 1996 IGC originated in the EPU IGC, when it
became apparent in late 1991 that decision-making procedures
(especially for the CFSP) would need to be reviewed shortly
after the proposed Treaty became operational, and that the

mid-1990s might be a calmer time than the heady days of late 1991 (with fierce fighting taking place in Croatia and the Soviet Union about to implode) to develop a common defence policy. Thus, the idea of holding a review IGC five years later slipped into the draft treaty with the Commission's acquiescence, not at its instigation. Nevertheless the Commission and like-minded Member States looked forward to an opportunity to rectify what they considered to be a seriously flawed TEU.

Preparation

The preliminaries to the 1996 IGC were different to the earlier IGCs in that formal preparatory work was undertaken by the Reflection Group (see above). Prior to the 1996 IGC the Commission's first formal involvement in the IGC process was to produce an opinion; for the 1996 IGC the opinion was produced after the Reflection Group reported.

The opinion customarily includes an overview of the IGC's scope and importance, and an explanation of the Commission's objectives. The drafting process is an opportunity to mobilise enthusiasm and support within the Commission for the negotiations ahead. Reflecting Delors' operational style, however, the Commission's pre-SEA, EMU, and EPU opinions and general preparations were a product of a small Delorist clique rather than of the Commission's services. Delors' team included the Commission's Secretary General (Emile Noel until 1987, David Williamson thereafter); Pascal Lamy, Delors's *chef de cabinet*; Francois Lamoureux, Lamy's deputy; and Claus-Dieter Ehlermann, head of the Commission's Legal Service and, later, head of the Competition Policy Directorate General. On EMU, Delors depended especially on Joly Dixon, the member of his *cabinet* responsible for monetary policy (Ross, 1995, pp. 32, 81, 90, 91). In any event, the swiftness with which the Commission had to produce its 1985 and EPU opinions, and the thoroughness with which Delors had mastered the EMU brief, effectively precluded the involvement of more than a handful of Commission officials. The Commission's preparations for the EMU IGC also included a cost–benefit analysis, *One Market, One Money*, which sought to generate public support for EMU rather than stake out a negotiating position (Commission, 1991a).

Although the Commission's preparations for the SEA and Political Union IGCs were both rushed, the radically different purposes and scope of the IGCs put the Commission in a markedly different position at the outset of the two sets of negotiations. In 1985, the Commission was well prepared to tackle institutional and policy issues with which (apart from foreign policy) it was thoroughly familiar. Accordingly, the Commission went into the 1985 IGC with a number of well-crafted demands, including more qmv, greater legislative power for the EP, and an extension of Community competence in such areas as environmental policy, industrial policy, research and development policy, monetary policy, and economic and social cohesion.

In 1991, by contrast, the Commission was weaker politically, and was poorly positioned to tackle foreign and security policy, an area hitherto almost exclusively the preserve of national governments. Preoccupied in 1990 with a variety of pressing problems (managing East Germany's absorption into the EC, coordinating international assistance to the newly-independent countries of Central and Eastern Europe, trying to conclude the contentious Uruguay Round of the GATT, tackling CAP reform, and negotiating a 'European Economic Area' with the EFTA countries), the Commission was unable to devote sufficient time and effort to preparations for the Political Union IGC. The Commission knew what it wanted to come out of the IGC (more qmv; more legislative power for the European Parliament; more Community involvement in areas such as the environment, social policy, industrial policy, and research and development; and Community competence in the realm of foreign policy, security, and even defense), but was ill-prepared when the negotiations began to argue its case and advance its positions.

In the run-up to the 1996 conference, as in the prelude to the EMU negotiations, the Commission had ample time to prepare. As with the other two conferences, however, the Commission's approach to each was markedly different. This was partly because of the content of the IGCs themselves, partly because of changed circumstances in 1995–6, and partly because of different Commission leadership. The broadening scope of the 1996 IGC (notably in the context of impending enlargement to the East), the Commission's political retreat during and after the Maastricht ratification crisis, and the appointment in January 1995 of a more unassuming and collegial President, had an obvious impact on the Commission's IGC preparations. Whereas Delors had monopolised the Commission's involvement in other IGCs, his successor, Jacques Santer, deliberately involved more colleagues and officials in the Commission's preparation for 1996.

Santer asked Commissioner Marcelino Oreja to coordinate the Commission's approach to the IGC and to represent the Commission in the Reflection Group. A former Spanish Foreign Minister and a former chairman of the EP Institutional Affairs Committee, Oreja was an ideal choice, not least because Spain held the Council Presidency during the latter part of 1995 and a Spaniard (Carlos Westendorp) chaired the Reflection Group itself. The Commission's official submission to the Reflection Group suggested a more restrained Commission approach and indicated lower expectations for constitutional reform in the minimalist post-Maastricht environment (Commission, 1995c). In marked contrast to Commission position papers in the run up to previous IGCs, and perhaps also in keeping with the nature of the Reflection Group itself, the Commission's submission to the Group was analytical and conceptual rather than assertive and concrete.

By contrast, the Commission's opinion (1996b), which came out after the Reflection Group's final report, was forthright. While acknowledging that the Commission neither wanted nor expected a big leap forward, and while advocating mostly greater coordination and consolidation of existing policies and procedures, the Commission nevertheless made a number of proposals to bring the EU closer to its citizens, to make the EU's presence felt more in the world, and to adapt the EU's institutional system in light of impending enlargement. The Commission also called unequivocally for a 'transfer of justice and home affairs (Pillar III) to the Community framework (Pillar I), with the exception of judicial cooperation in criminal matters and police cooperation'.

Perhaps the Commission's most striking preparations for the 1996 IGC, however, took the form not of mandated documents and submissions, but of other, seemingly non-IGC related, activities and programmes in 1995 and early 1996. Indeed, the Commission's work at that time must be seen as part of a pre-IGC strategy to regain credibility with the EU's citizens and national governments, and thereby strengthen the Commission's position during the IGC itself (Dinan, 1996). To that end, the Commission advocated 'less action, but better action',[5] encouraged greater deregulation and competitiveness, tried to consult and inform as widely as possible, launched a campaign to combat fraud in the Union, and took steps (such as reorganising DGs and revising procedures for promotion) to put the Commission's unruly house in order. These were necessary initiatives in their own right, but assumed added importance in the run-up to an IGC taking place at a time of rampant Europhobia.

Negotiation

Although an IGC is, by definition, a conference of national delegates, Members States have not objected to the Commission's participation in the IGCs. On the contrary, in the first of the IGCs in 1985 national governments expected the Commission, with its institutional memory and commitment to Community action, to play a prominent role. By submitting a number of position papers to get the discussions going, the Commission acquired a central IGC role in setting the agenda of the negotiations themselves. The Commission assessed Member States' willingness to share more sovereignty, and pitched its proposals at what it judged to be the level of the highest common denominator. As Ross commented about the Commission's role in the 1991 Political Union IGC, 'intelligent maximalism was its institutional duty' (Ross, 1995, p. 95). The Commission was more at home in the 1985 negotiations about Community competences and decision-making than in the parallel discussions about foreign policy coordination, a procedure in which the Commission was not centrally involved.[6]

In reality, the Commission's involvement in the 1985 negotiations meant Delors' involvement, or the involvement of a small team centred on him. This was due not only to Delors' approach, but to the pace of the negotiations and the high rank of the negotiators (formal sessions took place at the level of the Member States' Permanent Representatives, Foreign Ministers, and Prime Ministers/President, thereby limiting the Commission's representation to Delors and Emile Noel, the Commission's Secretary General). When the negotiations opened Delors had been Commission President for only nine months. He was known to his national counterparts because of his recent service as French Finance Minister, but was still unknown outside government and Commission circles. Indeed, Delors built his public reputation on the IGC, emerging from it as 'Mr. Europe' (Grant, 1994, pp. 70–7).

Delors' success owed much to his mastery of the subject matter, his full-time commitment to the IGC, and his ability to build coalitions and leverage support to bolster Commission positions. His skills were well suited to the personalised bargaining of the European Council, the IGC's ultimate negotiating session. Yet by the time the European Council convened in December 1985 Delors had little room to manoeuvre: as the stakes rose with the IGC's near completion, national governments took almost complete control of the agenda and became fully invested in the outcome. The Commission's diminishing influence as the negotiations neared an end became a feature of subsequent IGCs. Nevertheless, the Commission played a key part in shaping the 1985 outcome: on the new cohesion policy and the new cooperation procedure Commission texts accounted for much of what was included.

The EMU negotiations followed a similar path. Having prepared so thoroughly, the Commission (specifically, the Commission's small team centred on Delors and Dixon, his monetary policy adviser) was in an unusually strong position as the negotiations began. Moreover, Delors was at the height of his post-SEA fame and of his European Council prowess. His unequivocal support for German unification had cemented a close relationship with Chancellor Kohl: the decisive Franco-German driving force of European integration had seemingly turned into a Franco-German–Commission partnership, personified by Mitterrand, Kohl, and Delors. The unprecedented Paris–Bonn–Berlaymont axis provided a powerful impetus for deeper European integration.

Yet Delors's prominence and manifest ambition for EMU, together with the IGC's high political stakes, put the Commission in an awkward position even before the negotiations began. Not only was Britain avowedly hostile to EMU, but a deeply-divided Germany also opposed many of the Commission's proposals (the Bundesbank's reservations about EMU grew daily). Delors found himself fighting a rearguard action on several key points, notably the timing and procedure for moving to stage three of EMU and when the proposed European Central Bank would come into existence. The blueprint for EMU that emerged at Maastricht was far from what the Commission had proposed twelve months previously.

Compared to the Political Union negotiations, however, the Commission fared well with EMU.[7] Lack of time and inadequate attention dogged Delors and his chief advisers throughout the Political Union talks. Unveiled in April 1991, the Luxembourg Presidency's 'non-paper' (draft treaty), with its pillars and limited Community competences, represented an early setback for the Commission, which advocated bringing foreign and security policy into the Community and strengthening Community competence in other areas. Delors' aggressive efforts to revise and, later, to ditch the Luxembourg draft backfired badly. Only Belgium and the Commission supported a new draft treaty, introduced by the Dutch Presidency in September 1991, which scrapped the intergovernmental pillars and restored a unitary structure. The Member States' almost unanimous rejection of the Dutch draft at a fateful Foreign Ministers meeting on 'black Monday', September 30, 1991, not only ensured acceptance of the Luxembourg draft, but also isolated the Commission during the remainder of the IGC.

Delors' uncompromising advocacy of the Dutch draft treaty demonstrated a dangerous insensitivity to Member State concerns. Already, Delors' excessively maximalist position on the putative CFSP, a sensitive issue in national capitals, had weakened the Commission's input into the negotiations. With growing popular and political scepticism about supranational policies and institutions, the Commission was thrown on the defensive, to the point of having to protect some of its existing prerogatives. Delors was fortunate to be able to deflect an attack by some Member States (and by the EP) on the Commission's exclusive right to initiate legislation, and an overture to allow the Council to amend Commission proposals by qualified majority instead of unanimity. Under the circumstances, Delors also did well in the final stages of the negotiations to help settle a dispute between Kohl and Spanish Prime Minister Gonzalez over cohesion funds, and engineer the Social Protocol opt-out that saved the Maastricht Summit, and possibly the IGC itself.

As in the past, the Commission sought in the 1996 negotiations to advance its own and the EU's interests by making proposals, building coalitions, and brokering agreements. Although the Maastricht ratification debacle undermined the Commission's political effectiveness and persuasiveness, the Commission approached the negotiations in a positive and pragmatic way. The Commission did not look for greater power as a result of the IGC, and emphasised consolidation rather than expansion of Union competences. Nevertheless, judging from its SEA and EMU experience, the Commission will not play a subordinate role. (The final outcome of the IGC is unknown at the time of writing). As Oreja told the EP during his investiture hearing in January 1995, 'the Commission is there (at the IGC) to represent the Community interest. It should defend this interest and present proposals to Member States identifying problems and suggesting solutions . . . The Commission must, at all events, defend and promote the Union's past achievements and fundamental principles. It must also prevent any gulf from developing between the national governments' (Oreja, 1995, p. 4). The 1996 IGC negotiations were thus seen as giving the Commission a chance, after recent setbacks, to reposition itself at the centre of the Union.

Ratification

The Commission does not itself ratify the outcome of IGCs, but cannot avoid involvement in the crucial ratification stage. Inevitably, contending sides drag the Commission into Member State ratification debates, as happened in Denmark, Ireland, and France in 1992. Of course, the Commission is not a disinterested party, but events in 1992 show that the

Commission needs to pay careful attention to what it says and how it says it. Incautious utterances by Commissioners (including the normally precise Delors, whose statements during the Danish referendum campaign about greater Community competence were taken out of context), and a poor public image (the Commission was easily caricatured as aloof, technocratic, and undemocratic), lost the Commission considerable credibility throughout the Maastricht crisis and did little to help the Treaty's ratification prospects. Although circumstances may be different during the Maastricht II ratification debate, it is unimaginable that the Commission's performance will not be more nuanced and sophisticated.

Implementation

The IGCs' outputs directly affect the EC/EU's institutions, both in a strict legal sense (composition, decision-making role, formal authority, etc.) and in a less tangible but equally important political sense (prestige, influence, informal authority, etc.). Implementation of the SEA greatly boosted the Commission's institutional and political fortunes. Apart from acquiring new powers in the Act itself, the Commission gained in soaring prestige as integration accelerated in the post-SEA period. Delors reaped much of the benefit, using his newfound clout to launch the EMU initiative. Five years later, Delors and the Commission found themselves on the defensive, as the Maastricht Treaty ratification crisis generated a powerful anti-EC reaction among citizens. Implementation of the TEU did little to help, in formal or informal ways. Pushed to the periphery of the CFSP and Justice and Home Affairs pillars, and effectively excluded from the final stage of the new co-decision procedure, the Commission could rejoice only in the Treaty's espousal of EMU, albeit an EMU not entirely to its liking. The Treaty's widespread unpopularity worsened the Commission's predicament in the run-up to the 1996 negotiations.

ASSESSMENT

The Commission's participation in an IGC alters the dynamics of what would otherwise be an almost exclusively intergovernmental process. The Commission is not just another Member State: its positions are based not on domestic political, economic, and bureaucratic interests, but on a perception of the common (EU) good shaped by an institutional commitment to deeper integration. Of course, the Commission's positions are constrained by various factors, not least its judgment of how much sovereignty Member States are willing to cede at any given time and on any given issue.

The Commission's success in influencing an IGC's outcome depends essentially on how successfully it judges Member States' permissiveness for greater integration, how closely its own goals coincide with those of the large Member States, how it plays its hand at the IGC, and the prevailing political and economic climate. These factors obviously change over time; the lessons of the 1985, 1991, and 1996 IGCs are varied, making it difficult to draw general conclusions.

In 1985, political and economic circumstances were propitious for deeper European integration. The Commission's main goals – the SEM and the extension of qmv – coincided with the goals of several Member States, most notably France and Germany. Neither France nor Britain wanted greater parliamentary power, but Germany backed the Commission. On monetary policy and cohesion policy, by contrast, the Commission's preferences for progress were somewhat at odds with the preferences of large Member States which were mainly for minimal action in both areas. Hence the limited elaboration of these in the SEA. Yet in the Europhoric SEM environment, the Commission cleverly exploited the SEA's provisions by later fleshing out a potent cohesion policy (the Delors I budgetary package) and setting the stage for EMU.

In 1991, the Commission's preferences for EMU exceeded those of Germany and Britain, and its preferences for CFSP exceeded those of France, Germany, and Britain. Clearly, the Commission had miscalculated or disregarded the large Member States' thresholds for deeper integration. The Commission's overreach on Political Union culminated in the

Dutch draft treaty debacle, and severely curtailed the Commission's influence in the ongoing negotiations. Thereafter lowest-common-denominator state interests prevailed in the absence of a credible supranational input.

In 1996, the Commission's aspirations and expectations were low, in keeping with the prevailing post-Maastricht gloom. The Commission's modest objectives generally approximated those of France, Germany, and even Britain. Hence the likelihood after the IGC of institutional streamlining, simplification of treaty provisions and language, more meaningful and comprehensible subsidiarity, and greater inclusion of the Union's citizens. The Commission moderated its objectives in the key areas of decision-making, CFSP, and the Union's pillars, bringing them into line with what France and Germany were most likely to concede. Precisely because its goals were unambitious and its credibility was gradually recovering, however, the Commission was able to play a surprisingly active role in the negotiations.

Whatever happens during and after the 1996 IGC, the record of the Commission's involvement in earlier IGCs shows that the Commission's impact has been far from negligible. A full assessment must necessarily await the release of all relevant archival material. In the meantime, while acknowledging the highly state-centric nature of EC/EU constitutional reform, it seems reasonable to assert that the contribution of the Commission, and specifically of its leadership, is sometimes decisive. The observable impact of Delors and his formidable team at the SEA and EMU IGCs poses a challenge to the anti-supranationalist, liberal intergovernmentalist explanation of the EC's revival in the late 1980s and early 1990s.

Commission participation in the IGC process is also noteworthy because of its impact on the Commission itself. The Commission's IGC involvement is limited to a handful of key individuals, the most prominent of whom is the Commission President. Despite Delors' setbacks in the Political Union negotiations and in the subsequent ratification crisis, IGCs have greatly strengthened the Commission Presidency. In particular, Delors usually masterful performance in the European Council, the IGC's ultimate decision-making body, has raised the Presidency's visibility, status, and authority within the Commission. The exclusivity of IGC negotiations has put another nail in the coffin of Commission collegiality. Although Delors arguably carried presidentialism and individualism too far, the reality of the post-SEA and post-Maastricht EU makes it impossible even for the more egalitarian Santer to be a truly collegial Commission President.

As for the institution itself, the Commission's prominence in the late 1980s, as a sequel to the SEA, engendered a popular and political backlash in the post-Maastricht period. This highlights one of the Commission's greatest difficulties as an EU actor. Unlike the Court of Justice, whose relative anonymity reflects that of national constitutional courts; unlike the EP, whose agitation for greater power can be understood in terms of its elected status and the ubiquitous struggle between national parliaments and executives; and unlike Member State governments, which represent well-defined national interests, the Commission lacks a reference point in the state-centric framework in which most people regard European integration. Accordingly, in the public mind the Commission tends to be confused with the EU for better or for worse: for better when there is a general permissiveness about further integration (as in the late 1980s); for worse when support for integration erodes (as in the early 1990s). Indeed, the Commission's prominence during the former phase almost guaranteed that the Commission's image and authority would suffer during the latter phase. As a motor of European integration, the Commission inevitably splutters when the enterprise runs out of economic and political steam. Following the Maastricht ratification crisis, the tick of the EU's engine slowed down. The 1996 IGC, however, gave to the Union and to the Commission an opportunity to shift back into gear – although not necessarily into high gear.

Notes

1. The debate can be followed in Sandholtz and Zysman (1989), Moravcsik (1991, 1993), Wincott (1995), and Moravcsik (1995).
2. For an overview of the history of European integration in the 1980s and early 1990s, see Dinan. (1994), pp. 99–198.

3. Two participants in the Milan European Council, Garret FitzGerald (Ireland's Prime Minister) and Margaret Thatcher (Britain's Prime Minister), give interesting accounts of the summit in their respective memoirs. See FitzGerald (1991) and Thatcher (1993).
4. Moravcsik plays down Delors contribution to the report that bore Delors' name: Moravcsik (1995), pp. 619–20. Ross plays up Delors' contribution: Ross (1995), pp. 81–3.
5. Santer often uses this phrase, or a variation of it, to explain what subsidiarity means in practice.
6. For an insider's account of the SEA negotiations, see de Ruyt (1987).
7. For an insider's account of the Maastricht Treaty negotiations, see Cloos *et al.* (1993).

14 The Role of the Commission: A Theoretical Discussion
Janne Haaland Matláry

INTRODUCTION

There is a substantial body of empirical work demonstrating that the Commission plays a major role in the EU's policy-making processes. The influence of the Commission was especially important in the 1985–92 period, when it did much to expand European-level policy competences under the general internal market umbrella (see, for example, Sandholtz, 1993a; McGowan, 1993; Matláry, 1997a).

However, despite its important influence, relatively little systematic theoretical work exists on the role of the Commission. Theories are required to account for the activist role that the Commission clearly plays at certain times and, more generally, new conceptualisations are required to allow us to study the Commission's formal and informal roles within the EU. This chapter seeks to make a contribution to these requirements. It does so firstly by considering the weaknesses of traditional integration theories – intergovernmentalism and neofunctionalism – in dealing with the Commission, and secondly by looking at recent attempts – founded largely on network theory, leadership theory, and more broadly on the so-called 'new institutionalism' – to theorise about the Commission's role as a political actor.

THEORETICAL APPROACHES TO THE COMMISSION: THE TRADITIONAL INTEGRATION THEORIES

The two main theoretical approaches to the study of European integration – neofunctionalism and intergovernmentalism –

offer insights into the role and functioning of the Commission, but their explanatory record and capacity is limited.

Neofunctionalism was the 'mainstream' theoretical approach in the early years of European integration. Its foremost proponents were Ernst Haas (1958) and Leon Lindberg (1963). Neofunctionalism portrays European integration as an incremental and almost automatic process, positing that integration in one policy area will result in 'spillover' to other policy areas. This spillover can be intended as well as unintended, with the former giving considerable potential for non-state actors such as the Commission to exercise important policy roles. Policy-making is seen as a process and not as a series of independent bargains, and in this process the Commission's role as agenda-setter can be extremely important.

The many criticisms which have been made of neofunctionalism as a theory of integration have tended to concentrate on its complexity, its lack of specificity, and its heavy reliance on non-political, functional, driving forces. The slowing down of the integration process at certain points – notably from the late 1960s to the early 1980s – has been seen by many commentators as showing that integration does not necessarily take the form or follow the path that neofunctionalism implies. Above all, neofunctionalism is seen by its critics as neglecting the *political* nature of integration processes and the two-way mutual influences between EU-level and state-level actors.

However, notwithstanding its perceived weaknesses as a macro theory of integration, neofunctionalism is still seen by many as being a theoretical approach from which useful explanatory ideas can be drawn. Certainly it is an approach which has contributed much to some of the newer theoretical approaches to European integration and EU decision-making. Indeed, commenting on one of the most influential of such approaches – 'historical' or 'new' institutionalism (which is considered later in this chapter) – Pierson (1995) argues that 'historical institutionalist analysis greatly strengthens and expands the analytical foundations of neofunctionalism' (p. 26). From the viewpoint of our particular interest in the Commission, neofunctionalism is seen by many as being especially useful in the emphasis it gives to the importance of supranational actors in the integration process and the role it assigns to experts and professionals in policy definition and problem solving. In this context, it is pertinent to note that empirical research in many policy areas in the post-1985 period seem to bear out some of the insights provided by neofunctionalism into the potential role of the Commission in fostering integration (see, for example, Marks [1992], Cameron [1992], and Sandholtz [1993a]).

Intergovernmentalism, which was developed from the 1960s as a neo-realist corrective to neofunctionalism, has little to say about the role of the Commission in the integration process, other than to dismiss it as being of minor importance. For intergovernmentalists, states are the key EU actors. EU institutions, including the Commission, are, at best, facilitators of bargaining between states and have virtually no independent impact. Intergovernmentalists view actors as static in the sense that the theoretical emphasis is on one bargain or policy event at a particular time. There is little consideration of the actor structure problem or of the possible effects of EU actors on state actors. Moravcsik (1993), the main current proponent of intergovernmentalism, argues that 'EU institutions appear to be explicable as the result of conscious calculations by Member States to strike a balance between greater efficiency and domestic influence' (p. 507). He thus views EU institutions such as the Commission as the creatures of Member States and as essentially passive and neutral agents. They do not have an independent impact on the political process. The Commission is regarded as a facilitator and source of 'neutral' proposals: 'As a reliable source of independent proposals, the Commission ensures that technical information necessary for decision is available' (p. 511). He admits, however, that 'the ability to select among viable proposals grants the Commission considerable formal agenda-setting power, at least in theory' (p. 512).

With such a conceptualisation, the role of the Commission is assumed away. When the Commission is found to exert some influence, the empirical evidence is written off as being exceptional and as being of no general importance in the sense that it invalidates the theoretical assumptions of intergovernmentalism: 'independent actions by the Commission ... do not constitute decisive evidence against the intergovernmentalist view ... only when the actions of supranational leaders systematically bias outcomes away from the long-term interests of Member States can we speak of serious challenge to an intergovernmentalist view' (Moravcsik, 1993, p. 514). But what constitutes 'systematic bias'? The term implies that states' long-term interests underlie their preferences, and that these can be detected prior to the involvement of states in EU policy-making. Thus, it is regarded as being possible to isolate persistent state interests, but not possible to do so for EU actors. As we shall see, challenges to intergovernmentalist assumptions can be posed on both these counts.

A general critique of intergovernmentalism will not be developed here, since its assumptions have been sufficiently criticised elsewhere, both directly in theoretically based critiques (see, for example, Wincott, 1995, rejoinder by Moravcsik, 1995; Pierson, 1995), and indirectly in several empirical studies which show that the Commission has played a major role in policy-making. The position expounded here is not that an intergovernmentalist approach is irrelevant for studying, for instance, the 'major intergovernmental bargains' about treaty revisions, but rather that it is of little help when we are interested in the role of the Commission. However, the intergovernmentalist model serves as a reference point for the discussion in this chapter because its assumptions are the starting point for much research on the Commission.

Intergovernmentalism typically tells us something about bargaining power at a given moment in time, but we need to study the impact of the Commission not only in this way, but also over time. Fuchs (1994) remarks that although one can, for instance, study the Treaty on European Union (TEU) outcomes with an intergovernmentalist approach, 'the expansion of powers and competencies by the Commission was already going on for years before the treaty ...' (p. 178), and he cites empirical studies in various issue areas as evidence of this. Marks (1992) likewise concludes that 'the treaties are not representative of the ongoing process of agenda-building' (p. 23), and Pierson (1995) points out that historical analyses largely miss the point of Commission influence as it is the evolving practise of interpreting and applying policy mandates that is of importance.

Neofunctionalism and intergovernmentalism are thus of only limited help in seeking to explain the role of the Commission in the EU system and within the integration process more generally. Intergovernmentalism generally dismisses any significant role for the Commission, and neofunctionalism does not account for periods of relative inactivity on the part of the Commission. We therefore have to look elsewhere for theoretical building blocks.

RE-CONCEPTUALISING THE EU SYSTEM OF GOVERNANCE AND THE COMMISSION

The newer approaches that are emerging to the study of the Commission tend either to be derived inductively from empirical case studies or to be drawn from one of several theoretical traditions or sub-fields of political science. Significantly, these approaches are essentially 'middle range' in character in that they do not seek to establish a macro theory of European integration or of EU-Member State interactions, but rather are interested only in 'parts of the whole'. Significantly, too, most of the approaches recognise the shortcomings of the hitherto dominant neo-realist approach to the study of international organisations and are exploring new conceptualisations. Prominent amongst these conceptualisations is the EU as a complex system of multi-level governance (Cram, 1994; Kohler-Koch, 1996; Jachtenfuchs, 1997). In this conceptualisation, the Commission is seen as being a differentiated actor which plays different roles in different situations. To understand the Commission it is necessary, as Cram (1994) argues, to 'de-compose' it, as in the study of bureaucratic politics at the national level, and to examine the various policy styles and policy goals of its many parts.

Conceptualising the EU in multi-level terms implies that there is no privileging of the state as an actor (this is also consistent with transnational and transgovernmental mod-

els in international relations), but that there is an openness
to actor structure. It also implies that there is no positing
of a domestic-international divide (here domestic–EU divide).
The state as actor becomes the government as actor, and
other actors do not necessarily reflect national or domestic
interests. Actors are thus 'freed' from territory. With such
an 'agnostic' starting-point in terms of actors and structure,
interests also can fruitfully be 'opened up' as an analytical
category.

Re-conceptualising actors

When we look for new conceptualisations of actors we can
draw on several sub-fields of political science: in particular,
comparative public policy, organisation theory, and international relations.

Taking, for example, international relations theory, there
are several elements that constitute fruitful points of departure. One is the regime literature which investigates the impact
of international regimes on the outcomes of decision-making (see, for instance, Rittberger, 1993; Haas, 1993; Young
and Osherenko, 1993). Here we most often deal with
multilateral cooperation between state actors, but this work
is also useful for understanding the role of the Commission
because it attempts to study whether such cooperative arrangements – regimes – do in fact have an independent
impact on the cooperation between states. When we remem-
ber that the EU is 'much more' than a non-legally binding
regime, and that it has sanctioning power in some issue areas,
the findings from the regime literature should be relevant
for our purposes. Put simply: if international regimes matter for states' interest formation, then the EU, and especially
actors like the Commission, should matter considerably because of their formal powers.

Regime theory thus operates with a very different conceptualisation of actors than does intergovernmentalism, and
in order to meaningfully study the role of the Commission
from this viewpoint approaches are needed that deal with
non-state actors and non-formal political resources. The latter, for instance, can include access to expert knowledge,
intimate command of decision-making procedures, agenda-

setting ability, ability to define the policy 'problem' and to time its emergence on the agenda, and an ability to have some control over participants in the policy-making process.

Empirical developments in the EU in the post-1985 period show that there are indeed many actors that have been influential in policy-making – at both the sub-national level and at the EU-level – in addition to state actors. Moreover, sub-state actors do not always channel their policy-making through the state executive, but form links and alliances directly with the Commission. The Commission has been shown to initiate and encourage such links, thus bypassing the national executive in a 'pincer' movement (Marks, 1992). As a corollary of this, it may not make much sense to speak of 'high' and 'low' politics anymore. Risse-Kappen (1996) remarks that the literature on comparative foreign policy analysis shows that this distinction is flawed since executive control of 'high' politics depends very much on political institutions; viz. that the state controls and channels domestic policy-making.

When, in analysing the EU, we do away with the traditional assumptions about the Weberian state, we are left with a much more open field of enquiry. It is possible that various types of actors cluster in networks, but only empirical analysis will show whether state actors predominate in any given case. There is reason to believe that this will often be so, but we should not assume this at the outset. The Commission is an actor like any other, with its own political resources: formal powers, expert knowledge, right of initiative, and so on. The crucial empirical question then becomes that of actor *capacity*: how do the formal and informal resources of a given actor add up in a policy area or in a specific negotiation? We can infer that formal state actor capacity brings power with it, but this does not mean that other actors are powerless. Being a formal actor is important at the formal negotiating stage of a decision, but this is only one political resource among many. Non-state actors proliferate in a political world where traditional territorial politics means less and less, especially in the West. It is necessary to rethink what it means to be a political actor, and to look closely at the changing balance of what constitutes viable political resources in international and EU politics today.

Re-conceptualising interests

Where do interests come from, and of what do they consist? How are they formed, and how are they changed? The
conceptualisation of interests is a major problem with intergovernmental approaches and with much international relations theory in the neo-realist tradition. Here actors are
seen to promote 'national interests' which concern political
and/or economic power. Interests are not generated at the
EU level, and the EU process of policy-making is not seen
as important in this regard.

Rationalist regime theory has been the main approach to
studying interest formation, but there is also a growing interest in a different approach within regime theory. Recent
international relations theorising is about what many call
'the constructivist' challenge to mainstream theory, for want
of a better term (Jørgensen, 1997). It is, perhaps, better
thought of as a hermeneutic and historical understanding
of the importance of norms and rules that are particular to
an organisation, a culture, or a nation (Matláry, 1997b). This
bears directly on the understanding of human action and
of its motivations. The problem with a simple neo-realist
approach to human motivation and the determination of
interests in the EU context is not that actors do not act in
goal-oriented ways, but that these goals can be much broader
or different from 'maximation' of national economic or political interests, and that they are not necessarily generated
domestically but may also be generated at the EU level. It
is analytically very difficult to separate 'national' interests
from EU-specific ones, but in an increasingly interdepen-
dent world it should not be assumed that interests are always
'national' interests. Tonra's (1997) study of foreign political cooperation between the EU states clearly shows that
national representatives think in terms of a European logic
as well as in terms of national interests. There are, of course,
cases of 'hard' national interests, but they are relatively few
and far between. Most of the time, national diplomats at
the EU level work closely in order to try and achieve common positions; they do not usually come to Brussels with
fixed national interests.

Norms and rules within a political institution and culture

influence interest-formation. Learning in the context of decision-making may be very important in this respect (Sjøstedt, 1994). These aspects of potential Commission influence have not yet been studied systematically, but research is underway (Laffan, 1995). When the assumption that interests are exogenous to the policy process is abandoned, the relevance and impact of the types of political resources that both formal and non-formal actors possess can be better evaluated. This perspective on interests implics that the Commission may profoundly influence the positions or interests that states adopt, since it is not only the exclusive agenda-setter of EU policy, but it is also the agent that largely designs the policy process in terms of which procedures to use, which actors to include, and how to define policy issues.

A central issue regarding the Commission's role is not only what kind of interests actors have, but also where the interests are formed. Intergovernmentalism assumes that they are 'national interests', formed at the domestic level. Yet increasingly scholars question this assumption. Recent empirical scholarship shows that interests are also formed in the interactive policy process between the national and the EU level, and that they are not always instrumental economic interests. So, for example, Sandholtz's (1993b) study of the EMU negotiations found that some governments did not have interests *prior* to EU-level decision-making, but that they developed such interests in the negotiations over policy. The study also showed that the German policy choice was explained more by the general political stance on German integration than by hard economic interests. Likewise, in the sphere of energy policy from the late 1980s, where there were clear structural national interests, states did not come to the EU with a prior preference. Rather, the Commission's definition of the energy policy-problem constrained states' choices of viable interests (Matláry, 1997a).

As with conceptualising actors, it thus seems wise to adopt an 'agnostic' approach to conceptualising interests: in some cases there are structural national interests, whilst in other cases positions are taken after discussion, learning, and persuasion. The role of ideas and identities in this process is potentially very important, but cannot be taken into account

if interests are conceptualised as being exogenously determined prior to policy-making, and fixed. In order to study
the influence of policy ideas and the framing of the political problems it is necessary to depart from the instrumental
version of interest conceptualisation as well as from the assumption that interests are primarily 'national'.

Re-conceptualising the Commission

The Commission can thus be conceptualised as an actor
with its own interests, with various informal and formal powers,
and with the capacity to influence states' interests through,
particularly, the setting of the agenda. The agenda-setting
stage is of particular importance in the EU since policy deals
with problems defined technically and/or legally. As Peters
(1994) has noted ' . . . the prospects for agenda-setting appear to be almost the opposite of the rather gloomy sce-
nario for implementation' (p. 21). The general importance
of the agenda-setting phase and the potential for the Commission to exercise a key role therein is underscored by
general research in regime theory where it is clear that states'
interests are influenced by the international regime itself
and by its function as an arena for agenda-setting (Rittberger
et al., 1993).

Depending on the assumptions which are made about
interests, the roles of ideas, of knowledge and of persuasion in the political process, interests are viewed differently.
(On the importance of these aspects of the political process,
see Haas, 1990; Goldstein and Keohane, 1993; Sjøstedt, 1994).
However, even if one operates with a strict concept of instrumental interests, these may nonetheless be heavily influenced and constrained by factors over which the
Commission has considerable influence: the framing of policy
problems, the selection of decision-making procedures, the
choosing of arenas and participants, and so on. Héritier's
major study of environmental policy in the EU (1994 and
1995) showed that governments promoted their interests best
when they could influence the policy definition of the
Commission: 'The relative success of a Member State in imposing
its policy approach on the European level depends on the
cooperation with European institutions, especially the Commission.

In the period under investigation, Germany and Great Britain, respectively, fitted in better with the problem perspective of the Commission at different times' (1995, p. 299). It was the policies of these states that influenced the outcome of the EU regime. This is because the Commission 'functions as a gate-keeper and largely determines the chances of the member states regulatory proposals to influence the European agenda' (Héritier, 1996, p. 164).

If furthering one's interests is conditioned by the framing of the problem and the setting of the agenda, the Commission is in a perfect position to yield such influence: 'Although knowledge and expertise are an important factor in any policy process, it could be argued that they play a particularly central role in the EU policy process ... the Commission uses knowledge in a very sophisticated manner' (Laffan, 1995). The Commission's framing of the policy problem and its selection of participants in the policy processes, through for instance the many permanent and working committees which surround it, may be assumed to influence national interest formation and thus also the largely intergovernmental negotiation phase. Tonra (1997) found that even in the intergovernmentally based policy sphere of foreign policy, national interests were heavily influenced by the process of participation: 'So ingrained is the process of consultation and cooperation that where there is ever any new foreign policy initiative in the making, the first reflex is European' (p. 6).

So, if we leave the neo-realist assumptions of intergovernmentalism and the automatism of neofunctionalism we can start to build new theory about the role of the Commission. 'Building blocks for this are gleaned inductively from empirical studies, often of cases of issue-specific policy, as well as from theoretical traditions other than integration theory. Depending on how interest formation is conceptualised – as endogenous or exogenous to the political process – it has been argued here the Commission may exert great influence on policy-making.

But it is not necessarily true that empirical studies bring out which perspective is the 'right' one. Studies can usually be so designed that the analyst finds what he or she looks for – it is, for instance, usually possible to find a 'national interest' that 'explains' an outcome of an international negotiation (Green and Shapiro, 1994). Likewise, it is hard to agree on criteria for determining the extent of influence that agenda-setting amounts to. Much invariably depends on assumptions, conceptualisations, and philosophy of science in a very basic sense. This is too complex an issue to develop here; suffice it to state that finding 'systematic bias' in favour of Commission interests in EU policy-making, as Moravscik calls for, is hardly possible. Rather, it is necessary to develop empirical analyses that are sufficiently rich with information about different stages of policy-making processes so as to be able to specify if, where, and when the Commission is a strong actor. It is probable that the Commission is very important in agenda-setting. The issue then is how much this stage influences further policy stages, especially decision taking. At a minimum, it seems clear that it is near to impossible to reshape the agenda in the EU once it has been set – as the British found, for example, when, in the context of Economic and Monetary Union, they proposed a so-called 'hard ecu' far too late to have any real chance of altering the agenda (Dyson, 1994).

Intergovernmentalism has been used here as a key point of reference because its neo-realist assumptions still provide the 'mainstream' approach to the study of EU and international politics. The empirical findings on the Commission's role that are presented in this book and elsewhere are unlikely to convince adherents of intergovernmentalism that their approach is inappropriate. After all, inductively generated theoretical insights do not add up to a theory of integration that answers questions such as: under which conditions is the role of the Commission prominent? in which types of issue areas? how do the formal and informal powers of the Commission interact? when is the Commission a unitary actor, and when is it not? and how does the Commission, as a policy entrepreneur, use knowledge and ideas more effectively than state actors? As can be seen, there is no theory in the general political science literature that yields answers to all of these questions, let alone agreement on the best conceptualisation of the Commission. This unsatisfactory situation makes the intergovernmental model appealing because of its simplicity and parsimony.

TOWARDS A THEORY OF THE COMMISSION'S ROLE?:
LEADERSHIP THEORY, NETWORK THEORY, AND THE
'NEW INSTITUTIONALISM'

Given the limitations of established theories in facilitating
useful theorising on the Commission, it is necessary to ask
whether there are signs of any helpful alternative theoretical approaches emerging.

Leadership theory

A promising path may be found in the literature on leadership in international negotiations. Rosenthal wrote the classic study of 'the men behind the decisions' (1975), and
recently Ross has documented the very clear leadership of
Delors and his *cabinet* within the Commission (1994 and 1995).
These studies focus on persons as leaders. However, there
is also a growing literature that looks at institutional actors
as leaders. Young (1991) has developed the concept of entrepreneurial leadership, which refers to the ability to forge
mutually acceptable deals in international organisations – a
very important explanatory variable in studies of international
regime formation.

Some scholars have applied this literature from international
negotiations to the Commission's role in EU bargaining.
Sandholtz (1993a), for example, has attempted to theorise
about the Commission as leader, and Vahl has drawn up a
set of hypotheses about this (1992). In Vahl's view, the
Commission is most likely to provide effective leadership when
it is in possession of more expertise and information than
the Member States, can use existing principles, norms, rules,
and procedures (routinized decision-making), can define its
policies in apolitical terms, can facilitate agreement among
Member States, and takes into account explicit national
interests. Sandholtz reasons in much the same vein and
defines similar conditions, though he makes a distinction
between *necessary* conditions for effective leadership, and
sufficient conditions.

The methodological problem with the leadership approach
is, however, that we may agree that someone or some institution acts as leader, but what does this amount to? Is the

leader an autonomous political actor who wields an independent impact on decisions? When we use leadership as an analytical approach, we need to specify what we mean by autonomous actor influence. Take the example of EMU: the empirical studies of this process bear out the leading role of Delors, who was bent on putting EMU on the agenda from the beginning of his Commission Presidency and who used every opportunity, formal and informal, to do this. It was largely he who managed to have EMU as a political goal inserted in the Single European Act and it was he who chaired the so-called Delors Committee that was mandated to develop the EMU. However, at a critical point it seemed impossible to make the Germans accept EMU, despite various moves on Delors' part to make it more attractive to them. It was probably the unexpected possibility of reunification with East Germany that made the Germans accept EMU 'in return for' French support for reunification (Dyson, 1994; Lund, 1995; Sandholtz, 1993b). This example shows that leadership from the Commission or its President may be a main explanatory variable of successful policy-making, but that Member State support remains a *sine qua non*. Studies that seek to ascertain whether the Commission plays a leading role in a given issue area or policy process must thus discuss not only the criteria for leadership, but also what leadership means. An autonomous role for the Commission can only be established by positing the historical counter-factual, which is very difficult to do (Biersteker, 1993), or by finding cases where the Commission's interests differ from those of Member States.

A further difficulty is that we lack ways of assessing the importance of various types of political resources. The logic sketched here is really an intergovernmentalist logic which seeks to contrast Member States' influence with other actors' influence. The leadership approach should therefore be combined with a policy analysis approach that extends from agenda-setting to the final phase of decision-making in the Council. If Member States accept the policy design that emerged in the agenda-setting phase, this implies that the Commission's influence was very significant, even if we cannot prove that Member States would have differed in their preferences if the agenda were set differently. However, it must be admitted that we lack a sound method for assigning relative weight to various actors in the policy process if we work without mutually exclusive or at least conflicting preferences, the alternative to the historical counter-factual.

In sum, the usefulness of leadership theory applied to the Commission is that it offers insights into how institutional actors may use various non-formal political resources to enhance their own agenda. This focus is very relevant in the study of EU policy-making because EU policy tends to be highly technical, to be based on an intricate set of rules, procedures, and routines, to be long-term in character, and to largely concern the construction of new common policies and institutions. In other words, it is atypical of traditional interstate politics in the sense that it is not primarily about the defence of traditional national interests. Its mode of policy-making is cast in terms of problem-resolution and innovation, demanding extensive cooperation rather than zero-sum political games. Leadership theory is useful in dealing with this type of policy-making, but it does not offer any theory of the Commission's role within the EU.

Network theory

The network approach to policy analysis provides a conceptualisation of political actors that goes beyond state-centredness (Kohler-Koch, 1996).

Network theory has been developed in various sub-fields of political science, such as organisation theory, international relations, and policy analysis. It has been used as an analytical tool in major studies of EU–states interaction, such as the major study of environmental policy by Héritier *et al.* (1994). In the network approach, governance is de-coupled from the hierarchical organisation of the traditional state and the focus is on the interaction between various types of actors in issue-specific networks where state actors are not privileged. The approach makes a rigid distinction between the national level and the EU-level superfluous and, as such, it allows analysts to study the policy process without the prejudices of state-centredness, which is 'eine Verstandnissbarriere' ['an obstacle to understanding'] (Kohler-Koch, 1996, p. 8).

The importance of the network approach lies in its qualities of embraceability and openness. This puts it at some advantage over intergovernmentalism and neofunctionalism, both of which, but especially the former, rely on conceptualisations that emanate from a state-centred model of governance. In intergovernmentalism this reliance becomes almost a caricature when important actors such as the Commission are dismissed as being of little significance, but in neofunctionalism there is also an implicit state-centredness that posits some type of federal state as the blueprint or model for what the EU could, or should, become.

A valid criticism of network approaches is that they often lack hypotheses and treat all actors on a par – it is relatively easy to *map the actors* in a given network; the hard task is to explain *why they are relevant*. After all no-one wants to study all actors and all processes. Further, there is a need to explain why *issue-specific* networks are important, and whether networks are always issue-specific. Thus, there is a clear need to develop the network approach into a theory which, in the EU context, can be used to explain which actors (including the Commission), in which circumstances, are important.

The 'new' institutionalism

The third of the newer conceptual approaches to be considered here – 'new' or 'historical institutionalism' – offers a more fully fledged theory of the role of the Commission than the other two approaches. The approach has been developed in particular by March and Olsen (1989). A useful synopsis of the approach is presented in Thelen and Steinmo (1992b). Pierson (1995) has used the approach to offer the beginnings of a theory of the Commission.

There are many different aspects to new institutionalism. One important aspect is that political decisions, however they are made, are seen as having unintended consequences, as generating 'sunk' costs, and as evolving in unanticipated directions. Another important aspect is that institutions, which are broadly defined, are seen as attaining their influence in a variety of ways, as having resources beyond their formal powers, and as outliving the initial interests that created them.

This all implies that the influence of non-state actors, like the Commission, is best studied over time. In studies of formal EU intergovernmental negotiations, such as treaty revisions, the only formal actors are the Member States. But over time the Commission interprets the treaties and applies them. Its power is thus less visible than that of the Member States, and is best shown via an analysis of the long-term evolution of the EU. The Commission's true influence can thus only be unearthed if an approach is adopted that allows us to see how it uses its formal and informal resources in a variety of situations.

A key point in the new institutionalist perspective is that institutions are assumed to be interested in taking advantage of whatever opportunities are available to them to strengthen and expand their positions and their roles. Applying this to the Commission, attention is directed to the considerable opportunities for institutional advantage which it has within the EU system. Amongst these opportunities are utilisation of the slack which Member States provide to the Commission in the interpretation of assorted norms, rules, and duties.

Pierson (1995) links opportunities for the Commission to limitations on the influence of Member States in the intervals between major intergovernmental bargains: exiting the EU becomes increasingly difficult; the evolving *acquis* imposes constraints; preferences may alter, perhaps as a result of changes of government; and intergovernmental bargains often have unintended and unanticipated integrationist consequences. The Commission is in a strong position to utilise such factors to its own advantage. It can, for example, forge issue linkages, define new policy priorities, and group policies under 'headings' where it has formal powers.

A new institutionalist perspective thus permits analysis of how the Commission uses its formal and informal powers over time. Not only is the Commission in possession of autonomous formal powers that enable it to be a party to interstate negotiations and an exclusive agenda-setter, but it can in some respects command the scene within the EU in *la longue durée*, through the shaping of norms, rules, and political culture. Thus, in a more evolutionary perspective, the role of the Commission turns out to be much more important than what is suggested in the studies which look at one or two bargaining situations (Bulmer, 1994a). As Pierson (1995) points out 'what one makes of the EC depends on whether one examines a photograph or a moving picture' (p. 6).

CONCLUSIONS

Empirical work undertaken on the activities of the Commission in the post-1985 period have led to reconceptualisations of its role in the EU system. These findings cannot be fitted into a theory of integration based on intergovernmentalist assumptions. To advance further down the theoretical path, studies with similar analytical design are needed that examine the role of the Commission over time, where assumptions about actors and interests are not derived from neo-realist conceptualisations of state power.

In this chapter it has been argued that a major obstacle to theory-building about the Commission's role remains the state-centredness of traditional theories that deal with the relationship between state actors and international regimes, as well as the EU specifically. It has been suggested that actors, interests, and the Commission in particular, need to be reconceptualised in order to start to build a theory of *when* and *in which ways* the Commission is important. Network theory was presented as a potentially fruitful alternative conceptualisation of EU actor structure, while leadership theory was shown as helping in specifying conditions under which the Commission is an independent actor. However, it is necessary to study not only 'one-shot' negotiations between states and EU actors to ascertain the Commission's role, for such an approach is likely to distort the view. The Commission's influence must be studied over time. To this end, it has been argued that the new institutionalist perspective is useful, as it focuses on how intended agreements between formal actors are always subject to interpretation, application, and implementation. Actors such as the Commission which are in charge of day-to-day policy-making are central to the processes which shape real policy. Empirically rich studies that focus not just on final decision-making but also on other decision-making stages and processes are required to distill just where and when the Commission exercises these influences most. Theory about the Commission's role can ultimately only come from induction.

15 Themes and Prospects
Neill Nugent

THEMES OF THE BOOK

Running alongside the specific focus of individual chapters, a number of themes and issues have recurred through this book. Three of these themes and issues merit particular comment.

The influence of the Commission

It was noted in Chapter 1 that in the now long-standing debate on the nature of the European integration process much attention has been focused on the impact of the Commission. There is no doubt that the Commission is a very active EU actor, but does it, as those who emphasise the importance of supranational forces argue, exercise a significant autonomous influence on events? Or is it, as those who take a more intergovernmentalist view contend, confined to being essentially little more than a facilitator for the decisions and actions of national governments?

This key question about the autonomous impact of the Commission raises a number of difficult methodological problems. Mark Pollack explicitly addresses some of these problems in his chapter. Of particular concern to him is the problem of anticipated reactions: is it not the case, he asks, that many of the Commission's perceived successful initiatives have been successful because they have been based on rational anticipation of what will be received favourably by the governments of the Member States? Insofar as this is the case, the Commission should be seen, Pollack argues, as agent more than principal.

For the most part, the other contributors in the book who address the question of the influence of the Commission do not look at methodological issues in such an explicit way as Pollack. Insofar as they touch on such issues, it is in an essentially implicit manner. Concerning, for example, the anticipated reactions problem, several contributors make the point that the reactions are themselves at least partly shaped by Commission proactivism in agenda-setting.

Pollack is the only contributor to take a somewhat sceptical attitude towards the influence of the Commission. The other contributors lean decidedly towards 'a significant autonomous influence' viewpoint. They present evidence which they believe shows that, via the undertaking of a variety of roles and the use of a range of resources, the Commission exercises an influence that is real enough. The extent and nature of this influence is seen as taking many different forms. These forms include: playing a leading part in getting new policy initiatives off the ground, as, for example, Tom Lawton demonstrates in respect of industrial policy; being instrumental in effecting major reforms to existing policies, as Liesbet Hooghe shows in respect of the structural policies; and setting in place and managing mechanisms designed to try and ensure that policies are implemented properly, as Roger Levy illustrates in respect of the implementation of EU spending programmes.

An important point to emerge from the chapters which consider the influence of the Commission is that its significance varies not only between, but also within, issue areas. Variations between issue areas are, of course, to be expected, given that the factors which shape and determine the Commission's influence themselves vary so much from one policy area to another. These factors were outlined in Chapter 1 and include the extent of EU involvement in a particular policy area, the Commission's position in relation to that policy area, and a wide range of power resources. Where such factors favour the Commission, as for example they do in some Single European Market (SEM)-related policy areas, there is considerable scope for the Commission to exercise real power and influence. Where, however, such factors are not so favourable to the Commission and are tilted more towards the intergovernmental institutions and the Member States, as in policy areas such as justice and home affairs and social welfare, then the Commission's powers and influence are limited.

Variations within policy areas are less expected, but can also be significant. They are explained, naturally enough,

by changes in determining factors. An example of a variation within a policy area is seen in the sphere of competition policy where, as Lee McGowan shows in his chapter,
the SEM programme and the presence of strong Competition Commissioners were amongst the factors which produced
a major advance in Commission activity and influence from
the mid-1980s, whilst disappointment and dissatisfaction with
aspects of the Commission's performance were amongst
the factors which resulted in a slowing down in the
momentum from the early 1990s. Another example of such
variation is seen in the sphere of treaty reform where, as
Desmond Dinan demonstrates, variations in factors such as
the climate of the times and the priority attached to political
as distinct from socio-economic reforms, have resulted in
the Commission exercising different degrees and different
types of influence within Intergovernmental Conferences
(IGCs).

The large number of factors which combine to determine
the influence of the Commission, coupled with the many
different forms which such influence takes, has created difficulties not only for empirically-based studies of the Commission but also for more theoretically-based studies. Janne
Matlary considers some of these difficulties in her chapter
on the Commission and integration theory. Her main concern is with the difficulties which stem from the state-
centredness of much integration theory, for this, she believes,
has served to prevent an accurate assessment of the influence of the Commission. A state-centred approach is, in her
view, not warranted in the light of evidence which has established that the Commission plays a major role in EU policy
processes. The greater use and development of new conceptual approaches and theoretical models will, she argues,
help to clarify and demonstrate the position of very considerable importance that the Commission holds in the EU system and the very real influence that it exercises therein.

Evolving within an evolving system

The EU is a young political system. Its responsibilities, its
powers, its structures, and its methods of functioning are
all still very much evolving. Within this process of evolution

the Commission too is necessarily still evolving. As it does so, it seeks to ensure that its position at the heart of the Union is maintained and, where possible, is strengthened.

The evolution of the EU is occurring in a manner that results in three, in practice overlapping, issues receiving much attention from EU practitioners and commentators. These issues have been taken up in several chapters in the book. The issues, and their ramifications for the Commission, are, in outline, as follows:

1) *The balance between efficiency and accountability, and the location of legitimacy.* These are classic problems for all democratic and would-be democratic political systems.

When the EC was constituted in the 1950s the balance between efficiency and accountability was struck very much in favour of the former, with elites (both in the Council and the Commission) being given extensive powers, whilst not being much subject to direct forms of EC-level accountability. Insofar as legitimacy was considered, it was assumed to lie primarily with the national governments, each of which could make (greater or lesser) claims to having a popular mandate emanating from national elections.

Over the years, these elitist arrangements have increasingly come to be seen as unsatisfactory. Pressures for reform have stemmed particularly from the growth of policy responsibilities at EC/EU level, and from perceptions of extensive powers being in the hands of appointed and unelected officials in the Commission on the one hand and indirectly elected politicians in the Council on the other (indirect in the sense that ministers in the Council attain their position via national, not European, elections). Many different types of proposals have been advanced to rectify the perceived imbalance between efficiency and accountability and to increase EU-level legitimacy, most of which have involved granting greater powers to the directly elected EP.

The Commission has sought to engage with the debates about efficiency, accountability, and legitimacy and has attempted, where possible, to influence the debates to its advantage. The most obvious way in which it has done this has been at the time of IGCs when, as Desmond Dinan shows in his chapter, it has pressed for more powers for itself, especially more autonomous executive powers, and has also supported expansions in the role of the EP in the belief that this could assist Commission–EP relations which, in turn, could help to underpin Commission legitimacy.

Legitimacy has been a major problem for the Commission, as both Guy Peters and Helen Drake show in their chapters. There have been various reasons why the Commission's legitimacy has been queried, of which the most important is that it is expected to exercise political leadership as well as bureaucratic management responsibilities even though it is 'non national' and 'non democratic' in its composition. The Commission can certainly lay some claims to legitimacy, but if it seeks to exercise power in ways governments of the Member States dislike, such claims risk being contested and being contrasted unfavourably with the electoral base of national governments. The Maastricht Treaty reforms, which gave the EP the right to be consulted on the nominees for Commission President and the right of confirmation over the College of Commissioners, went some way to dealing with this legitimacy problem, but they certainly did not wholly resolve it. It can, therefore, be expected that the debate will continue to run – with proposals for such reforms as the direct election of the Commission President and the individual responsibility of Commissioners to the EP continuing to be heard.

2) *The balance, and the relations between, the executive, legislative, and judicial arms of government.* The differing arms, or branches, of government in the EU are much more fused than is normal in national political systems. A rudimentary separation of powers system could be said to be embodied in the Founding Treaties – the Commission proposes, the Council decides, the Parliament advises, and the Court interprets – but this separation has lost much of its intended impact as operating practices and treaty reforms have brought overlap and blurring in respect of which EU institution is responsible for, and does, what.

The lack of much of a separation of powers is witnessed in the wide variety of roles that the Commission exercises. Several chapters in the book have borne witness to this variety, not least Lee McGowan's chapter which shows the Commission acting in the sphere of competition policy, in legislative, executive, and judicial capacities: legislative in that it both proposes and (under Article 90 EC) makes laws; executive in that it carries both direct and indirect (supervisory) implementation responsibilities; and judicial in that, particularly in respect of merger control legislation, it has such extensive powers of interpretation that it plays the role not just of policeman but also of judge and jury.

The wide variety of roles and functions exercised by the Commission is, of course, the main reason why it is such an important institution. It is also one of the main reasons why it is such a controversial institution, for many of its activities are of a kind which are normally undertaken – both at national governmental levels and in other international organisations – by elected politicians rather than by appointed officials. Despite its supposed neutral and non-partisan position, the fact is that the Commission is constantly undertaking responsibilities and making judgements which are inherently political in nature. Moreover, as Lee McGowan and Mitchell Smith show in their chapters, these responsibilities and judgements can cover policy matters which are highly sensitive in nature.

The perceived political activities of the Commission frequently attract criticism. They do so not just from Eurosceptic quarters but from most quarters where particular Commission actions and decisions are disliked. A clearer separation of powers is sometimes called for in which the Commission's powers are curbed and in which it is confined to activities which are essentially executive, and non-political, in character. Most observers would see such curbs as unrealistic and undesirable given the institutional framework of the EU, but they are a part of the attitudinal climate in which the Commission functions. It is a climate which obliges the Commission to play a sensitive political game, in which its decisions must often be finely balanced and in which the exercise of its powers must be carefully measured. When the Commission fails on these counts – as, for example, it did by overstretching with its 1991 IGC proposals – it is likely to find itself in difficulties and to suffer what amount to institutional and policy defeats.

3) *The balance between EU and national levels.* Since the EC was founded, there has been a major shift of policy responsibilities from the national to the European level. Such has been the extent of the shift that there are now few areas of public policy in which the EU does not have an involvement of some kind. The nature of this involvement ranges from policy areas where the EU has taken over most policy-making responsibilities, such as external commercial policy and competition policy, to policy areas where its policy-making responsibilities are still very much secondary to the responsibilities of the governments of the Member States, such as education policy and health policy. In between these two 'poles' of policy responsibility are a host of policy areas where responsibilities are shared. Included amongst such policy areas are regional policy, industrial policy, research policy, social policy, and – increasingly in the context of EMU – important spheres of macroeconomic policy.

This expansion of EU-level responsibilities has naturally increased the responsibilities and tasks of the Commission. Several of the chapters in the book have looked at the nature of these increased responsibilities and have considered their implications. One of the more important implications is that the Commission is increasingly obliged to act as a broker between the EU and its Member States – by, for example, identifying courses of action in competition cases which are less than ideal in strict EU competition policy terms, but which provide some measure of political comfort to a national government that is faced with domestic political difficulties.

This brokerage role is being made more difficult to exercise by virtue of the fact that a growing feature of EU governance is that it is not only two-level – the EU and the Member States – but in some policy areas is also multi-level – the EU, the Member States, and regional and/or local governments. The development and greater activism of third and fourth levels of government in some Member States offers opportunities for the Commission to deal more directly than hitherto with users and operators of EU policies – especially distributive policies. It also offers some limited opportunities to sidestep national governments when these are judged to be adopting unhelpful attitudes on policy matters. However, such opportunities must be exercised with caution, since most governments have no wish to see their 'gatekeeper' positions transferred to subnational levels of government.

The growth in EU policy responsibilities and the increasingly multi-layered nature of the EU has done much to fuel debate about which policy functions should be undertaken at European level and which should be undertaken at national levels. It is a debate that has been brought into particularly sharp focus since the 're-launch' of the Community in the mid-1980s and the importance that has been attached to the concept of subsidiarity since the early 1990s. The Commission has, as several chapters in the book have shown, entered and sought to shape this debate, but its activities have also been much conditioned by it. The clearest example of such conditioning is the contrast between the bold policy expansionism offered by the Commission in the second half of the 1980s and the more cautious policy consolidations it has offered for most of the 1990s.

Internal weaknesses and problems

In addition to EU system framework weaknesses and problems to which the Commission is subject – of which the most important is its dependence on Council, and to a lesser extent EP, support for many of its activities – the Commission is also subject to various internal weaknesses and problems. Many of these internal weaknesses and problems have been noted and commented upon in the course of the book. Prominent amongst these internal weaknesses and problems are the lack of clear hierarchical relations between the Commission President and the rest of the College of Commissioners, the overlapping and sometimes competing policy responsibilities of DGs, and the suspicions and resentments which sometimes exist between Commissioners and *cabinets* on the one hand and DGs on the other. Such internal weaknesses and problems mean that some of the Commission's responsibilities are not undertaken in as effective a manner as possible, and mean also that the difficulties of adapting to an evolving system can be exacerbated.

Amongst the internal weaknesses and problems that are identified in the book, personnel matters are given the greatest attention. The most obvious issue here is that in many policy areas the Commission just does not have enough staff to undertake all of its responsibilities. Competition is an example of such a policy area and it exemplifies the sort of consequences that staff under-resourcing can bring: Member States are encouraged to deal with frontline policy implementation insofar as they can and to refer cases to the Commission only when it is absolutely necessary; the Commission's own frontline implementation responsibilities are undertaken on a partial, and largely spot-check, basis; and many tasks are contracted to outside consultants and agencies.

A different type of personnel problem concerns the composition of the College. In some respects this composition has been strengthened over the years, most notably, as Andrew MacMullen shows in Chapter 2, via the increasingly high status political background of its members. However, the fact remains that the composition of the College is a consequence of the balance of party political strengths in Member States at the time of the College's appointment. It is not a consequence of careful construction and deliberation designed to ensure that a cohesive and balanced team is formed. Nor is it a consequence of an election process which would give it a party political perspective and a collective electoral mandate. As a result, the College is not in a position to present itself as being, or to act as if it were, a clearly cohesive team with firmly democratic and legitimate credentials. The President of the Commission can, as Helen Drake shows in her study of Jacques Delors, seek to make use of his special position to advantage, and individual Commissioners can seek to make a mark in their spheres of portfolio responsibility, but the College as a body is not, and as presently constituted cannot be, a dynamic force in its own right.

'Below' the College, in the Commission's services, the personnel weakness and problem that receives most attention in the book is the lack of a clear and firmly established administrative culture grouped around shared norms, allegiances, and values. There can, perhaps, be said to be a Commission administrative culture of a kind, based on some commonly-used administrative practices and shared values. However, as both Maryon McDonald and Michelle Cini show, it is an administrative culture that can hardly be said to

have deep roots. Moreover, it is an administrative culture
that is cross-cut and fractured by particularistic attachments
and cultures.

FUTURE CHANGES AND CHALLENGES

It is highly probable that in the foreseeable future the EU
will be subject to major and rapid changes. Their impact
could be such as to transform the very nature of the EU in
important respects.

Three broad types of change seem especially likely to occur,
each of which will have significant implications for the Commission. These changes, and the challenges that they pose
for the Commission, are as follows:

- *The EU is likely to become less Western European and more pan-
  European.* The break-up of the Soviet bloc has had immense implications for the membership of the EU. It
  facilitated the 1995 accessions (in particular by making
  Finland and Sweden more relaxed about the idea of membership) and it paved the way for a stream of membership applications from Eastern European countries. The
  principle of Eastern European accessions has been accepted
  by the European Council, but accession dates – which will
  probably be staggered in batches – remain to be set. It is,
  however, quite conceivable that by around the turn of
  the century three or four of the more advanced Eastern
  European countries will be, or will be on the point of
  becoming, EU members.

  Eastern European accessions could well cause major difficulties for the Commission. Amongst such difficulties are
  likely to be: producing satisfactory and acceptable proposals for the reform of such policies as the Common
  Agricultural Policy and the structural policies, both of which
  will be too expensive to maintain in their current form
  when countries such as Poland and Romania become EU
  members; managing long transition periods and large
  numbers of policy derogations and special arrangements
  (these will be necessary for a number of reasons, not least
  to give Eastern European states the time and opportunity

to adjust to the requirements of the SEM); ensuring that national administrative agencies in Eastern Europe are properly implementing policies 'on the ground'; and incorporating into the Commission bureaucracy officials who are steeped in non Western administrative traditions.

- *The EU is likely to assume more responsibilities in politically-sensitive policy areas.* The EC/EU has never been a purely market integration organisation, but this has been its overwhelming focus. This focus is now broadening out as EMU furthers the degree of economic and monetary integration and as pillars two and three of the TEU further the degree of political integration.

  This broadening out has many possible implications for the Commission, for it is taking the form both of extending the EU's policy reach and of extending it into politically-charged policy areas. Under the TEU, the extensions into these areas were constructed largely on intergovernmental bases and the Commission's roles and responsibilities, though increased, were made subject to tight restrictions. In the future, these policies may well be put on a more supranational basis, the Commission's position in relation to them may well be enhanced, and as this occurs the Commission may well find not only that it has more to do but also that it has more politically sensitive and difficult things to do.

- *The EU is likely to become more multi-speed in character.* As the EC/EU has extended its policy reach, so has it become more multi-speed in character. Evidence of this is seen in the less than complete membership of the European Monetary System and the Schengen Agreement (the latter provides for the complete removal of border controls between acceding States), and the opt outs given in the TEU to the UK (from the single currency and the Social Chapter) and to Denmark (from the single currency). This movement towards a multi-speed EU seems likely to continue. Indeed, the pace of movement will probably increase, with 'fast stream' integration countries becoming less willing to be held back by 'slow stream' countries, with EU membership becoming larger and more heterogenous, and with more policy responsibilities being exercised at EU level.

The Commission has consistently opposed multi-speed ideas and proposals and has done what it can to keep all Member States abreast in policy terms. It has adopted this attitude partly because fracturing has been seen to be undesirable in itself, but partly too because fracturing makes it more difficult for the Commission to exercise its various roles in the EU system. Examples of ways in which it makes it more difficult include the Commission having to make decisions about when and when not to include 'non-participants' in policy deliberations, and having to make judgements about when 'non-participation' must be deemed to be unfair and unacceptable because of the consequences for 'participants'.

How well the Commission will respond to these changes and challenges remains to be seen. Predictions would certainly be unwise for, as has been shown throughout this book, the Commission's ability to deal with situations is determined by factors which can vary considerably in both nature and impact depending on context and circumstances. What can be said, however, is that there are grounds for at least some optimism, for prominent amongst the strengths which the Commission has long displayed are the character traits of flexibility and adaptability.

Annex: Directorates General and Special Units of the Commission*

DIRECTORATES GENERAL

DGI –   External Relations: Commercial Policy and Relations with North America, the Far East, Australia and New Zealand

DGIA –   External Relations: Europe and the New Independent States, Common Foreign and Security Policy and External Missions

DGIB –   External Relations: Southern Mediterranean, Middle and Near East, Latin America, South and South-East Asia and North-South Cooperation

DGII –   Economic and Financial Affairs

DGIII –   Industry

DGIV –   Competition

DGV –   Employment, Industrial Relations and Social Affairs

DGVI –   Agriculture

DGVII –   Transport

DGVIII – Development (Bilateral and development cooperation relations with Africa, The Caribbean and the Pacific; Lomé Convention)

DGIX –   Personnel and Administration

DGX –   Information, Communication, Culture and Audiovisual Media

DGXI –   Environment, Nuclear Safety and Civil Protection

DGXII –   Science, Research and Development Joint Research Centre

DGXIII – Telecommunications, Information Market and Exploitation of Research

DGXIV –   Fisheries

DGXV –   Internal Market and Financial Services

DGXVI –   Regional Policy and Cohesion

DGXVII – Energy

DGXIX –   Budgets

DGXX –   Financial Control

DGXXI –   Customs and Indirect Taxation

DGXXII – Education, Training and Youth

DGXXIII –Enterprise Policy, Distributive Trades, Tourism and Cooperatives

DGXXIV – Consumer Policy Service

SPECIAL UNITS

Secretariat-General
Forward Studies Unit
Inspectorate-General
Legal Service
Spokesman's Service
Joint Interpreting and Conference Service
Statistical Office
Translation Service
Informatics Directorate
Security Office
European Community Humanitarian Office
Euratom Supply Agency
Office for Official Publications of the European Communities

* Situation in February 1997

References

Abélès, M., Bellier, I., and McDonald, M. (1993) *Approche Anthropologique de la Commission Européenne*, unpublished report for the Commission.

Aberbach, J., Rockman, B., and Putnam, R. (eds) (1981) *Bureaucrats and Politicians in Western Democracies* (Cambridge, Mass.: Harvard University Press).

Adams, W.J. (1993) *Singular Europe: Economy and Polity of the European Community After 1992* (Ann Arbor: University of Michigan Press).

Allaire, Y. and Firsirotu, M.E. (1982) 'Theories of Organizational Culture', *Organization Studies*, vol. 5, no. 3, pp. 193–226.

Almond, G. and Verba, S. (1963) *The Civic Culture* (Princeton, NJ: Princeton University Press).

Alvarez de Cienfuegos, I.M. (1996) 'Adaptation and Change in the Spanish Administrative System as a Result of European Union Membership', paper presented at the Workshop of European Consortium for Political Research, Oslo, Norway, 30 March–3 April.

Anderson, J. (1996) 'Germany and the Structural Funds: Unification Leads to Bifurcation', in L. Hooghe (1996a).

Archer, C. (1994) *Organizing Europe: the Institutions of Integration* (London: Edward Arnold).

Aucoin, P. (1995) *The New Public Management: Canada in Comparative Perspective* (Montreal: Institute for Research on Public Policy).

Audretsch, D. (1993) 'Industrial Policy and International Competitiveness', in N. Phedon, (1993).

Bardach, E. (1977) *The Implementation Game: What Happens After a Bill Becomes a Law* (Cambridge, Mass.: MIT Press).

Bardach, E. and Kagan, R.A. (1982) *Going by the Book: The Problem of Regulatory Unreasonableness* (Philadelphia: Temple University Press).

Baun, M. (1996) *An Imperfect Union: The Maastricht Treaty and the New Politics of European Integration* (Boulder, Colo.: Westview Press).

Baylis, J. and Rengger, N.J. (eds) (1992) *Dilemmas in World Politics* (Oxford: Clarendon Press).

Beetham, D. (1974) *Max Weber and the Theory of Modern Politics* (London: George Allen and Unwin).

Bellier, I. (1994) 'La Commission Européenne: Hauts Fonctionnaires et "Culture du Management"', *Revue Française d'Administration Publique*, vol. 70, pp. 253–62.

Bellier, I. (1995) 'Une Culture de la Commission Européenne? De la Rencontre des Cultures et du Multilinguisme des Fonctionnaires', in Y. Mény *et al.* (1995), pp. 49–60.

Biersteker, T.J. (1993) 'Constructing Historical Counterfactuals to Assess the Consequences of International Regimes: The Global Debt Regime and the Course of the Debt Crisis of the 1980s', in V. Rittberger (1993), pp. 315–38.

Blok, A. (1981) 'Rams and Billy-Goats: A Key to the Mediterranean Code of Honour', *Man*, vol. 16, no. 3, pp. 427–40.

Boulay, J. du (1974) *Portrait of a Greek Mountain Village* (Oxford: Clarendon Press).

Bulmer, S. (1994a) 'The Governance of the European Union: A New Institutionalist Approach', *Journal of Public Policy*, vol. 13, no. 4, pp. 351–80.

Bulmer, S. (1994b) 'Institutions and Policy Change in the European Communities: The Case of Merger Control', *Public Administration*, vol. 72, Autumn, pp. 423–44.

Bulmer, S., George, S., and Scott, A. (eds) (1992) *The United Kingdom and EC Membership Evaluated* (London: Pinter).

Bundgaard-Pedersen, T. (1995) 'Recent Trends in Network Analysis: Alternative Conceptions and European Integration', unpublished paper (Oslo: ARENA).

Burley, A. and Mattli, W. (1993) 'Europe Before the Court: A Political Theory of Legal Integration', *International Organization*, vol. 47, no. 1, pp. 41–76.

Cafruny, A. and Rosenthal, G. (eds) (1993) *The State of the European Community. Volume 2: The Maastricht Debates and Beyond* (Boulder, Colo.: Lynne Rienner).

Calvert, R.L. (1995) 'The Rational Choice Theory of Institutions: Implications for Design', in D.L. Weimer (ed.), *Institutional Design*.

Cameron, D. (1992) 'The 1992 Initiative: Causes and Consequences', in A. Sbragia (1992), pp. 23–74.

Campbell, J. (1964) *Honour, Family and Patronage* (Oxford: Clarendon Press).

Caporaso, J. (1996) 'The European Union and Forms of State: Westphalian, Regulatory or Post-Modern', *Journal of Common Market Studies*, vol. 34, no. 1, pp. 29–52.

Cassese, S. (1987a) 'Divided Powers: European Administration and National Bureaucracies', in S. Cassesse (1987b).

Cassese, S. (ed) (1987b) *The European Administration* (Brussels: IISA).

Cassese, S. and Cananea, G. (1990) 'Procediementos de decision: Elaboracion y applicacion de medidas de integracion', in *Las implicaciones administrativas de la integracion economica regional: el ejemplo de la Communidad Europea* (Madrid: Ministerio para la Administraciones Publicas).

Cecchini, P. et al. (1988) *The European Challenge 1992: the Benefits of a Single Market* (Aldershot: Wildwood House).

Christiansen, T. (1997) 'Reconstructing Space: From Territorial Politics to European Multilevel Governance', in K.E. Jørgensen (1997).

Christoph, J.B. (1993) 'The Effects of Britons in Brussels: The European Community and the Culture of Whitehall', *Governance*, vol. 6, no. 4, pp. 518–37.

Cini, M. (1994) 'Policing the Internal Market: The Regulation of Competition in the European Commission', PhD thesis, University of Exeter.

Cini, M. (1995) 'Administrative Culture in the European Commission: The Cases of Competition and Environment', paper presented to the Fourth International European Community Studies Association Conference, Charleston, 11–14 May.

Cini, M. and McGowan, L. (forthcoming) *Competition Policy in the European Union* (Basingstoke: Macmillan).

Clergerie, J.-L. (1995) 'L'Improbable Censure de la Commission Européenne', *Revue du Droit Public et de la Science Politique en France et à L'Étranger*, no. 1, pp. 201–20.

Cloos, J. *et al.* (1993) *Le Traité de Maastricht: Genèse, Analyse, Commentaire* (Bruxelles: Bruylant).

Cockfield, Lord (1994) *The European Union: Creating the Single Market* (Chichester: Chancery Law Wiley).

Commission (1985) *Completing the Internal Market: White Paper From the Commission to the European Council*, COM (85) 310 final (Brussels: European Commission).

Commission (1988) *Research and Technological Development Policy*, periodical 2/88 (Luxembourg: Office for Official Publications of the European Communities).

Commission (1990a) *Draft Treaty on Economic and Monetary Union* (Luxembourg: Office for Official Publications of the European Communities).

Commission (1990b) *First Annual Report on the Implementation of the Structural Funds*, COM (90) 516 Brussels: European Commission).

Commission (1990c) *Industrial Policy in An Open and Competitive Environment*, Communication of the Commission to the Council and to the European Parliament, COM (90), 556 final (Brussels: European Commission).

Commission (1991a) *One Market, One Money: An Evaluation of the Potential Benefits and Costs of Forming an Economic and Monetary Union* (Luxembourg: Office for Official Publications of the European Communities).

Commission (1991b) *The European Electronics and Information Technology Industry: State of Play, Issues at Stake, and Proposals for Action*, SEC (91), 565 final (Brussels: European Commission).

Commission (1991c) *European Industrial Policy for the 1990's*, in *Bulletin of the European Communities*, Supplement 3/91 (Luxembourg: Office for Official Publications of the European Communities).

Commission (1992a) *Research After Maastricht: An Assessment, A Strategy*, Information Memo, Brussels, 8 April.

Commission (1992b) *Second Annual Report on the Implementation of the Reform of the Structural Funds* (Luxembourg: Office for Official Publications of the European Communities).

Commission (1993a) *Growth, Competitiveness, Employment. The Challenges and Way Forward into the 21st Century*, COM (93) 700 final (Brussels: European Commission).

Commission (1993b) *Fourth Annual Report on the Implementation of the Structural Funds*, COM (93) 530 (Brussels: Office for Official Publications of the European Communities).

Commission (1994a) *Twenty-Fourth Report on Competition Policy* (Luxembourg: Office for Official Publications of the European Communities).

Commission (1994b) *An Industrial Competitiveness Policy for the European Union*, Communication from the Commission to the Council, COM (94), 319 Final (Brussels: European Commission).

Commission (1995a) *The European Commission 1995–2000* (Brussels: European Commission).

Commission (1995b) *La Bonne Gestion Financiere, Texte F,* SEC (95) 477 (Brussels: European Commission).

Commission (1995c) *Contribution to the Reflection Group* (Luxembourg: Office for Official Publications of the European Communities).

Commission (1995d) *Fourth Survey of State Aid* (Luxembourg: Office for Official Publications of the European Communities).

Commission (1996a) *General Report on the Activities of the European Union 1995* (Brussels: Office for Official Publications of the European Communities).

Commission (1996b) *Intergovernmental Conference 1996. Commission Opinion: Reinforcing Political Union and Preparing for Enlargement* (Luxembourg: Office for Official Publications of the European Communities).

Commission (1996c) 'Green Paper on Innovation', *Innovation & Technology Transfer,* Special Issue, DGXIII, Luxembourg.

Commission Directorate General for Economic and Financial Affairs (1994) *EC Agricultural Policy for the 21st Century,* European Economy No. 4 (Brussels: European Commission).

Committee of Three (1979) *Report on European Institutions,* presented by the Committee of Three to the European Council, October.

Coombes, D. (1970) *Politics and Bureaucracy in the EC. A Portrait of the Commission of the EEC* (London: George Allen and Unwin).

Court of Auditors (1989) 'Annual Report Concerning the Financial Year 1988 Together With the Institutions' Replies', *Official Journal of the European Communities,* C312 vol. 32, 12 December.

Court of Auditors (1993) 'Annual Report Concerning the Financial Year 1992 Together With the Institutions' Replies', *Official Journal of the European Communities,* C309 vol. 36, 16 November.

Cram, L. (1993) 'Calling the Tune Without Paying the Piper? Social Policy Regulation: The Role of the Commission in European Community Social Policy', *Policy and Politics,* vol. 21, no. 2, pp. 135–46.

Cram, L. (1994) 'The European Commission as a Multi-Organization: Social Policy and IT Policy in the EU', *Journal of European Public Policy,* vol. 1, no. 2, pp. 195–217.

Cram, L. (1995) 'Rhetoric, Soft Law and Symbolic Politics in the EU Social Policy Process: Has the Commission Become a Victim of its Own Success?', paper presented to the Annual Meeting of the American Political Science Association, Chicago, Aug.–Sept.

Curzon Price, V. (1981) *Industrial Policies in the European Communities* (London: Macmillan Press for the Trade Policy Research Centre).

Davies, J. and Lavoie, C. (1993) 'EC Merger Control: A Half Term Report Before the 1993 Review', *World Competition,* vol. 16, no. 3, pp. 27–36.

Davis, J. (1977) *People of the Mediterranean* (London: Routledge).

Delamont, S. (1995) *Appetites and Identities. An Introduction to the Social Anthropology of Western Europe* (London: Routledge).

Delors, J. (1991) *La Reconversion des Régions Industrielles. Rencontre des 60 Régions Éligibles a L'Objectif des Fonds Structurels,* speech published by the Commission of the European Communities, Brussels, 8 July 1991.

Delors, J. (1993) *Pour Entrer Dans le XXIe Siècle. Emploi. Croissance. Compétitivité. Le Livre Blanc de la Commission des Communautés Européennes* (Paris: Michel Lafon/Ramsay).

Delors, J. (1995) 'Le Moment et la Méthode. Entretien Avec Jacques Delors', *Débat*, no. 83, pp. 4–23.

Dilley, R. (ed.) (1992) *Contesting Markets* (Edinburgh: Edinburgh University Press).

Dinan, D. (1994) *Ever Closer Union? An Introduction to the European Union* (London: Macmillan).

Dinan, D. (1995) 'The Commission, Enlargement and the IGC', *ECSA Newsletter*, vol. VIII no. 2, pp. 13–16.

Dinan, D. (1996), 'The Commission and the 1996 Conference', in G. Edwards and A. Pijpers, *The European Union: 1996 and Beyond* (London: Pinter).

Docksey, C. and Williams, K. (1994) 'The Commission and the Execution of Community Policy', in G. Edwards and D. Spence (1992), pp. 117–45.

Dodgson, M. (ed.) (1989) *Technology Strategy and the Firm: Management and Public Policy* (Harlow: Longman).

Donnelly, M. (1993) 'The Structure of the European Commission and the Policy Formation Process', in S. Mazey and J. Richardson, (1993a), pp. 74–81.

Donnelly, M. and Ritchie, E. (1994) 'The College of Commissioners and their Cabinets', in G. Edwards and D. Spence (1994), pp. 31–61.

Drake, H. (1995) 'Political Leadership and European Integration; the Case of Jacques Delors', *West European Politics*, vol. 18, no. 1, pp. 140–60.

Drake, H. (1996a) 'Jacques Delors and the Discourse of Political Legitimacy', in H. Drake and J. Gaffney (1996), pp. 233–58.

Drake, H. (1996b) 'The Legitimisation of Authority in the European Union. A Study of the European Commission with Special Reference to the Commission Presidency of Jacques Delors, 1985–1995', PhD thesis, Aston University.

Drake, H. and Gaffney, J. (eds) (1996), *The Language of Leadership in Contemporary France* (Aldershot: Dartmouth).

Duff, A. (ed.) (1993) *Subsidiarity Within the EC*, (London: Federal Trust).

Duff, A. (1994) 'The Main Reforms', in A. Duff *et al.* (1994), pp. 19–85.

Duff, A., Pinder, J., and Pryce, R. (1994) *Maastricht and Beyond: Building the European Union* (London: Routledge).

Dumont, A. (1990) 'Technology, Competitiveness and Cooperation in Europe', in S. Steinberg (1990), pp. 68–80.

Dyson, K. (1994) *Elusive Union. The Process of Economic and Monetary Union in Europe* (London: Longman).

Earnshaw, D. and Judge, D. (1995) 'Early Days: The European Parliament, Co-decision and the European Union Legislative Process Post-Maastricht', *Journal of European Public Policy*, vol. 2, no. 4, pp. 624–49.

Edwards, G. and Pijpers, A. (eds) (1996) *The European Union: 1996 and Beyond* (London: Pinter).

Edwards, G. and Spence, D. (1994) 'The Commission in Perspective', in G. Edwards and D. Spence, *op. cit.*, pp. 1–30.

Edwards, G. and Spence, D. (eds) (1994) *The European Commission* (Harlow: Longman).

Ehlermann, C.-D. (1994a) 'The Commission Standpoint', paper delivered to the conference entitled 'EC Competition Law: Procedural Aspects in Particular in the Light of the Select Committee of the House of Lords', Kings College, London.

Ehlermann, C.-D. (1994b) 'State Aids Under European Community Competition Law', *Fordham International Law Journal*, vol. 18, December, pp. 410–36.

Ehlermann, C.-D. (1995a) 'The European Administration and the Public Administration of Member States With Regard to Competition Law', *European Competition Law Review*, vol. 16, September, pp. 454–60.

Ehlermann, C.-D. (1995b) 'Reflections on the European Cartel Office', *Common Market Law Review*, vol. 32, no. 2, pp. 471–86.

Elmore, R.F. (1982) 'Backward Mapping: Implementation Research and Policy Decision', in W. Williams (ed.), (1982).

Euratom (1958) *Communauté Européene de l'Energie Atomique, Premier Rapport Général sur l'Activité de la Communauté* (Brussels: Services des Publications).

Eurobarometer: Public Opinion in the European Community (two issues each year) (Brussels: Office for Official Publications of the European Communities).

FitzGerald, G. (1991) *All in a Life: An Autobiography* (Dublin: Gill and Macmillan).

Fitzmaurice, J. (1994) 'The European Commission', in A. Duff *et al. Maastricht and Beyond*, pp. 179–89.

Freeman, C., Sharp, M. and Walker, W. (eds) (1991) *Technology and the Future of Europe: Global Competition and the Environment in the 1990s* (London: Pinter).

Freiherr von Gamm, O.F., Raisch, P., and Tiedmann, K. (1988) *Stafrecht, Unternehmensrecht, Anwaltsrecht, Festschrift fur Gerd Pfeifer* (Koln: Carl Heymanns Verlag).

Fuchs, G. (1994) 'Policy-Making in a System of Multi-Level Governance – the Commission of the European Community and the Restructuring of the Telecommunications Sector', *Journal of European Public Policy*, vol. 1, no. 2, pp. 176–94.

Fuchs, G. (1995) 'The European Commission as Corporate Actor? European Telecommunications Policy After Maastricht', in C. Rhodes and S. Mazey (1995), pp. 413–29.

Gaffney, J. (1989) *The French Left and the Fifth Republic. The Discourses of Communism and Socialism in Contemporary France* (Basingstoke: Macmillan).

Garrett, G. (1992) 'International Cooperation and Institutional Choice: The EC's Internal Market', *International Organization*, vol. 46, Spring, pp. 533–60.

Garrett, G. (1995) 'The Politics of Legal Integration in the European Union', *International Organization*, vol. 49, Winter, pp. 171–81.

Garrett, G. and Tsebelis, G. (1996) 'An Institutional Critique of Intergovernmentalism', *International Organization*, vol. 50, no. 2, pp. 269–99.

Garrett, G. and Weingast, B. (1993) 'Ideas, Interests, and Institutions: Constructing the European Community's Internal Market', in J. Goldstein and R.O. Keohane (1993), pp. 173–206.

Gellner, E. (1977) 'Patrons and Clients', in E. Gellner and J. Waterbury, (1977), pp. 1–6.

Gellner, E. (1983) *Nations and Nationalism* (Oxford: Blackwell).

Gellner, E. and Waterbury, J. (eds) (1977) *Patrons and Clients* (London: Duckworth).

George, S. (1991) *Politics and Policy in the European Community*, 2nd edn (Oxford: Oxford University Press).

George, S. (1995) 'The European Commission; Opportunities Seized; Problems Unresolved', paper presented to the Fourth International Conference of the European Community Studies Association, Charleston, 11–14 May.

Gerber, D.J. (1994) 'The Transformation of European Competition Law?', *Harvard International Law Journal*, vol. 335, Winter, pp. 97–147.

Gerus, V. (1991) 'Comitology within the European Community's Policy-Making Process: A Mechanism of Political Control in the Inter-Institutional Relations of the Council of Ministers and the Commission', unpublished manuscript, Harvard University, September.

Gilmore, D. (ed.) (1987) *Honour and Shame and the Unity of the Mediterranean* in Special Publication No. 22 (American Anthropological Association).

Giovanni, M. (1981) 'Woman: A Dominant Symbol Within the Cultural System of a Sicilian Town', *Man*, vol. 16, no. 3, pp. 408–26.

Goldstein, J. and Keohane, R.O. (1993) *Ideas and Foreign Policy: Beliefs, Institutions, and Political Change* (Ithaca, NY: Cornell University Press).

Goyder, D.G. (1993) *Competition Law in the EEC* (Oxford: Clarendon Press).

Grant, C. (1994) *Delors: Inside the House That Jacques Built* (London: Nicholas Brealey Publishing).

Graupner, F. (1973) 'Commission Decision Making in Competition Questions', *Common Market Law Review*, vol. 10, August, pp. 291–305.

Green, D. and Shapiro, I. (1994) *Pathologies of Rational Choice: A Critique of Applications in Political Science* (New Haven, Conn : Yale University Press).

Green, M (1993) 'The Politics of Big Business in the Single Market Program', paper presented to the European Community Studies Association Third Biennial International Conference, Washington DC, May.

Green Cowles, M. (1995) 'Setting the Agenda for a New Europe: The ERT and EC 1992', *Journal of Common Market Studies*, vol. 33, no. 4, pp. 501–26.

Grosser, A. (1980) *The Western Alliance* (London: Macmillan).

Haas, E. (1958) *The Uniting of Europe: Political, Social, and Economic Forces, 1950–57* (Stanford: Stanford University Press).

Haas, E. (1990) *When Knowledge is Power* (Berkeley: University of California).

Haas, P.M. (1993) 'Epistemic Communities and the Dynamics of International Environmental Co-operation', in V. Rittberger (1993), pp. 168–201.

Hallstein, W. (1973) *Europe in the Making* (New York: Norton).

Hanf, K. and Toonen, A.J. (1985) *Policy Implementation in Federal and Unitary Systems* (Dordrecht: Martinus Nijhoff).

Hansard, *Parliamentary Debates*, Various volumes.

Hart, K. (1992) 'Market and State After the Cold War. The Informal Economy Reconsidered' in R. Dilley, (1992), pp. 214–27.

Hayward, J.E.S. and Page, E.C. (eds) (1995) *Governing the New Europe* (Cambridge: Polity Press).

Héritier, A. *et al.* (1994) *Die Veranderung von Staatlichkeit in Europa. Ein regulativer Wettewerb: Deutschland, Grossbritannien, Frankreich* (Opladen: Westdeutscher Verlag).

Héritier, A. (1995) '"Leaders" and "Laggards" in European Clean Air Policy', in B. Unger and F. van Waarden (1995).

Héritier, A. (1996) 'The Accommodation of Diversity in European Policy-Making and Its Outcomes: Regulatory Policy as a Patchwork', *Journal of European Public Policy*, vol. 3, no. 2, pp. 149–67.

Herzfeld, M. (1980) 'Honour and Shame: Problems in the Comparative Analysis of Moral Systems', *Man*, vol. 15, no. 2, pp. 339–51.

Herzfeld, M. (1985) *The Poetics of Manhood* (Oxford: Clarendon Press).

Hjern, B. and Porter. D.P. (1980) 'Implementation Structures: A New Unit of Administrative Analysis', *Organisation Studies*, vol. 2, pp. 211–24.

Hood, C. (1976) *The Limits of Administration* (New York: John Wiley).

Hood, C. and Schuppert, G.F. (1988) *Service Delivery in Western Europe* (London: Sage).

Hood, C., Peters, B.C., and Wollmann, H. (1996) 'Sixteen Ways to Consumerise Public Services: Pick 'N Mix or Painful Trade-Offs?', *Public Money and Management*, vol. 16, no. 4, pp. 43–50.

Hooghe, L. (ed.) (1996a) *Cohesion Policy and European Integration: Building Multi-Level Governance* (Oxford: Oxford University Press).

Hooghe, L. (1996b) 'Building a Europe With the Regions: The Changing Role of the European Commission', in L. Hooghe (1996a).

Hooghe, L. and Keating, M. (1994) 'The Politics of EU Regional Policy', *Journal of European Public Policy*, vol. 1, no. 3, pp. 367–93.

Hooghe, L. and Marks, G. (1996) 'Birth of a Polity. The Struggle Over European Integration', paper presented at the Tenth Bi-annual Conference of Europeanists, Chicago, March.

Horn, M.J. (1995) *The Political Economy of Public Administration* (Cambridge: Cambridge University Press).

Hosli, M. (1996) 'Coalition and Power: Effects of Qualified Majority Voting on the Council of the European Union', *Journal of Common Market Studies*, vol. 34, no. 2, pp. 255–74.

House of Commons (1989–90) *House of Commons Papers 1989–90, Number 517 (i), Minutes of Evidence Taken Before the Trade and Industry Committee, 7 June 1989,* (London: HMSO).

House of Lords Select Committee on the European Communities (1989) *Fraud Against the Community*, Session 1988–89, 5th Report, HL paper 27 (London: HMSO).

House of Lords Select Committee on the European Communities (1991) *Regional Development Policy*, Session 1991–92, 4th Report, HL paper 20 (London: HMSO).

House of Lords Select Committee on the European Communities (1992) *The Fight Against Fraud (with Evidence)*, Session 1992–93, 13th Report, HL paper 44 (London: HMSO).

House of Lords Select Committee on the European Communities (1993a) *Enforcement of Community Competition Rules* (London: HMSO).

House of Lords Select Committee on the European Communities (1993b) *EC Development Aid*, Session 1992–93, 21st Report, HL paper 89 (London: HMSO).

House of Lords Select Committee on the European Communities (1994) *Financial Control and Fraud in the Community*, Session 1993–94, 12th Report, HL paper 75 (London: HMSO).

Howell, T.R. *et al.* (1992) *Conflict Among Nations: Trade Policies in the 1990's* (Boulder, Color.: Westview Press).

Hufbauer, G.C. (ed.) (1990) *Europe 1992: An American Perspective* (Washington, DC: Brookings Institution).

Huybrechts, L., Marchandise, D., and F. Tulkens (1994) *La Lutte Contre la Fraude Communautaire Dans la Pratique* (Bruxelles: Bruylant).

Jachtenfuchs, M. (1997) 'Conceptualising European Governance', in K.E. Jørgensen, (1997).

Jachtenfuchs, M. and Kohler-Koch, B. (eds) (1996a) *European Integration* (Opladen: Leske u. Budrich).

Jachtenfuchs, M. and Kohler-Koch, B. (1996b) 'Einleitung: Regieren im Dynamischen Mehrebensystem', in M. Jachtenfuchs and B. Kohler-Koch, (1996a).

Jørgensen, K.E. (ed.) (1997) *Reflective Approaches to European Governance* (Basingstoke: Macmillan.)

Journal of European Public Policy (1995) *The Single Market and Global Economic Integration*, special issue, vol. 2, no. 3.

Kartte, W. (1990) 'Die Politisierung der Europäischen Fusionskontrolle ist Programmiert', *Die Welt*, 31 December.

Kassim, H. (1994) 'Policy Networks, Networks and European Union Policy Making: A Sceptical View', *West European Politics*, vol. 17, no. 4, pp. 15–27.

Keohane, R.O. (1991) 'Sovereignty, Interdependence and International Institutions', Working Paper No. 1 (Harvard University: Center for International Affairs).

Keohane, R.O. and Hoffmann, S. (eds) (1991) *The New European Community: Decision-making and Institutional Change* (Oxford: Westview Press).

Kersbergen, K. van and Verbeek, B. (1994) 'The Politics of Subsidiarity in the European Union', *Journal of Common Market Studies*, vol. 32, no. 2, pp. 215–36.

Kiewiet, R. and McCubbins, M.D. (1991) *The Logic of Delegation: Congressional Parties and the Appropriation Process* (Chicago: University of Chicago Press).

Kingdon, J.W. (1984) *Agendas, Alternatives, and Public Policies* (Boston: Little, Brown).

Kohler-Koch, B. (1996) '*Regieren in der Europaischen Union. Vorschlag fur ein Schwerwertprogramm der DFG*' unpublished research programme prepared for German authorities.

Kok, C. (1989) 'The Court of Auditors of the European Communities: The Other European Court in Luxembourg', *Common Market Law Review*, vol. 26, pp. 345–67.

Korah, V. (1994) *An Introduction to EEC Competition Law* (London: Sweet and Maxwell).

Laffan, B. (1995) 'Knowledge and Expertise in the EU Policy Process', unpublished research brief.

Lane, J.-E. (1983) 'The Concept of Implementation', *Statvetenskaplig Tidskrift*, vol. 86, pp. 17–39.

Lavoux, T. (1986) *France, Water and Waste: A Study of the Implementation of EC Directives* (London: Graham and Trotman).

Lawton, T.C. (1995) *Technology and the New Diplomacy: The Creation and Control of EC Industrial Policy*, PhD thesis, European University Institute.

Lenaerts, K. (1991) 'Some Reflections on the Separation of Powers in the European Community', *Common Market Law Review*, no. 28, pp. 11–35.

Levy, R. (1990) 'That Obscure Object of Desire: Budgetary Control in the EC', *Public Administration*, vol. 68, no. 2, pp. 191–206.

Levy, R. (1991) '1992: Towards Better Budgetary Control in the EC?', *Corruption and Reform*, vol. 6, pp. 285–302.

Levy, R. (1994) 'Audit and Accountability in a Multi-Agency Environment: The Case of the Common Agricultural Policy in the UK', *Financial Accountability and Management*, vol. 10, no. 2, pp. 65–75.

Levy, R. (1995a) ' Subsidiarity, Accountability and the Management of EU Programmes', paper delivered at the Fourth International European Community Studies Association Conference, Charleston, 11–14 May.

Levy, R. (1995b) 'Managing EU Programmes: Subsidiarity and the Accountability Gap', paper delivered at the University Association For Contemporary European Studies Research Conference, Birmingham, 18–19 September.

Liefferink, D. and Lowe, P. (eds) (1993) *European Integration and Environmental Policy* (Scarborough: Belhaven Press).

Lindberg, L. (1963) *The Political Dynamics of European Economic Integration* (Stanford: Stanford University Press).

Lindberg, K. and Scheingold, S. (1970) *Europe's Would-Be Polity: Patterns of Change in the EC* (Englewood Cliffs, NJ: Prentice-Hall).

Linder, S.H. and Peters, B.G. (1989) 'Implementation as a Guide to Policy Formation: A Question of "When" Rather than "Whether"', *International Review of Administrative Sciences*, vol. 55, pp. 631–52.

Lipsky, M. (1980) *Street-Level Bureaucracy: The Dilemmas of Individuals in the Public Service* (New York: Russell Sage).

Lodge, J. (1994) 'Transparency and Democratic Legitimacy', *Journal of Common Market Studies*, vol. 32, no. 3, pp. 343–368.

Loizos, P. (1975) *The Greek Gift: Politics in a Cypriot Village* (Oxford: Blackwell).

Ludlow, P. (1991) 'The European Commission', in R.O. Keohane and S. Hoffmann, (1991), pp. 85–132.

Lund, C. (1995) *Changing Perceptions of the National Interest in Economic and Defence Policy under Mitterrand, 1981–1989*, PhD thesis, Cambridge University.

Lundquist, L.J. (1980) *The Hare and the Tortoise: Clean Air Policies in the United States and Sweden* (Ann Arbor: University of Michigan Press).

Macdonald, S. (ed.) (1993) *Inside European Identities* (Oxford: Berg).

McCubbins, M., Noll, R., and Weingast, B. (1989) 'Structure and Process, Policy and Politics: Administrative Arrangements and the Political Control of Agencies', *Virginia Law Review*, vol. 75, pp. 431–82.

McCubbins, M. and Schwartz, T. (1984) 'Congressional Oversight Overlooked: Police Patrols Versus Fire Alarms', *American Journal of Political Science*, vol. 28, no. 1, pp. 165–79.

McDonald, M. (1989) *'We Are Not French!' Language, Culture and Identity in Brittany* (London: Routledge).

McDonald, M. (1993) 'The Construction of Difference: An Anthropological Approach to Stereotypes', in S. Macdonald, (1993), pp. 219–36.

McDonald, M. (ed.) (1994) *Gender, Drink and Drugs* (Oxford: Berg).

McDonald, M. (1996) '"Unity in Diversity". Some Tensions in the Construction of Europe', *Social Anthropology*, vol. 4, no. 1, pp. 47–60.

McGowan, F. (1993) *The Struggle for Power in Europe: Competition and Regulation in the Electricity Industry* (London: Royal Institute of International Affairs).

McGowan, L. and Wilks, S. (1995) 'The First Supranational Policy in the European Union: Competition Policy', *European Journal of Political Research*, vol. 28, no. 2, pp. 141–69.

McKenzie, D. (1992) *The Horizons of Research. The Future of Cross-Border R&D in the European Community* (Brussels: Forum Europe).

Majone, G. (1989) *Evidence, Argument and Persuasion in the Policy Process* (New Haven: Yale University Press).

Majone, G. (1991) 'Cross-National Sources of Regulatory Policy-making in Europe and the United States', *Journal of Public Policy*, vol. 11, no. 1, pp. 79–106.

Majone, G. (1992) 'Regulatory Federalism in the European Community', *Environment and Planning C: Government and Policy*, vol. 10, no. 3, pp. 299–316.

Majone, G. (1994a) 'The Rise of the Regulatory State in Europe', *West European Politics*, vol. 17, no. 3, pp. 77–101.

Majone, G. (1994b) *The European Community as a Regulatory State*, lectures given at the Academy of European Law, European University Institute.

Majone, G. (1995) *The Development of Social Regulation in the European Community* (Florence: European University Institute).

Majone, G. and Wildavsky, A. (1978) 'Implementation as Evolution', in H.E. Freeman (ed.), *Policy Studies Annual Review*, vol. 2.

March, J. and Olsen, J.P. (1989) *Rediscovering Institutions: The Organizational Basis of Politics* (New York: The Free Press).

Marks, G. (1992) 'Structural Policy in the European Community', in A. Sbragia (1992), pp. 191–224.

Marks, G. (1993) 'Structural Policy and Multilevel Governance in the EC', in A. Cafruny and G. Rosenthal (1993), pp. 391–410.

Marks, G. (1996) 'Decision Making in Cohesion Policy: Describing and Explaining Variation', in L. Hooghe (1996a).

Marks, G., Hooghe, L., and Blank, K. (1997) 'European Integration From the 1980s: State-Centric Versus Multi-Level Governance', *Journal of Common Market Studies*, vol. 32, no. 3, pp. 341–78.

Marsh, D. and Rhodes, R.A.W. (eds) (1992) *Policy Networks in British Government* (Oxford: Clarendon Press).

Matlary, J.H. (1997a) *Energy Policy in the European Union* (Basingstoke: Macmillan).

Matlary, J.H. (1997b) 'New Bottles for New Wine', in K.E. Jørgensen (1997).

Mazey, S. (1995) 'The Development of EU Equality Policies: Bureaucratic Expansion on Behalf of Women?', *Public Administration*, vol. 73, no. 4, pp. 591–609.

Mazey, S. and Richardson, J. (eds) (1993a) *Lobbying in the European Community* (Oxford: Oxford University Press).

Mazey, S. and Richardson, J. (1993b) 'Conclusion: a European Policy Style?', in S. Mazey and J. Richardson, (1993a), pp. 246–58.

Mazey, S. and Richardson, J. (1993c) 'EC Policy Making: An Emerging Policy Style?', in D. Liefferink and P. Lowe (1993), pp. 14–25.

Mazey, S. and Richardson, J. (1994) 'Policy Co-ordination in Brussels: Environmental and Regional Policy', *Regional Politics and Policy*, vol. 4, no. 1, pp. 22–44.

Mendrinou, M. (1992) 'European Community Fraud and Institutional Development', The European Policy Research Unit (Manchester: University of Manchester).

Mendrinou, M. (1996) 'Non-Compliance and the European Commission's Role in Integration', *Journal of European Public Policy*, vol. 3, no. 1, pp. 1–22.

Mennens, E. (1986) 'Fraudebestrijing in de Europese Gemeenschap', *SEW 9/10*, pp. 624–40.

Mény, Y. (1993) *La Greffe et le Rejet: Les Politiques de Mimetisme Institutionnel* (Paris: L'Harmattan).

Mény, Y., Muller, P., and Quermonne, J.L. (eds) (1995) *Politiques Publiques en Europe* (Paris: L'Harmattan).

Metcalfe, L. (1992) 'After 1992: Can the Commission Manage Europe?', *Australian Journal of Public Administration*, vol. 51, no. 1, pp. 117–30.

Metcalfe, L. (1994) 'International Policy Co-ordination and Public Management Reform', *International Review of Administrative Sciences*, vol. 60, pp. 271–90.

Michelmann, H.J. (1978) *Organisational Effectiveness in a Multinational Bureaucracy* (Farnborough: Saxon House).

Middlemas, K. (1995) *Orchestrating Europe: The Informal Politics of the European Union 1973–1995* (London: Fontana Press).

Milward, A. (1992) *The European Rescue of the Nation-State* (Berkeley: University of California Press).

Moe, T.M. (1984) 'The New Economics of Organization', *American Journal of Political Science*, vol. 28, no. 4, pp. 739–77.

Moe, T.M. (1987) 'An Assessment of the Positive Theory of "Congressional Dominance"', *Legislative Studies Quarterly*, vol. XII, no. 4, pp. 475–520.

Moe, T.M. (1990) 'The Politics of Structural Choice: Toward a Theory of Public Bureaucracy', in O. Williamson (1990), pp. 116–53.

Monnet, J. (1978) *Memoirs* (London: Collins).

Moravcsik, A. (1991) 'Negotiating the Single European Act: National Interests and Conventional Statecraft in the European Community', *International Organization*, vol. 45, no. 1, pp. 19–56.

Moravcsik, A. (1993) 'Preferences and Power in the European Community: A Liberal Intergovernmentalist Approach', *Journal of Common Market Studies*, vol. 31, no. 4, pp. 473–524.

Moravcsik, A. (1995) 'Liberal Intergovernmentalism and Integration: A Rejoinder', *Journal of Common Market Studies*, vol. 33, no. 4, pp. 611–28.

Narjes, K.H. (1988) 'Europe's Technological Challenge: A View From the European Commission', *Science and Public Policy*, vol. 15, no. 6, pp. 385–402.

North, D. (1990) *Institutions, Institutional Change, and Economic Performance* (Cambridge: Cambridge University Press).

Norton, D. (1986) 'Smuggling Under the CAP: Northern Ireland and the Republic of Ireland', *Journal of Common Market Studies*, vol. 2, no. 4, pp. 297–312.

Nugent, N. (1991) *The Government and Politics of the European Community*, 2nd edn (Basingstoke: Macmillan).

Nugent, N. (1994) *The Government and Politics of the European Union*, 3rd edn (Basingstoke: Macmillan).

Nugent, N. (1995) 'The Leadership Capacity of the European Commission', *Journal of European Public Policy*, vol. 2, no. 4, pp. 603–23.

Obradovic, D. (1996) 'Policy Legitimacy and the European Union', *Journal of Common Market Studies*, vol. 34, no. 2, pp. 191–221.

Oreja, M. (1995) 'Written Answers to the Institutional Affairs Committee of the European Parliament', (Luxembourg: European Parliament).

Organisation for Economic Cooperation and Development (1982) *Innovation Policy Trends and Perspectives* (Paris: OECD).

Ostrom, E. (1991) 'Rational Choice Theory and Institutional Analysis', *American Political Science Review*, vol. 85, no. 1, pp. 237–43.

Ostry, S. (1990) *Governments and Corporations in a Shrinking World: Trade and Innovation Policies in the United States, Europe, and Japan* (New York: Council on Foreign Relations).

Page, E.C. (1985) *Political Authority and Bureaucratic Power* (Whitstable: Harvester Press).

Page, E.C. (1992) *Political Authority and Bureaucratic Power. A Comparative Analysis*, 2nd edn (Brighton: Harvester Wheatsheaf).

Page, E.C. and Wouters, L. (1994) 'Bureaucratic Politics and Political Leadership in Brussels', *Public Administration*, vol. 72, Autumn, pp. 445–59.

Page, E.C. and Wouters, L. (1995) 'The Europeanization of National Bureaucracies', in J. Pierre (1995).

Passas, N. and Nelken, D. (1991) 'The Legal Response to Agricultural Fraud in the European Community: A Comparative Study', *Corruption and Reform*, November.

Peristiany, J. (1965) *Honour and Shame: The Values of Mediterranean Society* (London: Weidenfeld and Nicolson).

Peters, B.G. (1992) 'Bureaucratic Politics and the Institutions of the European Community', in A. Sbragia (1992), pp. 75–122.

Peters, B.G. (1994a) 'Agenda-Setting in the European Community', *Journal of European Public Policy*, vol. 1, no. 1, pp. 9–26.

Peters, B.G. (1994b) *The Politics of Bureaucracy*, 4th edn (New York: Longman).

Peterson, J. (1991) 'Technology Policy in Europe: Explaining the Framework Programme and Eureka in Theory and Practice', *Journal of Common Market Studies*, vol. XXIX no. 3, pp. 269–90.

Peterson, J. (1992) 'The European Technology Community: Policy Networks in a Supranational Setting', in D. Marsh and R.A.W. Rhodes (1992), pp. 226–48.

Peterson, J. (1995) 'EU Research Policy: The Politics of Expertise', in C. Rhodes, and S. Mazey (1995), pp. 391–412.

Peterson, J. (1996) 'Policy Networks and European Union Governance', paper presented to the Tenth International Conference of Europeanists, Chicago, 14–17 March.

Phedon, N. (1993) *Industrial Policy in the European Community: A Necessary Response to European Integration?* (Dordrecht: Martinus Nijhoff).

Philip, A.B. (1988) 'The Application of the EEC Regulations on Drivers' Hours and Tachographs', in H. Siedentopf and J. Ziller, vol. 1, (1988).

Pierre, J. (ed.) (1995) *Bureaucracy in the Modern State* (Cheltenham: Edward Elgar).

Pierson, P. (1995) 'The Path to European Integration: A Historical Institutionalist Analysis', unpublished paper.

Pitt-Rivers, J. (1954) *People of Sierra* (New York: Criterion Books).

Pitt-Rivers, J. (1977) *The Fate of Schechem, or the Politics of Sex* (Cambridge: Cambridge University Press).

Pollack, M.A. (1994) 'Creeping Competence: The Expanding Agenda of the European Community', *Journal of Public Policy*. vol. 14, no. 2, pp. 95–145.

Pollack, M.A. (1995a) 'Regional Actors in an Intergovernmental Play: The Making and Implementation of EC Structural Policy', in C. Rhodes and S. Mazey (1995), pp. 361–90.

Pollack, M.A. (1995b) 'The New Institutionalism and EC Governance: The Promise, and Limits, of Institutional Analysis', paper presented at the American Political Science Association, Chicago, 31 Aug.–3 Sept.

Pollack, M.A. (1995c) *Creeping Competence: The Expanding Agenda of the European Community*, PhD thesis, Harvard University.

Pollack, M.A. (1996) 'The New Institutionalism and EU Governance: The Promise and Limits of Institutional Analysis', *Governance*, vol. 9, pp. 429–58.

Pollack, M.A. (1997) 'Obedient Servant or Runaway Eurocracy? Delegation, Agency and Agenda Setting in the European Community', *International Organization*, vol. 51.

Pollitt, C. (1993) *Managerialism and the Public Services: Cuts or Cultural Change in the 1990s?*, 2nd edn (Oxford: Blackwell).

Pope, D. (1993) 'Some Reflections on Italian Flat Glass', *European Competition Law Review*, vol. 14, no. 4, pp. 172–6.

Pratley, A. (1995) 'Auditing, Financial Management and Evaluation: An Interview with Alan Pratley', *Evaluation*, vol. 1, no. 2, pp. 251–63.

Pressman, J.L. and Wildavsky, A. (1974) *Implementation* (Berkeley: University of California Press).

Rengger, N.J. (1992) 'Culture, Society, and World Order in Politics', in J. Baylis and N.J. Rengger (1992), pp. 85–103.

Rhodes, C. and Mazey, S. (1995) *The State of the European Union. Vol. 3: Building a European Polity* (Harlow: Longman).

Richardson, J. (ed.) (1982) *Policy Styles in Western Europe* (London: Allen & Unwin).

Richardson, J. (ed.) (1996) *European Union: Power and Policy Making* (London: Routledge).

Risse-Kappen, T. (1996) 'Exploring the Nature of the Beast: International Relations Theory and Comparative Policy Analysis Meet the European Union', *Journal of Common Market Studies*, vol. 34, no. 1, pp. 53–80.

Rittberger, V. (1993) *Regime Theory and International Relations* (Oxford: Clarendon Press).

Rose, R. (1995) 'Dynamics of Democratic Regimes' in J.E.S. Hayward and E.C. Page (1995), pp. 67–92.

Rosenthal, D.E. (1990) 'Competition Policy', in G.C. Hufbauer (ed.), (1990), pp. 293–343.

Rosenthal, G. (1975) *The Men Behind the Decisions: Cases in European Policy-Making* (Lexington, Mass.: D.C. Heath).

Ross, G. (1993) 'Sidling into Industrial Policy: Inside the European Commission', *French Politics and Society*, vol. 11, no. 1, pp. 20–43.

Ross, G. (1994) 'Inside the Delors Cabinet', *Journal of Common Market Studies*, vol. 32, no. 4, pp. 499–523.

Ross, G. (1995) *Jacques Delors and European Integration* (Oxford: Polity Press).

Ruimschotel, D. (1994) 'The EC Budget: Ten Per Cent Fraud? A Policy Analysis Approach', *Journal of Common Market Studies*, vol. 32, no. 3, pp. 319–42.

Ruyt, J. de (1987) *L'Acte Unique Européen: Commentaire* (Bruxelles: Éditions de l'Université de Bruxelles).

Sabatier, P.A. (1986) 'Top-Down and Bottom-Up Approaches to Implementation Research: A Critical Analysis and Suggested Synthesis', *Journal of Public Policy*, vol. 6. Part 1, pp. 21–48.

Sabatier, P.A. (1987) 'Knowledge, Policy-Oriented Learning and Policy Change. An Advocacy Coalition Framework', *Knowledge: Creation, Diffusion, Utilization*, vol. 8, no. 4, pp. 649–92.

Sabatier, P.A. (1993) 'Policy Change Over a Decade or More', in P.A. Sabatier and H.C. Jenkins-Smith (1993b), pp. 13–30.

Sabatier, P.A. and Jenkins Smith H.C. (1993a) 'The Study of Public Policy Processes', in P.A. Sabatier and H.C. Jenkins-Smith (1993b), pp. 1–9.

Sabatier, P.A. and Jenkins-Smith, H.C. (eds) (1993b) *Policy Change and Learning: An Advocacy Coalition Approach* (Boulder, Colo.: Westview Press).

Sandholtz, W. (1992a) 'ESPRIT and the Politics of International Collective Action', *Journal of Common Market Studies*, vol. XXX, no. 1, pp. 1–21.

Sandholtz, W. (1992b) *High-Tech Europe: The Politics of International Cooperation* (Berkeley: University of California Press).

Sandholtz, W. (1993a) 'Institutions and Collective Action: The New Telecommunications in Western Europe', *World Politics*, vol. 45, no. 2, pp. 242–70.

Sandholtz, W. (1993b) 'Choosing Union: Monetary Politics and Maastricht', *International Organization*, vol. 47, no. 1, pp. 1–39.

Sandholtz, W. and Zysman, J. (1989) '1992: Recasting the European

Bargain', *World Politics*, vol. 42, no. 1, pp. 95–128.

Sandholtz, W. *et al.* (1992) *The Highest Stakes: The Economic Foundations of the Next Security System* (Oxford: Oxford University Press).

Santer, J. (1995) 'The Future of Europe: What Role for the Commission?', speech of President Santer at the Jean Monnet Conference, Florence, 20 October 1995, Ref: Speech/95/218.

Sbragia, A. (ed.) (1992) *Euro-Politics: Institutions and Policymaking in the 'New' European Community* (Washington: The Brookings Institution).

Sbragia, A. (1993) 'The European Community: A Balancing Act', *Publius*, vol. 23, Summer, pp. 23–38.

Sbragia, A. (1996) 'Institution Building From Below and Above: The European Union in Global Environmental Politics', paper presented at the conference on Supranational Governance, University of California, 1–3 November.

Scharpf, F.W. (1988) 'The Joint-Decision Trap: Lessons from German Federalism and European Integration', *Public Administration*, vol. 66, Autumn, pp. 239–78.

Scharpf, F.W. (1994) 'Community and Autonomy: Multi-Level Policy-Making in the European Union', *Journal of European Public Policy*, vol. 1, no. 2, pp. 219–42.

School for Advanced Urban Studies (1992) 'European Social Fund: Recent Developments', seminar held on 23–4 April and reported in *European Information Service*, No. 130, June 1992.

Scotland Europa (1996) *Monthly Report to Members (February)* (Brussels: SCOT-EUROPA).

Scott, A. (1992) 'Industrial Policy', in S. Bulmer *et al.* (1992), pp. 65–77.

Scott, A., Peterson, J., and Millar, D. (1994) 'Subsidiarity: A "Europe of the Regions" vs. the British Constitution?', *Journal of Common Market Studies*, vol. 32, no. 1, pp. 47–68.

Searing, D. (1991) 'Roles, Rules and Rationality in the New Institutionalism', *American Political Science Review*, vol. 85, no. 4, pp. 1239–60.

Searing, D. (1994) *Westminster's World. Understanding Political Roles* (Cambridge, Mass.: Harvard University Press).

Shackleton, M. (1994) *The Internal Legitimacy Crisis of the European Union*, Europa Institute Occasional Paper No. 1 (Edinburgh: Edinburgh University).

Sharp, M. (1989) 'Corporate Strategies and Collaboration: The Case of ESPRIT and European Electronics', in M. Dodgson (1989), pp. 202–18.

Sharp, M. (1991) 'The Single Market and European Technology Policies', in C. Freeman *et al.*, (1991).

Shaw, J. (1993) *European Community Law* (Basingstoke: Macmillan).

Shaw, J. (1995) *European Union Legal Studies in Crisis? Towards a New Dynamic*, European University Institute Working Paper RSC No. 95/23.

Sherlock, A. and Harding, C. (1991) 'Controlling Fraud Within the European Community', *European Law Review*, vol. 16, no. 1, pp. 20–36.

Shonfield, A. (1965) *Modern Capitalism. The Changing Balance of Public and Private Power* (London: Oxford University Press).

Siedentopf, H. and Ziller, J. (eds) (1988) *Making European Policies Work: The Implementation of Community Legislation in the Member States*, 2 vols (London: Sage).

Sjøstedt, G. (1994) 'The Development of Long-Term Strategies of the EU: "Externalisation" Through Consensual Knowledge', unpublished paper, Swedish Institute of International Affairs.

Smith, M.P. (1996) 'Integration in Small Steps: The European Commission and Member State Aid to Industry', *West European Politics*, vol. 19, no. 3, pp. 563–82.

Smyrl, M. (1995) 'A Policy Window, and What Came Through It: The European Community's Integrated Mediterranean Programs', paper presented at the 1995 Annual Meeting of the American Political Science Association, Chicago, 31 August–3 September.

Smyrl, M. (1996) 'Does EC Regional Policy Empower the Regions?', paper presented at the Tenth Bi-annual Conference of Europeanists, Chicago, March.

Snyder, F. (ed.) (1992) *European Law in Context: A Reader* (London: Dartmouth).

Spanou, C. (1996) 'Administrative Responses to Greece EU Membership', paper presented at Joint Sessions of European Consortium for Political Research, Oslo, Norway.

Spence, D. (1994) 'Staff and Personnel Policy in the Commission', in G. Edwards and D. Spence (1994), pp. 62–96.

Spierenburg, D. (1979) *Proposals for the Reform of the Commission of the European Communities and Its Services*, report made at the request of the Commission by an independent Review Body under the chairmanship of Mr Dirk Spierenburg, Brussels, September.

Steinberg, M.S. (1990) *The Technical Challenges and Opportunities of a United Europe* (London: Pinter).

Strasser, D. (1992) *The Finances of Europe: The Budgetary and Financial Law of the European Communities*, 7th edn (Luxembourg: Office for Official Publications of the European Communities).

Suleiman, E. (ed.) (1984) *Bureaucrats and Policy Making. A Comparative Overview* (New York: Holmes & Meier).

Suleiman, E. and Mendras, H. (eds) (1995) *Le Recrutement des Élites en Europe* (Paris: Éditions La Découverte (Collections 'Recherches'))

Sun, J.-M. and Pelkmans, J. (1995) 'Regulatory Competition in the Single Market', *Journal of Common Market Studies*, vol. 33, no. 1, pp. 07–90.

Sutherland, P. (1993) 'Progress to European Union: A Challenge for the Public Service', *Administration*, vol. 41, no. 2, pp. 105–19.

Taylor, P. (1991) 'The European Community and the State: Assumptions, Theories and Propositions', *Review of International Studies*, vol. 17, no. 2, pp. 109–25.

Thatcher, M. (1993) *The Downing Street Years* (London: HarperCollins).

Thelen, K. and Steinmo, S. (eds) (1992a) *Structuring Politics: Historical Institutionalism in Comparative Analysis* (Cambridge: Cambridge University Press).

Thelen, K. and Steinmo, S. (eds) (1992b) 'Historical Institutionalism in Comparative Politics', in K. Thelen and S. Steinmo, (1992a), pp. 1–32.

Tiedemann, K. (1988) 'Reform des Sanktionswesens auf dem Gebiete des Agrarmarktes der Europäischen Wirtschaftsgemeinschaft', in O.F. Freiherr von Gamm *et al.*, (1988).

Tömmel, I. (1992) 'System-Entwicklung und Politikgestaltung in der Europäischen Gemeinschaft am Beispiel der Regionalpolitik', *Politische Vierteljahresschrift, Sonderheft*, vol. 23, pp. 185–208.

Tonra, B. (1997) 'Practitioners' Assessment of Political Cooperation: Denmark, Ireland, and the Netherlands', in K.E. Jørgensen (1997).

Treaties Establishing the European Communities (1978) (Luxembourg: Office for Official Publications of the European Communities).

Treaty on European Union, Together With the Complete Text of the Treaty Establishing the European Community (1992), in *Official Journal of the European Communities*, C244, 31 August.

Tsebelis, G. (1994) 'The Power of the European Parliament as a Conditional Agenda Setter', *American Political Science Review*, vol. 88, no. 1, pp. 128–42.

Tugendhat, C. (1987) *Making Sense of Europe* (Harmondsworth: Penguin).

Tutt, N. (1989) *Europe on the Fiddle: The Common Market Scandal* (London: Croom Helm).

Tyson, L. and Zysman, J. (eds) (1983) *American Industry in International Competition: Government Policies and Corporate Strategy* (New York: Cornell University Press).

Tyson, L. D'Andrea and Yoffie, D.B. (1991) *Semiconductors: From Manipulated to Managed Trade*, Berkeley Roundtable on the International Economy (BRIE), Working Paper 47, August.

Unger, B. and Waarden, F. van (eds) (1995) *Convergence or Diversity? Internationalization and Economic Policy Response* (Aldershot: Avebury).

US Congress, Office of Technology Assessment (1991) *Competing Economies: America, Europe, and the Pacific Rim*, OTA-ITE-498 (Washington, DC: US Government Printing Office).

Vahl, R. (1992) 'The European Commission's Leading Role: The Conditions for Effectiveness', paper presented at the Inaugural Pan-European Conference in International Studies, Heidelberg.

Verney, S. and Tsakaloyannis, P. (1986) 'Linkage Politics: the Role of the European Community in Greek Politics in 1973', *Byzantine and Modern Greek Studies*, vol. 10, pp. 179–94.

Vervaele, J.A.E. (1992) *Fraud Against the Community: The Need for European Fraud Legislation* (Deventer: Kluwer).

Vogel, D. (1986) *National Styles of Regulation: Environmental Policy in Great Britain and the United States* (Ithaca, NY: Cornell University Press).

Weale, A. (1992) *The New Politics of Pollution* (Manchester: Manchester University Press).

Weber, M. (1964) *The Theory of Social and Economic Organization* (New York: The Free Press).

Weiler, J.H.H. (1993) 'After Maastricht: Community Legitimacy in Post-1992 Europe', in W.J. Adams, (1993), pp. 11–41.

Weiler, J.H.H. (1995) *European Democracy and its Critique. Five Uneasy Pieces*, European University Institute Working Paper RSC No.95/11.

Weimer, D.L. (ed.) (1995) *Institutional Design* (Dordrecht: Kluwer).

Weingast, B.R. and Moran, M. (1983) 'Bureaucratic Discretion or Congressional Control? Regulatory Policy-making by the Federal Trade Commission', *Journal of Political Economy*, vol. 91, no. 5, pp. 765–800.

Whish, R. (1993) *Competition Law* (London: Butterworth).

Wikan, U. (1981) 'Shame and Honour: A Contestable Pair', *Man*, vol. 16, no. 3.

Wilks, S. (1992a) 'The Metamorphosis of European Competition Policy', in F. Snyder (1992).

Wilks, S. (1992b) 'Models of European Administration: DGIV and the Administration of Competition Policy', paper presented to the European Group of Public Administration Conference, Pisa, Sept.

Wilks, S. and McGowan, L. (1995) 'Disarming the Commission: The Debate Over a European Cartel office', *Journal of Common Market Studies*, vol. 32, no. 2, pp. 259–73.

Williams, W. (ed.) (1982) *Studying Implementation* (Chatham, NJ: Chatham House).

Williamson, O. (ed.) (1990) *Organization Theory from Chester Barnard to the Present and Beyond* (Oxford: Oxford University Press).

Wincott, D. (1995) 'Institutional Interaction and European Integration: Towards an Everyday Critique of Liberal Intergovernmentalism', *Journal of Common Market Studies*, vol. 33, no. 4, pp. 597–609.

Wood, B.D. and Waterman, R.W. (1993) 'The Dynamics of Political–Bureaucratic Adaptation', *American Journal of Political Science*, vol. 37, no. 2, pp. 497–528.

Young, O. (1991) 'Political Leadership and Regime Formation: On the Development of Institutions in International Society', *International Organization*, vol. 45, Summer, pp. 281–308.

Young, O. and Osherenko, G. (1993) *Polar Politics. Creating International Environmental Regimes* (Ithaca: Cornell University Press).

Zimmerman, G.C. (1995) 'Implementing the Single Banking Market in Europe', *Economic Review, Federal Reserve Bank of San Francisco*, no. 3, pp. 35–51.

Zito, A.R. (1995) 'Integrating the Environment into the European Union: The History of the Controversial Carbon Tax', in C. Rhodes and S. Mazey (1995), pp. 431–48.

Index

320   *Index*

Directorates General (*continued*)
DGXV, 53, 295
DGXVI, 53–4, 93, 94, 95, 210, 213, 216–17, 295
DGXVII, 157, 295
DGXVIII, 295
DGXIX, 212, 214, 223, 295
DGXX, 210–11, 212, 213, 214, 216–17, 220–1, 223, 295
DGXXI, 295
DGXXII, 92–3, 94–5, 295
DGXXIII, 140, 141, 295
DGXXIV, 295
dirigiste approach (industrial policy), 140
discretionary powers, 80–2
Dixon, J., 253, 257
Docksey, C., 115, 198
domestic politics, 167–85
dominance, monopolies and, 148–9
Donnelly, M., 5, 74
Dooge Committee, 250
Drake, H., 4, 235, 236
Duff, A., 209
Dyson, K., 276, 278

Earnshaw, D., 120
Eastern Europe, 7, 292–3
Economic and Monetary Union, 3, 16, 18, 121, 126, 170–2, 182, 245–7, 251–4, 257–62, 273, 276, 278, 289, 293
Economic and Social Committee, 45
Edinburgh summit (1992), 210
efficiency, accountability and, 286–7
Eguiagaray, J.M., 180, 181, 182
Ehlermann, C.-D., 153, 155, 161, 163, 173, 253
electronics industry, 137–8, 139–40, 142
Elmore, R.F., 194
employees (of Commission), 104–5
empowerment, subnational, 90–3
energy policy, 24–5, 157, 273, 295

engrenage (intermeshing), 47
enterprise zones, 174, 176–9 *passim*, 183
environment policy, 274, 279
administrative culture and, 73–85
external constraints, 84–5
institutional autonomy, 81–2
path dependencies, 78–80
equal opportunities, 24, 53
ESPRIT programme, 125, 133, 135, 142
Eureka projects, 134, 142
Eurobarometer surveys, 107
European Atomic Energy Community, 27–8, 29, 31, 38, 40
European Cartel Office (ECO), 163–4
European Central Bank, 258
European Coal and Steel Community, 13, 27–30, 38, 40, 54, 146, 171, 173, 229, 231
European Community, 54–5, 76, 171, 245
Commissioners, 27–48 *passim*
Treaty, 9, 12, 25, 168, 172–3, 224
European Council, 7, 8, 11, 13–16, 21–2, 118–21, 124, 136, 138, 147, 198, 245–6, 250–2, 257, 262, 292, *see also under names of summits*
European Court of Auditors, 113, 204, 212, 214, 217, 220, 222, 224
European Court of Justice, 10, 20–1, 25, 29–30, 81, 113, 115, 149, 154, 156, 193, 205–6, 246, 263
European Development Fund, 213
'European Economic Area', 254
European Economic Community, 27–9, 31, 38, 40, 147
Treaty, 229, 235–6
European Environment Agency, 208
European Free Trade Association (EFTA), 254